Business Information Systems: a Process Approach

INFORMATION SYSTEMS SERIES

Consulting Editors

D.E. AVISON
BA, MSc, PhD, FBCS

*Professor of Information Systems
Department of Accounting
and Management Science,
Southampton University, UK*

G. FITZGERALD
BA, MSc, MBCS

*Professor of Information Systems,
Department of Information Systems and Computing,
Brunel University, UK*

This series of student and postgraduate texts covers a wide variety of topics relating to information systems. It is designed to fulfil the needs of the growing number of courses on, and interest in, computing and information systems which do not focus on the purely technological aspects, but seek to relate these to business and organizational context.

Business Information Systems: a Process Approach

Brian Warboys, Peter Kawalek, Ian Robertson
and Mark Greenwood

Informatics Process Group,
Department of Computer Science,
The University of Manchester, UK

THE McGRAW-HILL COMPANIES

London · Chicago · New York · St Louis · San Francisco · Auckland
Bogotá · Caracas · Lisbon · Madrid · Mexico · Milan
Montreal · New Delhi · Panama · Paris · San Juan · São Paulo
Singapore · Sydney · Tokyo · Toronto

Published by
McGraw-Hill Publishing Company
SHOPPENHANGERS ROAD, MAIDENHEAD, BERKSHIRE, SL6 2QL, ENGLAND
Telephone +44 (0) 1628 502500
Fax: +44 (0) 1628 770224   Web site: http://www.mcgraw-hill.co.uk

British Library Cataloguing in Publication Data
A catalogue record for this book is available from the British Library

ISBN 007 709464 6

Library of Congress Cataloguing-in-Publication Data
The LOC data for this book has been applied for and may be obtained from the
Library of Congress, Washington, D.C.

Further information on this title is to be found at
http://www.mcgraw-hill.co.uk/warboys

Publishing Director: Alfred Waller
Publisher: David Hatter
Typeset by: the Authors
Produced by: Steven Gardiner Ltd
Cover by: Hybert Design

McGraw-Hill

A Division of The McGraw·Hill Companies

1 2 3 4 5 CUP 3 2 1 0 9

Printed in Great Britain at the University Press, Cambridge

Contents

Part One Concepts

Part Two Practice

Chapter 5 The Nature of the Method

Chapter 6 Process Contexts

Chapter 7 Process Capture

Chapter 8 Process Design

Chapter 9 Process Managing

Chapter 10 Process Support Technology

Chapter 11 The OPM Case Study

Chapter 12 Conclusion

Acknowledgement

This book would not have been possible without all the people with whom we have worked over the years. First mention should go to those organizations who have collaborated with us on studies of their processes. Without them the approach described in this book would never have received the necessary testing to mature into its current publishable form. We should also mention our academic collaborators, and students, who have been both sources of useful ideas and helpful critics of our work. In particular, we are indebted to a number of people who have contributed to or reviewed earlier versions of this book: Ann Apps, Peter Kueng, Bob Snowdon, Martyn Spink, Philip Veasey and Phil White. The UK Engineering and Physical Sciences Research Council (EPSRC) has consistently supported our research. In particular the process approach described in this book was first developed as part of the EPSRC-funded Process Engineering Framework project.

In addition to studying organizations' processes we have also developed our ideas through experiments with process-based technology. We have had invaluable support from TeamWARE, formerly ICL, through their ProcessWise Integrator system. Ben Yeomans implemented the Process*Web* extension to ProcessWise Integrator, and has done the majority of the work on the interactive models accessible on this book's web site.

Series Forward

The Information Systems Series is a series of student and postgraduate texts covering a wide variety of topics relating to information systems. The focus of the series is the use of computers and the flow of information in business and large organizations. The series is designed to fill the needs of the growing number of courses on information systems and computing which do not focus on purely technical aspects but rather which seek to relate information systems to their commercial and organizational context.

The term 'information systems' has been defined as the effective design, delivery, use and impact of information technology in organizations and society. Utilizing this broad definition it is clear that the subject is interdisciplinary. Thus the series seeks to integrate technological disciplines with management and other disciplines, for example, psychology and sociology. These areas do not have a natural home and were, until comparatively recently, rarely represented by single departments in universities and colleges. To put such books in a purely computer science or management series restricts potential readership and the benefits that such texts can provide. The series on information systems provides such a home.

The titles are mainly for student use, although certain topics will be covered at greater depth and be more research-oriented for postgraduate study.

The series includes the following areas, although this is not an exhaustive list: information systems development methodologies, office information systems, management information systems, decision-support systems, information modelling and databases, systems theory, human aspects and the human-computer interface, application systems, technology strategy, planning and control, expert systems, knowledge acquisition and its representation.

A mention of the books so far published in the series gives a 'flavour' of the richness of the information systems world. *Information and Data Modelling, second edition (David Benyon)* concerns itself with one very important aspect, the world of data, in some depth; *Information Systems Development: A Database Approach, second edition (David Avison)* provides a coherent methodology which has been widely used to develop adaptable computer systems using databases; *Information Systems Research: Issues, Techniques and Practical Guidelines (Robert Galliers – Editor)* provides a collection of papers on key information systems issues which will be of special interest to researchers; *Multiview: An Exploration in Information Systems Development (David Avison and Trevor Wood-Harper)* looks at an approach to information systems development which combines human and technical considerations; *Relational Database Systems and Relational Database Design (Paul Beynon-Davies)* are two books which offer a comprehensive treatment of relational databases; *Business Management and Systems Analysis (Eddie Moynihan)* explores the areas of overlap between business and IT; *Decision Support Systems (Paul Rhodes)* places management decision-making in the perspective of decision theory; *Information Systems: An Emerging Discipline? (John Mingers and Frank Stowell – Editors)* debates the practical and philosophical dimensions of the field;

Why Information Systems Fail (Chris Sauer) looks at the reasons for IS failure and the problems of developing IS in organisations; *Human Computer Factors (Andy Smith)* emphasizes user-centred design, usability and the role of the users; *Transforming the Business: The IT Contribution (Robert Moreton and Myrvin Chester)* discusses the role that IS/IT can play in organizational change; and the second edition of *Information Systems Development: Methodologies, Techniques and Tools, (David Avison and Guy Fitzgerald)* provides a comprehensive coverage of the different elements of information systems development. *The Information Systems Life Cycle: A First Course in Information Systems (David Avison and Hanifa Shah)* covers the basic material necessary in a first course in information systems. It can be used as a 'prequel' to Avison and Fitzgerald but can also be used 'stand-alone' where the teaching of IS does not go beyond a first course. The most recent addition to the series is *Rapid Information Systems Development (Simon Bell and Trevor Wood-Harper)* in which rapid applications development is explored in a clear and friendly manner, with many examples to help readers in picturing how their real-world problems might be tackled.

We now welcome *Business Information Systems: A Process Approach* by Brian Warboys, Peter Kawalek, Ian Robertson and Mark Greenwood of the Informatics Process Group (IPG) at the University of Manchester. The book arises from concern for the effectiveness of organizations and, in particular, the issues around how software support relates to business goals. It believes that modelling the organizational process provides a key to the comprehension of, and the effective support of, business goals. In doing so the book draws upon systems concepts; understanding organizations as systems highlights the requirements of coordination and change, thus providing a refreshing vantage point from which to approach the design of software systems.

David Avison and Guy Fitzgerald

Preface

'An executive decision is a moment in a process'

Mary Parker Follett

This book is the product of a team rather than just several individuals. That is, its beliefs and prejudices have been fashioned over the decade during which the Informatics Process Group (IPG) has been in existence in the Department of Computer Science at The University of Manchester. It is the result of many case studies, Undergraduate, Master's and Ph.D projects, a Process Modelling Master's Course and research projects funded by the UK EPSRC and the EU Esprit/Framework programmes. A huge debt is owed to all those individuals, too numerous to mention, who have helped, sometimes unwittingly, to fashion our beliefs over this period. Hopefully many will read this book and be able to take pleasure in finding their contributions, however obscurely hidden in our theology.

The immediate origins of this book can be traced to the IPG's Process Engineering Framework Project which ran from October 1993 to October 1995. A large debt is owed to the UK national research council EPSRC which provided much of the funding for the project. This project sought to develop a framework for process engineering and was, in turn, based on previous work from the IPSE 2.5 project and its exploitation successor, the IOPT project, which ran during the late'80s and early'90s.

The IPSE 2.5 project had been a major component of the UK Alvey Programme's Software Engineering Strategy. The Alvey Programme is described and critiqued in the book of the project (Oakley and Owen, 1989). That book describes how, 'A unique experiment known as the Alvey Programme revolutionised traditional attitudes and mechanisms'. Well, perhaps, although it is worth noting that, 'In 1988 the government decided against an "Alvey 2" programme as such. The signs are that the Alvey community has survived that blow and is alive and well'. This was published in 1989 ... one wonders whether the observation would be the same today.

It is thus perhaps fitting that some not-too-distant child of the Alvey Programme, which set out to better integrate the technical (academic) and the sociological (industry), should concentrate on the issue of building social information systems.

The concern of this book is with the development of software support for modern organizations. In particular, the concern is for complex systems, where there are many people and many software applications, which get things done by interacting with each other.

We have taken the view that only by attempting to understand both the means of expression of business processes and the means by which this understanding may be translated into IT systems can one achieve the rewards promised by the ongoing IT revolution. There is no doubt that information and its ready availability to potentially all citizens will be a major driving force during the next millenium. The problem is not one of information access but rather of what to look for and where to find it. This general problem is one which faces us all, and successful people and enterprises are those which have sufficiently solved this problem.

The overarching issues which we seek to address are the themes of *interaction* and *evolution*. This process approach to the development of business information systems perceives the organization as a network of interacting components. Change is intrinsic to this network: patterns of interactions between these components change, new components are introduced, existing ones are removed.

In spite of numerous recent volumes concerned with business processes, most do not attempt to define the nature of process. It is taken as axiomatic that the *man in the street* definition of the term will suffice. We reason that not only do we need to understand the term properly but we need to do so in a number of different domains. Process technology needs to support the understanding, the representation and the performing of processes. Thus we set out to explain the term in a number of appropriate domains.

There are, of course, any number of fashionable current process initiatives. Most practitioners generally take the view that IT is a central concern, indeed is somehow pivotal to future developments and, yet, the nature of this IT system is not elaborated. IT is viewed as some fixed entity which, although central, is non-negotiable.

We thus attempt to elaborate the properties of IT systems which allow them to be better integrated with the modern business systems which result from an application of a modern process-centric initiative. In so doing we hope that the current notions and limitations of IT systems will become evident.

The book is, in some senses, borne out of frustration. Frustration that there has been a considerable lack of exploitation of the fact that software is after all *soft,* that it is *malleable.* Some 30 years of software engineering has largely been spent in trying to make software *harder,* that is more amenable to management in the same way that hardware has been controlled, rather than seeking to exploit its inherent softness. Our approach seeks to provide a framework within which software systems can be developed in such a way as to enable subsequent evolution throughout their useful lives. Further we actively seek to exploit software's ability to change in order that software systems can become more personalized, but even more significantly, can be used to liberate business processes so that they can better respect the creative rights of individuals.

Obviously a book such as this embodies many of the beliefs and prejudices of its authors. We believe that understanding business processes offers a way of developing a closer match between business objectives, the people involved, and the IT systems which support them. We believe that such improvements are needed to reap the full rewards of the ongoing IT revolution. Just as a process model which cannot evolve to cope with the inevitable business and technological changes is limited in value, so is this book. We hope that readers will take up the challenge of evolving our method in the light of their experience, just as we shall evolve it in the light of ours.

I owe an enormous debt of gratitude to my fellow authors. They provided the sweat and guile which both converted my arm-waving strategies into implementation reality and resulted in the majority of the text for this book.

Brian Warboys
Manchester, England, October 1998

Part One

Concepts

1

Introduction

This chapter provides a rough map of the rest of the book. First, the broad problem domain of organizations and their information systems is outlined. The chapters are described briefly, illustrating the relationship between the book's two parts: Concepts and Practice. There are also some hints which should prove useful to readers on their journey through the book.

1.1 Overview

A modern organization will typically involve many people and many business information systems. Both people and information systems are critical to an organization's effectiveness. The concept of *process* is a powerful way of understanding how an organization works. By identifying key objectives we can begin to discern patterns of activity, and understand the reasons for people working together, exchanging information and using specific business information systems. The broad concern of this book is with the development of organizations. Its focus is upon the development of the business information systems which support an organization's processes. The problem domain is seen to be one of complex systems made up of people and technology. This book describes an approach to the study of the relationships between people, between people and tools, and between tools.

1.2 Organizations and their Software

If we think about a modern organization, we probably picture a building filled with people at desks. These people interact with each other. They each have goals which they seek to fulfil by carrying out activities, by making requests of others, by delegating and by carrying out certain activities in order to satisfy some request. People interact with each other inside the organization; they also interact with many people outside the organization. They also interact with software systems.

Many organizations are software-rich. Their software systems are a critical medium for the interactions between people. This software-mediated interaction can be indirect. For example, one person places something in a database which another person makes use of in some other context. Increasingly software-mediated interaction can be direct. For example, two clerks in an insurance company might be linked by a workflow system; email may carry the hub of an organization's shared thoughts; a groupware system might be used to facilitate meetings. Then, of course, these days any organization is likely to be housed in more than one building. An organization might have different offices in different countries and continents, staff may work from home or on the road between the offices of clients. Telecommunications devices and software mounted on laptop computers might in effect *be* the infrastructure of the organization.

Organizations are increasingly dependent on a wide variety of software tools for their effectiveness. Organizations are complex systems made up of people and technology, and their effectiveness depends on the ways in which people and technology work together. People interact with people, people interact with software applications, software applications interact with software applications. Appreciating this complexity, we put great emphasis on the modelling of behaviour so that we can understand the contribution that software can make to help the people in an organization work effectively. Such modelling work is the core of this book. Our goals are business information systems which provide effective support for the process as a whole, rather than just assisting individuals with their tasks. The requirement for such systems will inevitably increase as people become more and more used to communicating and collaborating through their computers.

Organizations do not stand still. They change in response to commercial opportunities, advances in technology, and sometimes legislative changes. Recognizing that organizations are not only complex but dynamic, we appreciate that there is no such thing as the *right* system. A complex software system is cast according to organizational goals. Not only do we have to judge the software system against these goals but we have to consider the validity of the goals themselves. The fact that organizations are dynamic means that their goals change. We are faced with a conundrum. Discrete, static software systems must be shaped to serve explicit and implicit goals and yet these goals that they serve are dynamic and transitory. The conclusion must be that software systems should be evolvable so that they can be used satisfactorily in environments of changing circumstance. We introduce an approach to evolving processes.

The most common reason for organizations to model their processes is to understand where they are and to reflect upon where they might be. A process model can help individuals to identify how their contribution fits into the wider picture, and can enable potential new ways of working to be communicated and critiqued. Process models can also represent the relationship between an organization and the business information systems it uses. In this context a process model has two faces: it reflects the people involved and how their activities are coordinated, and it reflects the systems used and how they contribute. This enables people to look beyond how individual activities are supported by Information Technology (IT) and consider how business information systems could support the complete process.

1.3 Background

At the heart of this book is the mediation between organizational need and technical capability. We draw on a number of related areas and apply them to this crucial problem.

The relationship between the people doing the work and the business information systems which support them is obviously a socio-technical issue. There is a social system: the people doing the work, and a technical system: the IT systems they use. We draw on systems concepts to establish the rationale for the modelling work. This system focus clarifies the emphasis on the process as a whole, rather than on individual tasks within it.

There is a significant body of related work in software engineering, in particular in the evolution of large software systems, and in the modelling of the software development process. The use of models to communicate and critique different software development processes is well established. There has also been considerable experience of the use of software engineering environments to support the various parties in the software process.

Recently there has been considerable interest in process through so-called Business Process

Re-engineering (BPR) initiatives. Its practitioners generally take the view that IT is a central concern, indeed is somehow pivotal to future developments and, yet, the nature of these IT systems is not elaborated. IT is viewed as a fixed entity which although central is non-negotiable. This contrasts with our focus on the ongoing relationship between the business process and its business information systems.

We take the view that reaping the full benefits of IT depends both upon being able to express the business processes and understanding how these processes can be supported by business information systems. The problem is not one of recording and accessing information but rather of what to look for and where to find it. This general problem is one which faces us all. as the amount of accessible information grows.

An immediate and obvious approach is to employ some *browsing* system that does the hard work of retrieving what we wish to see. However, most of what we want to see is conditioned by the events which define the work or social context in which the search is made. Thus we might wish to discover the information which has lead to the current situation in which we find ourselves and further what information we might need to make the right decision in this situation. This is not a passive query, the situation is a dynamic one essentially conditioned by the processes which we and others have exercised previously. Our scope for future action is again conditioned by other processes. Thus we take the view that process is central to the management of information and hence central to our very business and social existence.

1.4 Readership

The target audiences of this book are students of information systems, process modelling and process-based technology in the broadest sense. This includes those with an IT background who are interested in the socio-technical problems of ensuring that IT solutions match organizational needs. It also includes those of a business background who want a better understanding of the dependencies between a business and its IT systems.

This target audience includes postgraduate students and researchers in the field of business process modelling and technology, and many in the fields of software engineering and information systems. Most of the material has been used on a M.Sc module which includes both students with an existing computer science background, and those who are enhancing their previous science-based degree with computing qualifications. The material has also been used by students in projects modelling organizations and their information systems. The practical element has made these projects popular with students.

1.5 Structure of the Book

This book is divided into two parts: Concepts and Practice.

The Concepts part describes the foundations on which the approach is built. The Positioning chapter describes the problem domain, and places process modelling in the context of systems thinking, information systems, and the evolutionary development of software systems. It distils two themes, interaction and evolution, which are central to our process approach. The Process Concepts chapter describes the different views of processes, and the different domains in which the term *process* can be defined. It discusses the differences between static models which represent a snapshot or overview of a process, and active models which represent the current state of a process in real-time. It also introduces the idea of process evolution and a *meta-process*.

The final chapter of part one, Engineering of Processes, explains the need for an engineering approach to producing effective information systems to support business processes, and the limitations of such an engineering approach are reviewed. These concerns are placed first in the book because it is easier to apply our approach effectively with an understanding of the ideas which lie behind it. This part will be of particular interest to those who wish to adapt the approach to their own particular circumstances, or to compare it with other approaches.

The core of the book is the Practice part. Practice involves understanding, and improving, the match between an organization's processes and its business information systems. The Nature of the Method Chapter introduces this as a socio-technical activity, and describes the implementation concepts of our approach: the Organizational Process Modelling (OPM) method, the co-ordination layer, and the Process for Process Evolution (P2E) meta-process. It also introduces the case study which is used throughout this part. The case study has been adapted from a number of studies which have been influential in developing the approach. The Process Contexts Chapter describes how the particular organizational circumstances influence the application of our approach. Understanding these influences is important because the effectiveness of the approach depends upon moulding it to the organization's circumstances. For this book the case study provides this organizational setting.

The OPM method is described in the chapters Process Capture and Process Design. Process Capture involves developing models which illustrate how people and software systems interact to address business goals. Process Design builds on process capture to develop active models which can be used to coordinate people and software tools within an organization. Such models can provide a process-sensitive coordination layer within an IT infrastructure. A distinctive feature of our approach is the aim that these models should be evolvable to cope with inevitable changes. The Process Managing chapter deals with this aspect and how it can be addressed through the P2E meta-process.

Providing a process-sensitive layer within an IT infrastructure involves using technology to support processes as a whole rather than simply the activities within them. The Process Support Technology chapter introduces the key features of process technologies. Our approach is essentially technology-independent. Indeed with the developments in multimedia, virtual reality intranet and internet systems, new and exciting possibilities are emerging. We exploit one specific technology to illustrate how a process-sensitive coordination layer can be realized. A key reason behind this choice is its ability to support controlled evolution.

The previous chapters have used the case study as a background for describing the approach. The value of the approach to an organization comes from the value of the results of its application. The OPM Case Study chapter provides a coherent view of the results of applying OPM to the case study.

1.6 Related Web Pages

There is a web site which has been developed in association with this book at:

http://www.mcgraw-hill.co.uk/warboys

These pages provide graphical user interfaces which enable interested readers to interact with a number of interactive models, some based on the case study in the book. This should give a flavour of what is possible with a business information system based on an active model. Some information about the technology involved and the models is given in Chapter 10. The up-to-date information on the interactive models will be available on the web site. As our process approach is technology-independent, readers do not need to access the web-based models to understand the book. However, we believe that many will find these models to be useful concrete examples.

We plan to develop the web site: making further examples available, providing links to related information which may be of interest to readers, and in response to feedback.

1.7 Using the Book

Readers will place more emphasis on specific parts depending on their interests. Those involved in modelling an organization and its information systems will concentrate on Practice. They could start with the practice part and dip into the concepts part when needed. However we would recommend at least a quick read of the Positioning chapter first.

Readers learning about systems thinking and process modelling will be interested in both parts; they might find it is useful to look through the case study at an early stage.

Readers who have some familiarity with process modelling and wish to evaluate our approach should read the concepts part to understand the thinking behind the approach.

2

Positioning

The focus of this book is upon the software support of organizations, the role that the software systems play in the organization and how their behaviour is attuned to the behaviour of the organization as a whole. This motivates an investigation of the nature of these organizations. The problem domain is conceptualized as being one of complex systems made up of people and technology. This chapter sets the scene for the description of an approach to the study of the relationships among people and tools. It promotes a process approach which, at its most simple, can be understood as giving a way of studying the behaviour of systems. Through process modelling, the approach looks at interactions, the goals they serve and the way in which these goals are fulfilled. This chapter introduces the concerns of the book and positions them amidst an array of other work. It makes reference to some well-known and some not so well-known thinking.

2.1 Introduction

Here the intention is to explore some fundamentals, beginning with a number of observations about organizations as they are today. Next we look outward to established views and to underlying theory. This chapter ends by noting some of the concerns which seem to be prominent in the modern organization as people develop new structures, new technologies and new relationships. Along the way we explore some concepts and develop a useful set of terms. It is a *positioning* chapter.

The ultimate concern of the book is the development of organizations. Organizations are fundamental to our lives as human beings. We belong to some and *interact with* many. The modern study of organizations is dominated by issues of complexity and change. Different organizational forms are advocated as the perceived environment changes. Indeed, organizations not only seek to adapt to their environment but also endeavour to define it. Organizations face the need to innovate, to replicate and to extemporize. These pressures seem to affect one and all; it is not just businesses but many kinds of organizations that find it necessary to define and then re-define their purpose and structure. Of course, in the open marketplace conditions can be especially acute. These days even big businesses, the household names, are vulnerable. Their successes can be short-lived, they make well-publicized mistakes and, sometimes, they fail spectacularly. It seems that today, in this uncertain world, the study of organizations is very important.

The direct lineage of this work comes not from organizational theory or management but from software engineering. The focus of the book is upon software systems and the design of their contribution to the organization. The need to relate software systems to broader issues of organization should not, actually, be surprising. Technology has always been utilized by organizations and by virtue of this has helped to shape the form of these organizations. Today, the most significant organizational technology is the computer.

Thus, it can be stated that any study of software systems in organizations has necessarily to be concerned with both the nature of software and the nature of the human organization which it serves. The form of the human organization affects the form of the software system, which in turn affects the process of its development. Interestingly, the principle is also true in reverse. The software system affects the form of the human organization and thence the process of its development. Whichever way you look at it, at some level the engineering of software systems must relate to the management and development of human organizational systems. Hence, from software engineering a connection is made to organizational theory and management just as, it is to be hoped, these and other disciplines link across to each other and to software engineering. This is actually a very obvious point; different disciplines must connect in the grander organization of learning and knowledge. The connections can be understood by *abstraction*, by understanding the problem as a greater whole. Mental abstraction is a sort of journey. It is akin to putting physical distance between your vantage point and the object you study; for example we can actually understand *some* aspects of the Earth's climate more easily from space than from the Earth itself. A more complete picture can then be drawn by synthesis of this abstract view with the detail of occurrences as they are experienced *on the ground*; that is, to understand both the rolling movement of the clouds and the sensation of the splash of rain.

2.2 Organizations

If we return to our depiction of a modern organization, we again see a building filled with people at desks. Observing that these people interact with each other, we are able to identify goals which they seek to fulfil by carrying out activities, by making requests of others, by delegating and by carrying out activities in order to satisfy some request. We feel confident that we can characterize organizations as purposeful structures of human collaboration. We note that equally, as people interact with each other inside the organization, so too they interact with many people outside the organization. They also interact with software. Of course, many of today's organizations are software-rich. Chapter 1 has described how software systems are a critical medium for the interactions among people. The daily operations of modern organizations might be carried out from different offices in different countries, from clients' offices, from people's homes and the hotel rooms of business travellers. Thus it can be seen that the increasing variety of software systems that are deployed in modern organizations (e.g. applications, databases, groupware, internet etc.), constitute a vital coordinative infrastructure for these organizations.

It is not just that software systems are becoming more significant in modern organizations, but that the form of the software system is changing. This in turn fuels, and is fuelled by, the drive to new ways of working, new strategies and new products. Today, many organizations' software systems, rather than converging towards some finely tuned ideal, are becoming increasingly large and diffuse. Commonly, they are constructed not only from many modules but from many programs. Discrete tools such as bespoke corporate applications, generic word processors and databases are called upon to serve routine and ad hoc activities. The high costs of developing bespoke software systems leads to a requirement that they be long-lived. This in turn means that their scope, functionality and the assumptions embedded within them are more likely to be breached by new needs which result from broader organizational changes. These changes occur, sometimes with rapidity, as the organization seeks to survive, to compete and to innovate. At the same time, the number of solutions available in some generic form *off the shelf* continues to multiply. As it becomes increasingly easy to obtain and apply software tools in organizations, so there are increased risks; integrity is endangered, there is a greater likelihood of redundancy between applications and there are new threats to usability through the necessity of working with several non-integrated and possibly heterogeneous devices. These several pressures suggest that when considered as a whole, organizational software systems may increasingly be characterized as heterogeneous, of different ages, part bespoke, part general purpose and dynamic.

Inevitably the concern for the software support of organizations translates into a need to understand complex systems where there are many people and many software applications that get things done by interacting with each other. People interact with people, people interact with software tools, software tools interact with software tools. Appreciating this complexity we put great emphasis on the modelling of behaviour so that we can understand the contribution that software can make to the people in the organization. Modelling is *intrinsic* to the comprehension of complexity. We have cognitive models (or maps) in our heads. The various processes of graphical modelling, discussion, writing and picture drawing serve as fodder to these cognitive models and help to align those of one team member with those of another. The comparison of mental models (as sets of assumptions) against perceptions of reality can lead to the revision of the cognitive models as well as precipitating and guiding some intervention in the *real* environment. Hence, learning is facilitated through modelling.

The definition of the behaviour of software programs is also intrinsically a modelling discipline. In one sense a program can be understood to be a statement of beliefs about the behaviour that should take place under certain circumstances. Logic allows us to verify the internal consistency of the program. However, the validity of the beliefs upon which this behaviour is founded will always, to some degree, be elusive. If our software system is to play a role in a human organization, it requires that the wider implications of the behaviour of the program within its environment be understood precisely. This is actually a most formidable task! It requires both the comprehension of extraordinary complexity and the gift of foresight. For not only may the environment be incomprehensibly complicated, it will also be unpredictably dynamic. In fact, we rely upon highly abstract models of the relationship between programs and their environment to guide the development of the program. As we can never be totally confident of the validity of these models, it seems vital that we are able to gather feedback from the domain of application and to revise the models. In other words, *we need to learn* and, as we do, the software systems under our control must evolve or be replaced.

This book describes a simple modelling approach. It relates a complex software system to the organizational goals which are sought through its use. The fact that organizations are dynamic means that their goals change. This raises the conundrum wherein discrete, static software systems must be shaped to serve explicit and implicit goals, and yet these goals that they serve are dynamic and transitory. This motivates us to introduce an approach to evolution in this book.

2.2.1 Interaction and Goals

As a starting position for our modelling of organizational behaviour, we can depict an organization as a complex system of interacting agents who each have goals. This may seem somewhat removed from the exhilarating, emancipatory, sterile, turgid or tempestuous organizational life that many will recognize. It is, however, a very useful starting point. We use the concept of a goal-seeking, interacting agent to describe the contribution of people to the organization. The level of concern being somewhat higher than the more humble notion of an *entity*.

At its most abstract, through the notion of interaction we understand the points of contact, what we can call the *relationship*, of different elements in a system. In a general systems context, by *element* we might mean cells in an organism or IT systems interacting through the world wide web. In fact, given our organizational remit, the elements which we believe to be *most important* are people. For example, bank customers interact with bank tellers, bank tellers interact with other bank tellers, with foreign currency clerks and with bank managers. These are observable patterns of behaviour which we all can recognize and can therefore give explicit form to in a model.

It seems certain that the physical act of standing in a bank waiting to interact with a human bank teller will in the future be a far less commonplace event than it has been in the past. This is, of course, due to the impact of various technologies, many of which have already revolutionized banking organizations. For example, automated tellers, telephone banking and card currency all diminish the need to interact over a counter with a bank teller, as pleasant or unpleasant as that experience may be. However, the goals served by our visit to the bank have tended to persist. People still need to open accounts, close accounts, make balance enquiries, request loans, make deposits and withdrawals, exchange currency, seek advice and request clarification. It is just that people are able to redefine their relationship with the bank, they are able to do these things using new means.

This brings us to a consideration of goals. If we want to understand more than just the existence and media of interactions, if we want to begin to understand their meanings, then we need to understand the goals that they serve. Goals are important to us here, in this book, because in developing complex IT systems which serve humans, we use goals as a way of understanding interactions and grouping like interactions. We can describe the interactions people enter into (with each other or with software tools) by describing the goals of the people involved. Thus, the system which we are investigating is made up of people who interact with each other and who undertake what we can consider to be *purposeful action*. The concept of the *purposeful system* from which our observations are derived is an important one. References will be made to it later. From here onwards we can take, in our terminology, the possession of a *goal* and the possession of a *purpose* to be synonymous.

What goal does a customer have when interacting with a bank teller? What goal does the bank teller have when interacting with a customer? By asking questions such as these we are able to describe interactions and, in so doing, we are able to take a participative approach wherein people are asked to summarize their goals for us. However, we can also usefully use goals to describe even non-human or inanimate systems. For example, even an interaction between cells in an organism might be said to serve some goal. Similarly, we might describe an interaction among IT systems over the world wide web as serving some goal. In these cases it is you, the observer, who describes the purpose of the non-human system.

This, in the simplest sense, has been a summary of the basis of our investigation of process. When we talk of using a process perspective we are talking of an investigation of agents that are interactive and goal-seeking. These agents represent people.

2.3 The Themes of this Book

The process approach espoused throughout this book is essentially concerned with codifying and modelling the behaviour of organizations. For the purposes of this book we can understand the term *process* to refer to some pattern of behaviour of a system. The subject domain is the *organization* where this is taken to refer to a special kind of system, i.e. one where many people are involved in a network of interactions with each other and with the technology that they use in their day-to-day activities.

Out of the many concerns which we have touched upon already, we can distil two themes to describe the heart of this book.

• Interaction – organizations are understood to be composed of elements which coordinate with each other. The notion of an interaction is used to explore this coordinative behaviour. Each interaction has a goal and a place in a network of interactions. Interactions can lead to activities which fulfil the goal of the interaction. In this way, interaction provides a goal-driven needs/capabilities framework for the investigation.

• Evolution – organizations are understood to be dynamic. The goals which motivate patterns of interaction may change. This leads to new patterns of interaction. Many organizations are dependent upon software systems. Software systems are static and discrete. Paradoxically therefore software *support* systems might in some circumstances thwart the dynamism of the organization. One response is that software systems should be developed within an evolutionary framework. A control process which relates goal change to technical capability is proposed. This is a meta-level consideration of process (a *meta-process*).

We shall return to these as we progress. The rest of the chapter looks briefly to contemporary debates and thinking about organizations and their software support.

2.3.1 The Rest of this Chapter

From here on this chapter does two things. It explores the basis of the process approach by reference to systems concepts. These give a rich taxonomy of ideas which can be used to describe observations and thoughts. The chapter then positions related and comparative work which is concerned with the development and use of software systems in organizations.

2.4 Systems Theory

The term *system* can be given many meanings. The development of systems theory has not led to an obviously consistent usage of the term. Amongst systems theoreticians there are a number of different definitions of the term *system*. Some of these will be explored later. In everyday language, the meanings of concepts such as *system, holism* and thence the *holon* have been transmuted for application in different contexts. In the computing sphere, there are domains of interest such as *information systems*, *systems analysis* and *systems engineering* which seem to adopt quasi-systems-theoretical stances. Within and among these interests the term *system* may be used to refer to different things. The *Oxford Dictionary of Computing* (1990) recognizes this in declaring of *system*: 'In computing the word is widely used with many shades of meaning. Most commonly, however, it may refer to a related set of hardware units, or programs, or both.'

The purpose of describing systems theory is to pursue a more general characterization of the properties a system has, and to understand this *process approach* as a *systems approach*. In doing this it will become possible to start to coalesce a shared understanding of process modelling.

The following sub-sections are presented:

• Origins. This describes the origins of systems theory in different fields and the attempts to unify the concepts in *General System Theory*.

• Criticisms and utility. The distillation of a General System Theory proved problematical and led to substantial criticisms. However it is noted that it is argued that systems concepts are likely to be useful and developed through application in discrete subject domains. The application of systems concepts to human organizational issues is noted with special reference to Soft Systems Methodology. It is concluded that this process-modelling approach is concerned with technical issues in social contexts and that it must interface to a consideration of *soft* issues.

- Characterizations of *system*. Through reference to a number of different definitions it is concluded that a system has elements, relations between elements, behaviour and purpose. These attributes form the basis for the process modelling approach adopted later in this book.

- The adaptive whole. Checkland (1981) describes a system as an adaptive whole and proposes that *organized* complexity is the subject matter of systems theory. A more detailed characterization of systems is then developed through reference to two pairs of ideas: hierarchy and emergence, communication and control.

- Open and autopoietic systems. The concept of an *adaptive whole* leads readily to that of an *open system* i.e. one which interacts with its environment. The open system concept is commonly applied as a metaphor for organizations. An autopoietic system is one which promotes its identity through a closed set of relations. Applying autopoiesis as a metaphor for organizations emphasizes that they must be structurally equipped to interact. The inference is that new interactions and revised identity rely upon structural change at a number of different levels, including that of software support.

- Systems theory and the investigation of organizational process. Using systems thinking, the organization can be characterized through the goals that precipitate interactions among people, the interactions which take place and the activities which result. In so doing the frame of reference for the process approach is enlarged to include the coordination of people and tools as a central element as opposed to traditional models of data and function.

2.4.1 Origins

At least in a formal sense, systems theory is still relatively new. Its origins stem principally from biology, for example through the early work of Weiss (Koestler and Smythies, 1969) in which he proposed a general systems theory of animal behaviour. However, von Bertalanffy (1971) is justified in stating that, 'Independently of each other, similar problems and conceptions have evolved in widely different fields.' Wilson (1990) suggests that alongside biology the particularly significant advances took place in systems engineering methodology in the post-war years. He describes how market pressures meant that manufacturing companies had to develop and operate processes that were highly efficient. The systems engineering methodologies that resulted attempted to, '...integrate the effects of interactions between the process units themselves, between the process being designed and others on which it depended and between the interacting set of processes and the market environment being served' (Wilson, 1990).

The idea of a general system theory is generally accredited to von Bertalanffy (1971), although the earlier work of the Russian scientist Bogdanov has recently received increased attention (Capra, 1996). To date, however, the progress of systems thinking in Western society is more often credited to von Bertalanffy's General System Theory (1971) than to Bogdanov's *tektology*. Through von Bertalanffy's work, systems theory took on a generalist stance, not confined to biology or even the natural sciences but also to social sciences, management and the like.

2.4.2 Criticisms and Utility

This generalist stance led to significant and sustained criticism of systems theory. This criticism focuses upon the failure to rigorously establish *general* system concepts beyond the laws of mathematics. Emery (1981) states that General System Theory, '...has so far failed to further its unifying mission.' Checkland (1981) proposes that, 'Progress in the systems movement seems more likely to come from the use of systems ideas within specific problem areas than from the development of overarching theory.'

Systems theory has been developed and extended by its application to human organizations. Notable works in this domain include those by Ackoff (1981) and Beer (1979). The work of Checkland (1981), Checkland and Scholes (1990) and Wilson (1990), extends the *hard* systems concepts which arise from engineering and biology to *soft* problems through Soft Systems Methodology (SSM). Thus systems thinking is applied to issues arising in human organizations where unequivocal solutions cannot be identified and where there is a requirement to reconcile competing perspectives. These developments have in turn have been referenced in the development of critical systems perspectives (Flood and Jackson, 1991).

A fundamental principle of this process approach is that the value of software systems has to be understood in social terms. For example, the success/failure/utility/uselessness of a software system in a government department has to be accounted for in relation to soft aspects such as the collective and individual goals of its users. In such a scenario, soft systems approaches permit the reconciliation of different views of purpose or the triumph of one particular statement of goals over alternatives. The significance of this work on soft problems has been widely noted. This book does not contribute to these concerns but starts some way further down the line. It starts where there is a statement of goals which are used to describe and define software capability. That these goals may themselves be reassessed and redefined is one of the reasons why an approach to evolution is introduced.

This process-modelling approach can therefore be characterized as being concerned with technical issues in social contexts. It interfaces to a gamut of other process and systems thinking where issues that are neglected here are given their due weight. It seeks flexible and comprehensible software systems that conform to the operational goals of the people in an organization but does not seek to tell you what the best process is for your business. Thus, the focus is upon the software support of an organization and, appreciating the systemic nature of the problem, how this contributes to the wider problem domain.

Some further thinking about systems should help to make this clear.

2.4.3 Characterizations of System

The biologist Weiss devised a simple formula to describe the systems character of a cell. He suggests:

> '...a complex is a system if the variance of the features of the whole collective is significantly less than the sum of variances of its constituents.'
>
> Weiss, 1969

Elsewhere, Wilson has described a system as:

> '...first of all a set; i.e. it contains elements that have some reason for being taken together rather than some others. But it is more than just a set, it also includes the relationships which

exist between elements of that set.'

Wilson, 1990

This is a simple, useful description. It gives us two fundamental aspects of a system; its elements and the relationships between them. Beishon and Peters take a similar position. They describe a system in the following way:

'a set of objects together with relationships between the objects and between their attributes connected or related to each other and to their environment in such a manner as to form an entirety or whole.'

Beishon and Peters, 1976

Ackoff (1976) gives a neat summary when he describes a system simply as, 'a set of interrelated elements.' Elsewhere (Wardman, 1994), he suggests that a system is not the sum of its parts, '...it is the product of their interactions.' He also stipulates three conditions to which a system must conform. First, the behaviour of each element has an effect on the behaviour of the whole. Secondly, the behaviour of the elements and their effects on the whole are interdependent. Thirdly, sub-groups of elements may be formed and these also must conform to the first two conditions (Ackoff, 1981).

These four definitions are all useful and help to make it obvious that the system has *behaviour*. It is not a static construction of elements but a dynamic whole in which different elements engage in different relationships under many different conditions. Beer (1979) highlights behaviour in his definition of a system. He describes a system as, 'a group of elements dynamically related in time according to some coherent pattern.' It is also important to him, as a management cybernetician, to add that a system has purpose. It is a difficult notion, admittedly, but for Beer purpose is accredited to a system by its human observer. To Checkland and Scholes (1990), purpose is intrinsic to human activity. Human beings attribute meanings to what they see and do. Therefore, systems of human activity are inherently purposeful.

Little by little a jigsaw is assembled: a system has elements, relations between elements, behaviour and purpose. These different pieces of the jigsaw define the basis for the process approach which is presented later.

2.4.4 The Adaptive Whole

Checkland (1981) utilizes each of these pieces of the jigsaw in developing an interesting summation of the nature of a system. He describes a system as an adaptive whole and proposes that *organized* complexity is the subject matter of systems theory. He characterizes systems through two pairs of ideas: emergence and hierarchy, and communication and control. These are important concepts. Checkland distils them from biology, control engineering and communication engineering.

Emergent properties exist at a certain level of a hierarchy but are meaningless at another, lower level. Biology gives the best basis for exploration of the concepts of emergence and hierarchy. In living things there is a recognizable hierarchy of structures in the sequence molecules, organelles, cells, organs and the organism. The organism itself is the apex of the hierarchy because it intuitively marks a boundary, that of the living whole, even though there may be transports across this boundary. Within the hierarchy the cell plays a special role as the power of reproduction is not available to any single molecule by itself but only becomes manifest in the cell. Thereby, we see that certain properties exist at one level of the hierarchy but not at a lower level. To develop the point, emergent properties are *meaningless* at a lower level of description. For example, the shape of an apple, although the result of processes which operate at the level of cells, organelles and molecules and ultimately explicable in terms of those processes, is a property which is meaningless at the lower levels of description. These lower-level processes result in an outcome which is a stable level of complexity having emergent properties, one of them being the apple's shape. Thus, although any arrangement of the organic bases is compatible with the laws of physics and chemistry, in biology the actual arrangement is crucial. Checkland goes on to suggest that this idea that, '...the architecture of complexity is hierarchical and that different languages of description are required at different levels has in recent years led to a developing interest in hierarchy theory.' He cites an argument from Simon (1981), which shows that the time required for the evolution of a complex form from single elements depends critically upon the numbers and distribution of intermediate forms which are themselves stable. Therefore Checkland concludes, 'Hierarchies are characterized by processes of control operating at the interfaces between levels.'

This leads to a consideration of Checkland's second pair of ideas: communication and control. To understand these ideas and why they are regarded as inseparable requires reference to the study of cybernetics initiated by Wiener (1950, 1961). Wiener classes communication and control together and justifies this position in the following way:

> 'When I communicate with another person, I impart a message to him, and when he communicates back with me he returns a related message which contains information primarily accessible to him and not to me. When I control the actions of another person, I communicate a message to him, and although the message is in the imperative mood, the technique of communication does not differ from that of a message of fact. Furthermore, if my control is to be effective I must take cognizance of any messages from him which may indicate that the order is understood and has been obeyed...in the future development of these messages and communication facilities, messages between man and machines, between machines and man, and between machine and machine, are destined to play an ever-increasing part.'

Wiener, 1950

Checkland describes how Wiener's research came to focus upon the importance and ubiquity of the concept of feedback. This stemmed from a research project undertaken by Wiener at the beginning of World War Two which aimed to improve the accuracy of anti-aircraft guns. Feedback is the transmission of information about the performance of any machine to an earlier stage in order to review, and possibly modify its performance. A distinction can be made between negative and positive feedback. Negative feedback acts to reduce the difference between actual and desired performance as when the increasing speed of a steam engine causes the flying pendulum of the governor to reduce the steam supply and hence lower the speed. Positive feedback induces instability through reinforcement of a modification in performance. For example, two people in a crowded room might conduct a conversation in louder and louder tones, inducing a higher level of noise in the room, making it increasingly difficult for them to hear each other, and causing them to speak more loudly. To Wiener these apparently dissimilar problems, the accuracy of anti-aircraft guns, the regulation of a steam engine and two people conversing in a noisy room, were all related to the abstract notion of a message and its transmission. Although the practical application of cybernetics research has focused upon controllers for man-made systems, Wiener recognized the consistency of the concepts across the mechanical and biological domains. Thus, Wiener defined cybernetics as, '...the entire field of control and communication theory whether in the machine or in the animal' (Checkland, 1981).

2.4.5 Open and Autopoietic Systems

The concept of an open system is amongst the most significant systems concept to come from biological research and to be used to represent human organizations. The concept can be used to describe how an organization engages in a critical, life-sustaining exchange with its environment. It is, again, an adaptive whole.

Morgan describes open systems in the following way:

> 'Organic systems at the level of the cell, the complex organism, and the population of organisms exist in a continuous exchange with their environment. This exchange is crucial for sustaining the life and form of the system, since environmental interaction is the basis of self-maintenance...Environment and system are to be understood as being in a state of interaction and mutual dependence...Towers, bridges, or even clockwork toys with predetermined motions are closed systems. A machine that is able to regulate its internal operation in accordance with variations in the environment may be considered a partially open system. A living organism, organization or social group is a fully open system.'
>
> Morgan, 1986

The open systems concept has crept into common usage as a metaphor for organizations. It describes organizations as undergoing decay if isolated from their environment. This simple point can be sustained by simple reference to the thirst of organizations for resources and custom in order that they can engage in the activity, that they can create the outputs, which give them meaning and identity. They depend upon interaction with their environment to sustain themselves. The dynamic of this interaction determines and then refines the form of the organization.

This is a very useful way of thinking about organizations and can be extended to consideration of the software system embedded within it. If software systems serve dynamic organizations then it follows that a change to the organizational environment represents a challenge to which the software system may be required to adapt. Clearly then, there is a need to be able to understand the mappings between the capabilities offered by the software system and the organizational context.

In so considering the nature of the organization, we have started to suggest that its identity is determined, at least to a degree, by the interactions it engages in with its environment. This position is worth emphasizing for it argues that the form of the organization itself is affected by its interactions with the environment and, by extension, the form of the each element of the organization is affected by its interaction with the environment.

The picture we are building, wherein organizational identity is founded upon environmental interaction, actually invites us to go beyond the open systems metaphor to the autopoietic. The open systems metaphor is useful but limited because it implies that the system is open to all stimuli. Organizations are clearly not like this. They respond only to those stimuli which they have the structure to recognize. The concept of *autopoiesis* describes the process of self-renewal wherein the identity of a system is maintained by a closed set of interactive behaviours. It is again a biological concept which was developed by Maturana and Varela (1980). They suggest that living systems are characterized by three principal features. These are autonomy, circularity and self-reference. Through these they contend that the aim of living systems is ultimately to produce themselves. The argument that living systems are autonomous means that we must understand that they seek to maintain their identity. All changes are linked to the maintenance of the structure of the living system as a given set of relations. They engage in circular patterns of interaction whereby a change to one element of the system is coupled with changes elsewhere. As the authors explain it:

'In a living system, the product of its operation is its own organization.'

Maturana and Varela, 1980

Maturana and Varela are cautious about the applicability of the concept of autopoiesis to social organizations. That caution accepted, we can refer to the concept of autopoiesis in undertaking a metaphorical exploration of an organization. For example, an insurance company can be described as engaged in a continuous pattern of interactions that are self-referential. It interacts with brokers, clients, re-insurance companies and so forth. Self-referentiality dictates that the organization cannot enter into a pattern of interactions that are not prescribed in the pattern of relations that define it as an organization. Thus, it cannot at a particular instant start interacting with people whose house is on fire because it is not internally defined as a fire-fighting organization. It cannot at a particular instant start interacting with people who want software products because it has not defined itself as a software providing organization. Thus, the interactions in which it does engage reflect and are part of the organization of the insurance organization itself. In other words, its environment is really a part of itself. The interactions which the organization engages in are defined in its structure and in this sense it is a closed system. In practical terms this forces us to consider how the interactions in which an organization engages are determined by the organizational structure. It also emphasizes the repetition of interactions and how, as a change in the environment occurs, there is a ripple effect as each component/sub-component responds through maintenance of its own structure in order to assert its identity. This ripple effect is circular. It can be observed on several levels. It is of a part and of the whole.

Applied as a metaphor for organizations, autopoiesis tells us how they must be *structurally equipped* to interact. New interactions and revised identity rely upon structural change.

2.4.6 Systems Theory and the Investigation of Organizational Process

Consider any organization: if we look at this organization externally in its context we will observe how it interacts with its environment. For example, if we again think about an insurance company we will note that it interacts with insurance brokers and with organizations of a special status (clients). That we can identify and classify the interactions of the insurance company leads us to infer that its external behaviour is somehow organized. The way in which it interacts with its environment is at least partially predictable. It is well worth betting that it will interact with insurance brokers far more often than it interacts with zoo keepers.

If we observe its internal behaviour we come to similar conclusions. We *lift the lid off it* and first of all note its complexity. Then we observe that it has elements which interact. For example, we note that there are risk-assessment experts who are known as *underwriters* and who interact with administrators. Many, though by no means all, of the interactions they engage in seem to conform to general patterns. For example, we note a regular occurrence of interactions between the underwriters and administrators. Each interaction is initiated by an underwriter communicating with an individual clerical assistant. This occurs in order that the details of a policy are logged in a database when they have finished negotiating a quote with a broker. This is a simple observation of goal ('in order that the details of a policy are logged in a database') and state ('when they have finished negotiating a quote with a broker'). We conclude that the insurance company is, to some degree, *organized*.

A longer study of this insurance company will reveal how these regular patterns of behaviour change. For example, the administrators might introduce a series of rationalizations of their work. One of these means that they will log all policies into the database in a batch. Although the underwriter still passes the policy details for the same purpose and at the same state, the clerical assistants no longer proceed to enter the details to the database there and then. Instead they put the policies together in a tray and in the afternoon, according to some rota, a particular clerical assistant enters all the details in one batch. In this example we see that an interaction is unaltered (between underwriter and clerical assistant) but that the activities which satisfy the goal of the interaction are changed. At another time, due to a fall in the share price of the organization, the operational management introduces a cost-cutting exercise. This is initially introduced as a pilot study to test its effectiveness. The clerical assistants are diverted to other duties and the underwriters are encouraged to log the policy details themselves. Here, at the point where previously an interaction existed, a number of additional activities are introduced to the underwriter's role.

This sketch has revealed a number of opportunities for us to characterize the insurance company as a system. We note that there are hierarchies (e.g. organization/ underwriting team/ underwriter) and that each level of a hierarchy has emergent properties (e.g. the organization has a share price, the underwriter does not). Communication is endemic (noted in all interactions, including those with software), and we can observe that there are examples of the action of control structures (e.g. in the action of some as yet unidentified authority which introduces and assesses the changes to the underwriters' role; the action of the clerical assistants who as a group rationalize their activities).

Throughout we observe the following general pattern:

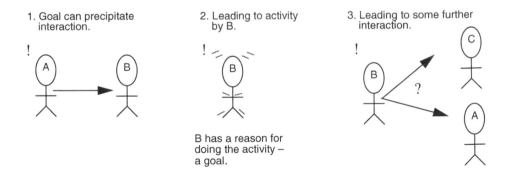

Fig. 2.1 A Goal, Interaction and Activity Model of Social Behaviour

This gives a broad basis from which to consider the contribution of software systems to an organization. The point is that the software takes part in and supports human activity. This embraces software support for interaction (communication and coordination of A and B) as well as activity (for example, the interaction with applications and databases used by B at point 2). The approach is hierarchical. There is a generic, recursive pattern of goals which precipitate interactions, which lead in turn to activities. Of course, throughout, as we try to understand the contribution software can make to the organization, much emphasis is placed upon the support of these activities. That is, what software capabilities does B need at point 2?

This little sketch of the insurance company should encourage us to unify our thinking about the organization as a structure and as a process. These two views are intimately related, indeed they are fundamentally bound together. As Capra puts it:

'Systems thinking is always process thinking.'

Capra, 1996

A useful accessory to this is given by the simple served and serving systems model proposed by Winter and Brown, (1994) and Winter et al., (1995). Software systems can be described as *serving systems* which serve human activity systems, *served systems*. For example, we can take an insurance office to represent a served system within which is located its information system, which is a serving system. Winter et al., point out that conventional views of the system development lifecycle are characteristically concerned with the development of just one system, the serving system. This is an unsustainable approach since, critically, the conceptualization of the served system affects the form of the serving system.

Winter et al. illustrate this through the example of a prison:
• If a prison is conceptualized as a system for rehabilitating law breakers then software systems may be required which assist the administration of counselling sessions, the booking of meaningful recreational activities and the learning and personal development of inmates.
• If a prison is conceptualized as a system for punishing law breakers then software systems may be required which assist the administration of punishment programmes (e.g. counting and recording the number of rocks broken!), the locking and securing of gates, and the policing of the environment to ensure that prisoners are quiet and obedient.

We can understand the relationship between served and serving systems through the activities that take place. In the insurance office example, activities such as 'acknowledge receipt of application', 'pass application to underwriter' and 'seek latest market information' may all be points of contact between the served and serving systems. In other words, each activity (e.g. 'acknowledge receipt of application') may be manifest as an interaction between served and serving systems (in this case perhaps between the clerical assistant and a word-processor).

The served and serving systems model has some similarity with the socio-technical model of organization. This describes the organizational system as being composed of two sub-systems, one which is social and the other which is technical. The central thesis is that changes to each sub-system may impact upon the other. Emery's phrase, 'joint optimization', neatly encapsulates this idea (Emery, 1959).

A constant in all that has been learned about software systems in organizations over many years is the fundamental idea that an IT system (or the technical part of an information system) is a thing that processes data. In taking this process approach and in drawing upon the socio-technical and served and serving systems models, the frame of reference for investigation is, to an extent, being redefined. Additional concerns are introduced and made central. These concern the ways in which software elements relate to the lives of people in the organization and even how software is applied to *knit* other software together into a meaningful support system for these people. Coordination is critical and hence, the frame of reference is made up of process coordination (many agents) as well as functions undertaken by single agents.

This can be expressed as a rich picture in the following way:

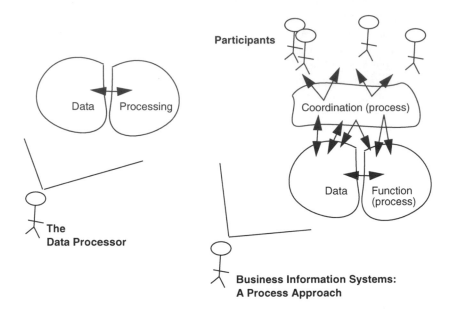

Fig. 2.2 Coordination, Function and Data

2.5 The Software Engineering Research Lineage

Software Engineering research and practice provides the direct lineage for this work and highlights several important issues and lessons. The discussion explores this lineage through the following sub-sections:

• Software process research. Reference is made to software process research where methods and technology for support of complex activities have been developed. This research has led to the development of process-centred software engineering environments (PSEEs) for the support of teams of programmers and designers.

• The enforcement versus flexibility debate. This presents an important design issue affecting software systems in general but which is particularly apparent in the design of PSEEs and workflow systems. It concerns the degree to which users should be given flexibility in using software systems or whether the systems should be used to enforce a process upon them.

• Evolutionary software systems. Theory relating to the evolutionary nature of software systems shows how the application of software systems can be intrinsically uncertain and affected by the dynamism of the application domain. This leads to the conclusion that a meta-level consideration of process is needed.

2.5.1 Software Process Research

The software development process (usually known simply as *the software process*) is an interesting, economically vital application domain characterized by the need to attain quality of output whilst working with a complex and malleable technology. In it we see the familiar pattern of people working with people, people working with software tools and software tools working with software tools.

The origins of the term software engineering are normally accredited to two NATO-sponsored workshops (Naur and Randell, 1969; Buxton and Randell, 1970). The motivation was the perception that software systems were becoming increasingly complex. It was suggested that an engineering method was necessary to guide their construction.

Since this time a number of important developments have taken place within software engineering. Lehman (1989) cites the advances gained through the development of high-level programming languages, the development and deployment of structured methods and then, in recognition of the need for rigorous specification of programs, the development and deployment of formal (mathematically defined) methods. Each of these advances is significant. However, Lehman (1991) argues that large programs have raised issues of variety, uncertainty, complexity and evolution that do not arise in the creation of small programs and therefore have not been extensively considered. Dowson (1993) concurs with this view and notes that although the discipline of an engineering approach became widely accepted in the 1970s, '...the industry's ambition – to producer larger, more complex systems – grew faster than its ability to manage larger projects and control the complexity of the systems they produced.' Thus, the study of the software process has become a discipline meriting considerable research effort within the broader software engineering domain (for example, Finkelstein et al., 1994; Derniame et al., 1999).

The IPSE 2.5 project was among the most UK prominent projects in this area. It sought the development of a support system which raised the level of integration above, '...the store-plus-tools' model (Snowdon, 1989). The supporting software system acts as an envelope to the stored data modules and various support tools which are used by team members, by serving these components to the users when the process achieves an appropriate state. It achieves this through what can be described as an *encoded process model*. This determines who can do what and when. This process model has enabled the development of understanding of, and ultimately support of, some of the various coordinative behaviours that take place among different software developers, software developers and their tools and among different tools. Clearly then, integration of activities and tools through coordinative software technology was the central concern of the IPSE 2.5 project. The lessons and concerns of this project have been discussed in a number of places (e.g. Warboys, 1990, 1991) and have been taken beyond the software process itself (e.g. Ould, 1995).

IPSE 2.5 is one of the earliest examples of a technology genus often known as the process-centred software engineering environments (PSEEs) (Lonchamp, 1993). According to Curtis et al., (1992) the motivation for the PSEE is the provision of 'embedded support for an orderly and defined software development process.' Thus the thinking is to extend the store-plus-tools level of support by an encoded process model (i.e. a definition) which is enactable, and thereby make the process orderly. A number of commentators have noted the similarity between this approach and the better-known workflow systems which are used in the general organizational context (Conradi et al., 1994; Fernström, 1992; Gruhn, 1994).

2.5.2 The Enforcement Versus Flexibility Debate

Summarizing the software process research domain, Wastell and Arbaoui (1996) are concerned with human issues, such as flexibility at work. The human issues centre upon the still-developing debate about whether it is useful to prescribe and enforce a detailed prescription of process though the support system. In some ways this is a test case for a broader battleground. Already, commentators such as Miers (1994) have raised concern about the programming-in of detailed business rules to some workflow applications in a diverse range of organizations. Workflow systems vary considerably, but the archetypal model has been of automated bureaucracy wherein the computer software is used to enforce a Taylorist paradigm (Taylor, 1911) on the office. Such a system provides a networking capability amongst users, routing tasks to these users and requiring their completion of standard forms and templates. Judged from the perspective of most users, such systems might dictate the progress and pattern of work. The end result can be that the user has little or no operational flexibility but is required to input to an externally defined quota of business cases. The battery-user has been invented!

A knee-jerk reaction is to argue that neither workflow, PSEE's nor any other type of software system should be used to enforce such a working regime on its users. A rationalization of this instinctive response can be forged from a number of empirical studies which suggest that operational flexibility is an indispensable part of work (e.g. Rodden et al., 1994; Sommerville and Monk, 1994; Wastell et al., 1994). Cybernetic theory (Beer, 1974, 1979) can also be used to expose the irrationality of highly constraining software systems. In brief, the theory shows that operational flexibility is always necessary, because from the perspective of the regulator the activities of the regulated cannot be understood in detail. These activities are too complex. However, conversely, freedom can also be lost in the absence of regulation. For example, it is globally reported that where governments seek to maximize the personal mobility of the individual and promote car ownership to do so, traffic congestion results. The net result may then be that personal mobility is hindered and not helped. This is because the design for freedom (promote car ownership) is poor. A better design relies on a slightly higher level of intervention and might use the car plus real-time traffic routing, the train, tram, bus and bicycle. Therefore whilst overly constraining users has obviously undesirable effects, so too under-constraining users (having no coordination or cohesion in the system) can also be detrimental. From these dual pressures comes the requirement that freedom be *designed*. In this we allude to another debate which we cannot touch upon here. It asks: *Who does the designing?*

These design issues have been highlighted in relation to the support of the software process and to workflow but actually affect *all* forms of software systems employed in organizations. To the PSEE and workflow the issues are clearly fundamental (this may in a way be a benefit as the designer is forced to recognize them). It seems that to be able to use any form of software support in a flexible and contingent manner can be highly beneficial (or vital?) to users and organizations. The usability, applicability and effectiveness of systems can be heightened by allowing user discretion and choice. In a small way this might contribute to people having control over their own life. However, there are certain aspects of a software system's functionality where flexibility might willingly be sacrificed so as to attain some other benefit (e.g. robust preservation of data integrity). There are also contexts and circumstances in which imposition of procedure is deemed beneficial (e.g. a nuclear power plant).

There is a balance to be struck between the degree of control given to the software system and that retained by the human users. It can be a difficult decision. One thing is certain, however: the deployment of IT in organizations is an exercise in social change. The evidence is overwhelming. The following quote is taken from the report of the inquiry into the London Ambulance Service following the devastating failure of its computerised dispatch system:

'Management were misguided or naive in believing that computer systems in themselves could bring about such changes in human practices...any attempt to force change through the introduction of a system with the characteristics of an operational "strait-jacket" would potentially be doomed to failure.'

Report of Inquiry into the London Ambulance Service, 1993

2.5.3 Evolutionary Software Systems

It can be said that a system does things and adapts its doings. This maxim is coined from the coupling of the concepts of communication and control in cybernetics. Software systems, on the other hand, do things. Their adaption is subsumed into the part-bureaucratic and part-technical phase known as *maintenance*. In other words, a software application seems to be much like any other product. It is designed, tested, implemented and maintained. For it to be adaptable is not, seemingly, a central concern.

It can be strongly argued that software applications should not be seen in this way. Rather they should be seen as evolutionary in that they affect the form of the organization and are affected by it. Design, testing and implementation are not stages that start and then finish, but phases that commence, pause and recommence within an overall evolutionary framework. The rationale for this rests principally upon two pillars. First, it cites the inherent uncertainty of the process of developing applications for organizations. Can requirements be *right*? Secondly, the organizations into which software systems are applied are themselves dynamic. Indeed the act of developing and applying a software system will itself change the organization. Earlier in section 2.4.3, Ackoff's three behavioural conditions of system behaviour were outlined. They tell of the interdependence between the behaviour of the whole and the behaviour of elements. Surely then, the splash of introducing a software system into an organization induces a ripple effect. The organization is not quite the same after as it was before.

Today, many organizations are dependent upon their software systems. These organizations are dynamic, however, generally, the software systems are static and discrete. This is why it can be said that there is a paradox wherein software *support* systems may actually thwart the dynamism of the organization. There are many everyday examples of this: a manager who wishes to introduce new practices but is forced to wait for the next raft of IT updates; users who could rationalize and innovate but for the particular way of work that is programmed into the IT; a whole company working with a legacy system they no longer find convenient nor especially useful.

Several responses have been proposed. Kawalek and Leonard (1996) posit a 'scratch formula' for evolutionary systems based upon research into organizational complexity. Elsewhere, drawing upon the 'Design Paradigms in Computer Science' put forward by Dasgupta (1991), Warboys (1995) proposes the Theory of Evolutionary Design Paradigm. This acts as a framework to other, better-known design paradigms (e.g. algorithmic, formal design). The paradigm takes as its starting position the view that the software design process is evolutionary. It accommodates change and failure through the proposing and assessment of hypotheses. This means that in practice designers are forced to resort to satisfactory rather than optimal designs and through this there can be a recognition of both the evolutionary and error-prone nature of software development. As the design of software is regarded as an evolutionary process, any design is itself always a tentative solution to the problem posed. Thus, clearly the Theory of Evolutionary Design Paradigm draws upon an empirical scientific tradition. It encourages us to recognize the strong link between natural and artificial sciences, the use of testable hypotheses as a method, the nature of evolutionary systems and hence the need for an incremental development approach.

There is resonance between this position and that taken by Lehman's (1991) well-known work. A central concept is the E-type program, the *E* stemming from evolution. An E-type program is one which required to solve a problem in a real-world domain. The acceptability of the program is determined by its consequences. Such consequences might be the information conveyed to human users or the way in which the program induces behaviour in attached or controlled artefacts. As an E-type program is judged by the satisfaction it yields, correctness cannot be included amongst the criteria of its assessment. It is the relationship with the real-world domain that is critical. Thus, the acceptability of the system is entirely dependent on subjective human judgement. It cannot be judged against some separate specification or problem statement but is understood in relation to needs and expectations which arise in the domain of which it is a part.

An E-type system is not entirely formal. Lehman notes that validation techniques such as testing, prototyping and simulation are available to address the uncertainty which is induced by the non-formal parts of the system. However, whilst validation techniques are of value they are always themselves incomplete and imprecise. This leads to a consideration of the uncertainty itself, and the positing of the uncertainty principle of computer application:

'The outcome, in the real world, of software system operation is inherently uncertain with the precise area of uncertainty also not knowable.'

Lehman, 1991

Later, in Chapter 9, a control process which relates goal change to technical capability is proposed. This control process constitutes a meta-level consideration of process (a *meta-process*). Through *meta-level* we refer to the useful distinction between operational activities and those activities which are themselves concerned with activities, i.e. performance monitoring and controlling activities. This distinction between an operational and a meta level is a characteristic of systems approaches (e.g. Beer, 1979; Checkland, 1981).

The concept and application of meta-process has been a major theme in software process research. The thesis here is that as development projects progress it can be necessary to introduce changes to a product (with implications for the process of its development) or to the process directly. Hence, this profile of the Research Lineage returns to where it started with the concerns of the software process.

There are many other areas of research that are for many other reasons relevant to us and our broad concern for organizations and software systems. A few of these areas are sketched out in the following section. They are drawn from a variety of different systems analysis enquiries into the application of software systems.

2.6 The Wider World

It is interesting to reflect that data-modelling techniques have risen to become the dominant techniques employed in systems analysis today. Process modelling and data modelling are not mutually exclusive. To suggest that you use one or the other would be nonsensical. It would be a little like using nouns but not verbs or verbs but not nouns. Nonetheless, the usefulness of each of data modelling and process modelling is stratified by the use of the other.

This review considers some research issues arising beyond the domain of process modelling and software engineering under the following headings:

• The dominance of data modelling. The established place of data modelling in the modern organization is critically assessed. In particular it is noted how data modelling has risen to become an influential technique, not only amongst system developers but in the boardroom too. It is argued that in so doing the inherent subjectivity of the problem domain has been neglected.

- The nature of the organizational context. Information systems research has highlighted the subjectivity of organizational analysis and design. The consequence is that there must be, at some level, a concern for the subjective aspects of the design process.
- Business Process Re-engineering. The idea that business processes should be radically redesigned in order to tap the full potential of IT has been popularized as *Business Process Re-engineering*. It is noted that this has been a seductive message for businesses seeking to survive in turbulent operational conditions but that, from a software engineering point of view, it does not contribute to an understanding of how the software systems should be constructed and adapted to their environment.

2.6.1 The Dominance of Data Modelling

It has been noted that the earliest systems analysis methods focused upon processing rather than data structure (Wood-Harper and Fitzgerald, 1982; Lewis, 1994). Today the situation is radically different. There is a plethora of systems analysis methodologies almost all of which, according to Lewis, include a component of data analysis. Lewis suggests that the risen importance of the data perspective can largely accounted for by the opening up of the technical possibility of the database, as products such as IBM's IMS software became commercially available. This led in turn to a concern for the efficient use of software and hardware resources. The work of Codd (1970) and Chen (1976) is generally accredited with being of special significance. The reason for this is that in developing the principles of normalization and entity-relationship modelling respectively, these two authors laid the foundation of an approach which focused upon the intrinsic structure of the data itself rather than the means of storing it. It is arguable that almost all of today's systems analysis techniques, including the powerful object oriented modelling techniques such as the Unified Modelling Language (e.g. Fowler and Scott, 1997), draw in some way upon the respective works of Codd and Chen.

Lewis does not question the value of data analysis in the design stage of creating new software information systems but raises concern over its use in a much earlier stage, that of designing the organization itself, through enterprise modelling and the like. A number of factors have motivated the use of data analysis techniques at this much earlier stage. For example, Lewis proposes that the statement, 'data is a resource of the modern organization' is not testable as such but has become an influential part of the 'mythology' of data analysis. This mythology exploits the ability given to data analysts by Codd and Chen, to construct and develop conceptual data schemas independently of the means of their implementation. Furthermore, structured methods have been developed which seek to align organizational plans and strategies with information systems development. These methods import techniques which were created to promote the efficient use of computing resources to a very different, more strategic context. The problem with this, Lewis argues, is that there is a discrepancy between on the one hand the theory and philosophy of data analysis and on the other the practical application of it. Lewis warns that the theory of data modelling embodies an assumption of an *objective reality* composed of entities, relations and attributes, whilst the practical reality is that analysts make many *subjective judgements* about what constitutes an entity, relationship and attribute. This discrepancy is particularly consequential where data analysis techniques are being used to shape strategy and thereby mould the perceived problem domain that is considered later in the development process.

Thus, Lewis describes how data modelling has grown from a restricted role to be the primary component of most modern systems analysis methods. It would be wrong to imply that Lewis argues for a process-oriented approach. His concerns are different. However his account provides an interesting backdrop upon which to consider the relationship which data modelling has with process modelling. The rise of data modelling has proceeded in tandem with the rise of the database. Today the most common use of computing technology amongst organizations is for database purposes (e.g. Li's and Rogers' 1991 survey of U.S. firms). In order to understand why process modelling is being given a renewed emphasis it is necessary to appreciate the ever-changing nature of the problem being addressed. In society at large software is afforded a position of great significance. For increasing numbers of organizations there is a critical dependency upon software. Operational (and hence financial) success is entrusted to the capabilities and reliability of software. Software helps to support the global market which in turn imposes a change imperative on thousands of organizations. Business practice and methodology exhorts the need for innovation and flexibility. Individual businesses respond by buying the latest generation of software products and platforms. Many of them gain critical advantage over their competitors. Many of them do not. Users are able to load and program software on local machines. This facilitates tactical innovation and flexibility. It endangers integrity and useability. The software applications of today are more complex than their predecessors. As a whole, the corporate system becomes more complex as databases and applications are added to the network. We are left with questions such as the following:
• How does this system fit together?
• How do the parts interact?
• How are the people served by the system?
• How do people innovate?
• What requirements are placed on the technical system by organizational innovation?
• How can the system be evolved?
The process approach set out in this book seeks to provide a way of answering these questions.

2.6.2 The Nature of the Organizational Context

Information systems research presents a growing body of work which reminds us that the organizational context for software systems is complex and problem-laden. The complexity of software application within the organization brings an increased imperative for a recognition of the connectivity between organizational function and other important aspects such as capabilities, culture and stakeholders. It suggests, then, that technical information systems development must interface to a higher level consideration of social issues.

Much new work challenges the philosophical foundations of conventional systems analysis. The charge is that rationalist, positivist approaches are naïve in social organizations; that problem situations and solutions can only be understood in terms of their social meanings (see also Chapter 4). The interpretative approach as described by Walsham (1993) is a movement away from the natural science type approaches to research in information systems development. Lewis (1994) has shown that utilizing the interpretative stance has pragmatic implications for systems analysis and design in organizations. The approach proposes that a problem situation can only be investigated, 'as it is understood by those who perceive it as problematical'. The investigative methods can therefore be described as reality creating methods. Objective facts are not somehow captured by the analyst, in a way akin to the butterfly collector with his net, but are agreed upon by all those involved.

Related themes are to be found in the user-centred approach of Ethics (Mumford, 1981; Mumford and Weir, 1979). This emphasizes the importance of autonomy, job satisfaction and empowerment for people within organizations. The method allows users to be directly involved in the design of their own work activities and technology. Hence the locus of control is moved out of the hands of the technically expert systems analyst and into the hands of the domain expert users. By so doing, users are likely to feel more empowered and more able to raise their level of performance (e.g. Rotter, 1966). It is argued that the overhead in time and money in producing a participative design of a system is compensated by the reduction in subsequent system maintenance and user dissatisfaction (Mumford, 1981).

In these ways systems analysis is increasingly seen as a social science. Factors such as the socio-political, cultural and psychological aspects within organizations need to be understood. Many structured methods have been criticized for making sweeping assumptions about the operation of the organization, its power structures, user requirements and the stability of these requirements. These methods have been dominated by assertions that technical activities such as data modelling are objective and rationalist exercises. The data is seen as static, and the human processes and the resulting designs for software were thereby also understood to be fixed.

The lessons seem to be:
- The development and deployment of complex software systems can be seen to be an exercise in organizational change.
- Organizational change is a multi-disciplinary exercise.
- The acceptability of any *solution* can be only be evaluated in social terms.
- The acceptability of software applied in the real world is not fixed. There is therefore no such thing as a right solution.

2.6.3 Business Process Re-engineering

During the 1990's the management change initiative Business Process Re-engineering (Hammer, 1990; Hammer and Champy, 1993; Harrington, 1991; Davenport, 1993) became a popular topic amongst academics and business practitioners. It is related to this book's process-modelling approach by the use of the process concept as a fulcrum of organizational change initiatives. In other ways it is quite different. It is primarily a management initiative and therefore its concern is for the form of the social system (as opposed to the technical). A principal concern is to facilitate radical change at organizational and process levels rather than through organizational functions (Hammer, 1990; Hammer and Champy, 1993; Davenport, 1993). Thus the concept of process is used almost exclusively at a high level. It is not seen to be a scalable concept with which consideration can be given to user tasks. In much of the literature, the power of IT is a central theme (e.g. Hammer and Champy, 1993), but even then the form of the IT system is not considered. There are no words on the use of modelling, languages and architecture. IT plays a cameo role as something of great power but fixed form. The evolution of organizational systems is considered at least in a partial sense in some of the literature (e.g. Harrington, 1991) through a development of the principles of Total Quality Management.

Faced with a climate of competition and uncertainty, BPR represented a promising treatise for many organizations. It subverted traditional systems analysis which seeks to fit IT to the business by presenting case studies where the business was designed to exploit IT. It encouraged the use of technology to radically redefine social systems and thus mirrored the way social systems have shaped technology. It tapped a broad perception that the true power of IT has not yet been realized. Hammer (1990) suggests that thus far systems analysis has only succeeded in, '...embedding outdated processes in silicon and software'.

2.7 Conclusion

This chapter started with the intent of creating a positioning chapter and in doing so has covered a lot of ground. The focus is upon the development of software support for modern organizations. In particular, the concern is for complex systems where the refrain is of many people and many software tools which get things done by interacting with each other. The approach does not seek to consider the software issues separately from the development of the organization as a whole. There is a complex relationship between social and technical systems. This book is concerned with the technical mediation of the two.

The foundations have been described through reference to concepts established in systems theory. It is concerned with a system of many elements that interact with each other and adapt their patterns of interaction. The organization can be understood to have social and technical sub-systems where the social system is a served system and the technical system is a serving system.

Two themes have been distilled. These are a concern for interaction (i.e. coordination of people, people and software applications and among software applications) and a concern for evolution. These can be considered as related problems which are akin to the characteristics of communication and control in systems. Later chapters will show how this process modelling approach tackles the problems by relating them to the structure of organizations (i.e. *What are the elements that interact?*).

Using systems concepts, the organization can be described as an adaptive whole. Thinking of it as an autopoietic system fuses the concepts of its identity and its structure. Its ability to adapt must then depend to some degree on the creation of new structures for interaction. Elements of the system must be able to coordinate with each other in new ways or new elements must be introduced into the coordinative network.

That the ability to adapt software systems can be a crucial component of adapting the organization is reinforced by software engineering work which highlights the the uncertainty of applying software systems. Software engineering also provides a body of research concerned with the support of the software process. Here, as in the workflow domain, important issues are highlighted which describe the need to balance enforcement and flexibility in the operation of software systems.

It can be suggested that for many organizations it is often futile to try and distinguish between, on the one hand, the activities which people seek to carry out and on the other, the support technology upon which these actions rely. If we change one we are likely to affect the other. This is the basis of the reasoning that the development and deployment of complex software systems is an exercise in social change. User-centred approaches (e.g. Mumford, 1981) require that domain experts are able to shape this social change. Elsewhere, attention is being given to the development of philosophical stances which appreciate the essentially subjective nature of the deployment of technology in organizations (e.g. Walsham, 1993). There has been criticism of positivist approaches which encourage the analyst to capture subjective assertions as though they are objective facts. It is not the direct concern of this book to address social issues but it is important that these issues are given due appreciation and set the context for a process approach to business systems engineering.

3

Process Concepts

This chapter introduces concepts that are needed for the exploration of the domain. Some are useful, and some are essential. It builds on the ideas introduced in the last chapter and forms the basis for the modelling methods which are introduced in Part 2 of this book. After a discussion on the process phenomenon, a new view of process is proposed which is aimed at better understanding the relationship between goal, activity and interaction in organizations. Following this, there is a description of the different kinds of models that are in use, and a unique model, the active model, is introduced and discussed. The distinction between automated processes and human activity processes is clarified with reference to various process domains. The chapter concludes with a brief introduction to the concept of the meta-process.

3.1 Introduction

Chapter 2 has introduced a number of concepts that were used to describe a particular view of the world of organizations. This chapter builds on these concepts, and introduces many more that are specific to the concerns of industry professionals, managers, process modellers and researchers, and which form the basis of the methods that are introduced later in Part 2 of the book.

Recent years have seen an increasing focus on the business process in management science through movements such as Total Quality Management (Bank, 1993) and Business Process Re-engineering (Scott Morton, 1991; Hammer and Champy, 1993). On the other hand interest in software process modelling, with its emphasis on the active support of the process through IT, has evolved independently and in parallel with such concerns. Both the business process practitioner and the software process modeller have much in common, although the former is seeking new ways of delivering products with or without new technologies, and the latter is seeking how best to support process-centred activity using IT. They both need to understand the processes of their organizations and how they relate to organizational information systems. One has to design dynamically changeable and efficient processes, and the other the process knowledgable software to support them.

The emerging common ground is that the processes cannot be considered in isolation from the information systems that are potentially available, systems as applications and tools, and systems as infrastructure. This more recent focus complements those process aspects of businesses that have been understood for many years and are embedded in conventional Information Systems.

Any method, as opposed to a set of heuristics, ought to have a coherent theoretical base. Process modelling today still, to an extent, lacks such a theoretical grounding. A great deal of practical work has been carried out with mixed results, but an essential cohesion is absent. This chapter is intended as a remedy for this shortcoming.

A theory is a conceptual net for structuring phenomena. Ideally it should provide both explanatory power (a route to understanding), and also predictive power (a way of anticipating likely future situations based on current conditions). The latter aspect is extremely important when seeking to adopt an engineering approach to the solution of real-world problems. This work does not try to develop a predictive theory; it will focus on a description and analysis of concepts which might at some time contribute to the building blocks of a process theory. We will examine in detail the essential constituents of a process so that it is possible, in any given situation, to identify processes, to say that this entity is a process and this is not, and to be able to argue the identity of a process. We will examine the different kinds of models that are available and in use.

An important dimension to this study of processes is that of change. This issue has, as yet, hardly been addressed by research workers. Change is variously viewed as both a strength and a weakness of the organization process. On the one hand, activity can be modified to address a situation which has not been anticipated, but on the other hand processes tend to ossify as individuals forget the original reasons behind them. All too often the answer to the question, 'Why do you do it like this?' is, 'We've always done it this way'. Reluctance to effect change can arise because the reasons underlying the process are obscure, so there is a very real possibility of change having undesirable impacts. Successful process change entails an understanding of business objectives, of process in general, of the particular process under consideration, what it is intended to achieve, and the reasons why it is the way it is. The latter point is particularly important for consideration of evolutionary rather than radical change.

There is a brief overview of the process phenomenon in Section 3.2, followed in Section 3.3 by a description of the interactional view of the organization process. Section 3.4 describes some different kinds of processes that are found in organizations. Associated concepts needed for discussing these processes are identified in Section 3.5. Models, particularly active models, are examined more closely in Section 3.6, and in Section 3.7 a clear distinction is drawn between human activity processes and those of machines by identifying the different domains of process. Section 3.8 identifies the need for a meta-process and the kinds of requirements placed upon it.

3.2 The Process Phenomenon

In the previous chapter, our attention was drawn to the interactive behaviour evident in organizations, between people, between people and machines and between machines. We assume that they all contribute to the achievement of the goals of the business. Much of this behaviour is not random, but in fact conforms to a pattern of some kind, and this constitutes our working definition of the term process. There are many shades of meaning to the term *process*, and the scope of its usage is very wide, as demonstrated in the range of definitions quoted later in this section.

In its loosest sense *process* relates to flux in the real world, to observable progressive changes of state of the world. A process (in its abstract sense) can exist through time, but a process example, or occurrence, only unfolds through time. A process is structured change, i.e. there is a pattern of events which an observer may recognise across different actual examples (or occurrences) of the process, or which may be made manifest, or implemented, in many different occurrences. The process may be a description of occurrences, or it might in fact shape these occurrences.

To begin to focus on our particular area of interest, an immediate distinction can be made between natural processes and artificial processes. An example of a natural process changing the state of the real world is that of fossilization – the series of steps by means of which primeval vegetation was converted into coal deposits which we have been able to exploit. We know that such processes exist and have existed, but we can only speculate as to *why?*. On the other hand artificial processes, those that are constructed by people, invariably exist for an acknowledged purpose to change the state of the real world or to constrain it in some way to suit human needs. The process of constructing a building is an example of the former, and the process of law, which minimizes the occurrence of undesirable human behaviour, is an example of the latter. Artificial processes do not simply occur as do natural processes, they need to be articulated by an agent of some kind to effect the transformations.

Where the agent is a machine, there is a regularity, predictability and determinism in the process which permits relatively easy and precise description. With human agents, however, there is no guarantee that an anticipated event will in fact take place. They are non-deterministic. On the other hand, people have an adaptive capacity. An individual may perceive a fault or error in a process definition and take the initiative of working around it. Thus the objectives of the process can be achieved even though the original process was wrong. This illustrates the essential difference between the human and machine worlds which is illuminated in the distinctions drawn between the different domains of process described later in Section 3.7.

Organizational processes are artificial processes, usually hybrids of the above, in that some parts may be articulated by humans and other parts by machine. Examples of such processes can exist over a period of time, days or months or longer, and involve interaction between individuals, between individuals and machines, and between machines. These are the processes by which many organizations achieve their objectives. As organizations exist for a purpose, so their processes also exist for a purpose. The process steps are not so much executed by an agent, as they are enacted, or played, or performed by an agent. In business processes the agent is of course frequently human, but machines (in the form of software systems, applications and tools) are being used to articulate more and more aspects of business process activity. Of course humans are concerned with, and interact with, many social processes within organizations, but as mentioned above, our concern is solely with purposeful processes, i.e. those which are collectively directed toward satisfaction of organization objectives.

We are concerned about changes needed or wanted in the real world, and the mechanisms which bring about desired changes. The mechanism in which we are interested is the one that involves a progressive change of state. It has to be pointed out that not all organizations achieve their (tacit and overt) objectives by articulating processes. In different organizations the balance varies between the process – the structure of regularities, and the articulation – the context-dependent actions of individuals or machines that flesh out the structure in order to achieve productive outcomes. The execution of the process brings about successive changes of state that result in the original need being satisfied. In this way, for example, a customer's need for insurance cover is satisfied by the policy sales process being carried out in an insurance company. Thus the process is a method for addressing a need in the real world and, in a way, it can be viewed as a solution to a problem.

Within the group of organizational processes, our primary concern is with information processes, those that manipulate data or information, rather than those that manipulate materials in the well-known factory production processes. That is to say, the change of state of the real world consequent to the process being performed is one of an informational nature, rather than the changes of a physical nature brought about by manufacturing processes (although this is arguable). Within informational processes, our concern for the organizational dimension focuses on those processes which involve interaction or coordination among people and groups.

All organizations, to a greater or lesser extent, coordinate the activities of their members in order to achieve their objectives. Much non-productive effort is expended in unifying the outputs across an organization in order to achieve objectives, and it is a major issue which has confronted organizations for some time:

'The problem of coordination is ... the crux of the business organization.'

Follett, 1941

The nature of this coordination covers a spectrum from the very loose, where individuals are aware of the objectives that have to be attained, and are left to proceed by whatever means they see fit, to, at the other extreme, individuals being given explicit descriptions of what tasks they have to accomplish, how to obtain needed inputs from others, and what deliverables are needed from them. Academic research groups are typically representative of one end of the spectrum (the generation of ideas being of paramount importance), and government bureaucracies that are intent on minimizing risk and maximizing accountability lie at the other end. Thus, how processes are interpreted depends very much on their context: the culture of an organization.

What makes the study of business process particularly difficult (and interesting) is this human dimension from which emerges issues relating to creativity, intuition, ability to learn, ability to make mistakes, ability to improvize, ability to anticipate, awareness of intentionality, and the limits to understanding expressed as our bounded rationality (Simon, 1981). Organization process are usually badly defined: details are ignored in the definition, they get out of date quickly, definitions are corrected only infrequently. Yet this does not mean that processes are performed badly, since humans, being aware of intention, can adapt to this by inventing activity that allows the objectives to be reached anyway. Furthermore the process may not be fully defined until the the ocurrence is almost complete: the definition may only unfold as the process is followed through (projects are like this). Human activity can appear chaotic and in attempting to understand a process there may be a temptation to impose an order which might be self-defeating. In many cases we do not really understand the conditions that have to pertain for activities to take place. In addition, process structures are often dynamic, in the sense that the patterns of activities themselves will be changing. Processes themselves may change in either structured or unstructured ways, i.e. there may be a process of process change.

There are many definitions of organization process in existence, perhaps reflecting its imprecise nature and the manifold ways in which it can be considered. In order to give an indication of their variety, some are quoted below:

• A set of partially ordered steps intended to reach a goal (Feiler and Humphrey, 1993).
• The transformation of something from one state to another state through partially coordinated agents, with the purpose of achieving certain goals that are derived from the responsibility of the process owner (Platt, 1994).
• A specific ordering of work activities across time and place, with a beginning, an end, and clearly identified inputs and outputs: a structure for action (Davenport, 1993).
• A bundle of goal directed actions that are performed by actors (Bauer et al., 1994).
• A collection of activities that takes one or more kinds of output and creates an input that is of value to a customer (Hammer and Champy, 1993).
• A set of purposeful activities performed by agents supported by logistical means (Halé, 1995).
• A group of related tasks that together create value for a customer (Hammer, 1995).
• All the real-world elements involved in the development and maintenance of a product (i.e. artefacts, production support tools, activities, agents, process support) (Conradi et al., 1994).
• Any work that meets these four criteria: it is recurrent; it affects some aspects of organizational

capabilities; it can be accomplished in different ways that make a difference to the contribution it generates in terms of cost, value, service, or quality; and it involves coordination (Keen, 1997).

• A set of partially ordered process steps, with sets of related artefacts, human and computerized resources, organizational structures and constraints, intended to produce and maintain the requested software deliverables (Lonchamp, 1993).

Curtis, Kellner and Over (1992) adopted the last of these definitions in their seminal work which proposed an insightful way of addressing the problems arising from inherent complexity. This was to distinguish between the different process views which could be of interest. These views were:

• Functional – considering what process activities are being performed, and the relevant flows of information entities.

• Behavioural – considering when they are performed, as well as aspects of how they are performed (conditions, sequence, iteration etc.).

• Organizational – considering where and by whom in the organization the activities are performed.

• Informational – considering the informational entities, including structure and relationships produced or manipulated in the process.

These were recognized at the time as not being comprehensive and since then another view has emerged, one which is particularly relevant to the methods described later in Part 2. That is the *interactional* view that is explored in the following section.

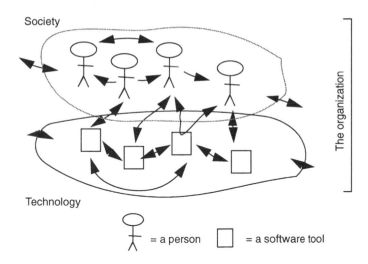

Fig. 3.1 Interactions Within an Organization

3.3 The Interactional Basis of Process Activity

Concern for issues related to coordination has been raised in Chapter 2. Such concerns led to the development of the *interactional* view of process activity, which combines the behavioural and organizational views referred to in the last section. This can be explained by developing an interactional view of the system expressed in Figure 3.1. If the organization is considered to be a kind of box, what can be seen when the lid is lifted off? The modeller will see that it is composed of many different components. Some of the components will be human and some will be technological. These components interact with each other. The interactions may appear to be random or even chaotic; however, the modeller will learn that they are all related to invisible and sometimes ephemeral phenomena called goals. These induce a certain amount of regularity, the degree of which is variable.

So Figure 3.1 can be taken as a representation of an organization. It is possible to identify the usual pattern of people interacting with other people, people interacting with software applications and software appllctions interacting with other software applications. It could be a bank, a government department, a software team, a car manufacturer or any number of other types of organization. For the purposes of this chapter it can be taken to representative of the insurance industry.

The interactions that take place between people will always be subject to a degree of negotiation. Their usefulness, meaning and procedure will be subject to the motivations, intentions, wants and whims of those who participate. Interactions are always significant however, for it can be argued that in the most fundamental sense organizational goals are achieved by the interaction of people with one another. This might be illustrated through a customer–provider (or transactional) relationship. For example, a secretary interacts with a travel agent in order to book a business flight. The travel agent undertakes certain activities (e.g. look up alternatives, make the booking) in order that the goal precipitating the interaction is fulfilled. An alternative example (shown in Figure 3.2) could be a manager interacting with the secretary in order to send a letter. The manager asks a secretary to prepare the letter. The secretary then carries out certain activities (e.g. word-process the letter, print it) in order that the goal is fulfilled.

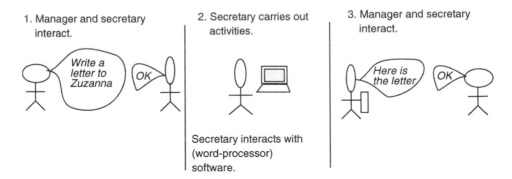

Fig. 3.2 An Example of Interaction as the Basis of an Organizational Behaviour

These examples give us a picture of human interactions (i.e. secretary and travel agent, manager and secretary) spawning dependent actions which satisfy a goal. However, it is useful to develop this a little further and to consider interactions in a broader sense. In the technological, software-rich environment of today it is vital to consider the interaction of humans with Information Systems in their various forms, and the interaction of these software packages with other systems. Thus, it may be observed that the travel agent interacts with an airline booking system to look up flight details and make the booking. The secretary interacts with a word-processor in order to create the letter. The word-processor may, in turn, interact with a database in order to read the address fields for entry on to the letter. Thus the notion of interaction gives us a basis for the exploration a broader range of coordinative issues in a complex organization. In so doing it is possible to distinguish *collaborative* interactions (i.e. between people) from *integrative* interactions (i.e. involving software applications).

3.3.1 The Role–Activity–Interaction Paradigm

Organizational goals are achieved by means of work being done by people and machines, and for this work to be unified by coordination between them. The coordination is achieved through interactions.

When work is done, some transformations take place, intermediate artefacts or services are produced and made available to others, and if the work is properly coordinated, ultimately the business goals are achieved. Interactions convey such intermediate products (partial results) as well as the other communications needed to ensure coordination. However, in addition to knowing what is conveyed, we need to express between whom or what the interactions occur. It has been mentioned earlier that one of the main purposes of process modelling is to identify and study just how best such transformations can come about – the *how* of a data or state transformation and goal achievement. When activities have to be undertaken or handled by people or by machine, it is essential to know what characteristics or capabilities are needed of them. In the case of a person it is their experience and skills, and in the case of a machine its capacity and performance. A concept that is of great help in exploring this issue is that of *role*. A role serves the organizational function of associating or binding individual agents (machines, people, or groups of people) to a particular objective or purpose, and, under some circumstances, also to certain activities and interactions with other roles.

Role theory (Biddle and Thomas, 1966) furnishes a definition that a role is, 'a behavioural repertoire characteristic of a person or position', and, 'the set of standards, descriptions, norms held (by anyone) of a person or position'. Thus it indicates what will be required or expected of the agent, what professional skills, experience, authority, and managerial abilities are needed. Viewed another way, we expect certain behaviour from a role, thus it can be thought of as encapsulating certain activity. This reflects the two aspects to roles: a responsibility (rights, powers, duties), and a pattern of actions, some of which involve interacting with other roles. Although expressed in human terms here, the role concept can usefully be adopted in regard to work undertaken by machines. For example, it is probably true to say that the role of ticket selling at a railway station could be articulated either by a person or by a machine.

A responsibility is a duty to handle certain types of situation, to produce results in line with given objectives, and to be accountable to seniors and customers for them. A role confers bounded autonomy on the agent – they have an organizationally circumscribed freedom of action in accomplishing the duties of the role. The empowerment of the individual is limited by this scope plus the limits on their power to command resources to accomplish actions.

It is necessary to distinguish general responsibilities from particular responsibilities, that is responsibility for certain types of situation or pieces of work from responsibility for particular pieces of work. Both these kinds of responsibilities can be modelled, the former as a set of problem-solving activities, and the latter as a pattern of specific activities.

In organizations, roles are often initially synonymous with an individual's job title, such as secretary or manager in the previous example. However the notion can usefully be applied at higher and lower levels in the organization structure. A department can have a role in an organization, and a job title can subsume further roles. A manager can, at different times, be a planner, leader, trouble-shooter, or father-figure, each a role with its own characteristic behaviour. These roles can subsume others. The planner for example can be involved in researching, coordinating etc., depending upon the situation. Roles may be delegated from one agent to another, or subsumed. Roles can give varying amounts of scope for interpretation or creativity, and they also recognize that certain situations demand certain skills. Interactions establish the purposeful relationships between them.

The role concept is central to any discussion on organization process modelling, and the role–

activity–interaction paradigm is the basis of the method described in Part 2 of this book.

3.4 Kinds of Process

Processes in organizations exist in a huge variety of forms, from explicit steps carried out almost automatically (such as a typical staff expenses-claiming process in a business), to software processes which might only indicate a strategy which ought to be followed, and which depend for their success on the expertise, knowledge and cooperation of the developers. This section serves as a reminder of different kinds of process that can occur in organizations.

Operational process or production process. This is the process that directly sets out to achieve organizational objectives (e.g. the efficient production of insurance policies). All operational processes in organizations have outputs which are either physical or textual objects, or a behaviour (i.e. a service) which is of value to someone else either within or outside the organization. They are examples of a goal-attaining process. Any particular example of the operational process ceases to exist once the goal of the process has been achieved.

Control process. The goals of a control process are continuously to maintain a state which relates to another process, rather than to achieve a specific state and then conclude. Such a state might be one of showing a profit. This means that the control process exists for the life of all the ocurrences of that process, and it may cycle through its definition many times. It must have certain specific features, such as some provision for feedback, for its analysis, and the means of manipulating the operational process to achieve desired results. The control is usually effected by manipulating the resources of the operational process. In addition a control process can be an intrinsic component of the operational process, as well as exerting overarching control over all aspects of an operational process.

Generic process. The term *generic* means that something is applicable to any member of a group. Generally it refers to some kind of abstraction, a simplified description exposing the essentials of a process, so avoiding obfuscation by implementation details. However, the term is relative. As an example, both the insurance process and construction process are examples of a generic bidding process. This is a template process that structures the search for and the finalization of a commercial relationship. It covers the soliciting of inquiries for a product or service, developing interesting ones, bidding for them, negotiating the bid, and if successful, ultimately providing the service in exchange for a payment. A generic process exists only as a model, as it does not possess sufficient information for it to be used directly in the real world. However it can be adapted and associated with, or bound to, people and machines for carrying out the work of the process. In this context, generic processes might be viewed as *patterns* (Alexander, 1964): architectures of potential solutions to certain types of problem.

Customized process. An adaptation of a generic process to suit specific objectives and using identified resources in an organization.

Enactable process. A process which is defined in such a way and in such a medium that it can be executed using process technology such as a process-centred environment referred to in Section 2.4. It interacts with users to coordinate their activities in such a way as to progress the instance (see the following sub-section) of the process to its conclusion. When implemented, and thus capable of interacting with users as a part of the real world, we will refer to it as an *active* model which is explained later in this chapter.

Meta-process. The term was first used in the domain of software process modelling. The prefix implies *about*, and this can be interpreted as a process that is concerned with another process or processes. In the context of process modelling we consider this concern to be that which brings a process into existence, is responsible for continuous adaptation or evolution of the process, and which brings about its eventual termination. To ensure distinction, the process which is the immediate concern of the meta-process can be called an operational process, or a production process. The control process already referred to (and exemplified in everyday management activity) can be considered to be a specialization of this concept, where the concern is to ensure the satisfactory functioning and performance of an operational process. Section 3.8 is devoted to the concept of the meta-process.

3.5 Associated Concepts

There are many concepts which appear in any dialogue on the subject of business processes. They are taken mainly, but not exclusively, from management science.

Activity is an item of behaviour which is of interest. The granularity of the behaviour has a very wide scope, from the elemental movements of an individual to the behaviour of a whole organization. A choice has to be made as to the suitable granularity for modelling purposes. A **task** is a managed activity, i.e. one whose properties such as start time and duration are of managerial interest.

Agent is the means of accomplishing the activity or the task. The agent articulates the task and can be human or machine (physical or software).

Behaviour is usually taken as a synonym for activity, and this is the usage in this book. However there are other views such as those of Turski (1991), for whom behaviour is activity whose preconditions are too subtle to be usefully defined.

Cases. These are succeeding process occurrences for which certain aspects of the context are dissimilar and thus require slightly different activity in order to achieve the desired outcomes. However they are not sufficiently dissimilar as to merit organizational re-arrangement to deal with them.

Cybernetics. The study of control and communication in natural and artificial systems. It is particularly focused on self-regulating, self-maintaining systems (Beer, 1974, 1979).

Plan. This is typically a chart of a route through activities for an instance of a process. A plan states or shows how an objective will be realized, not in terms of a general method, or theory, although it may make use of these, but in practical terms. It consists of specific sub-goals, which often delineate tasks which need to be achieved in order to achieve the main objective. It is a way of anticipating problems in complex activity, and focusing discussion on future activity. It is used where specific guidance is needed, and can be a basis for commitment and coordination of resources. Plans can be dynamic, in the sense that they can be modified by the feedback of information about current activities in the real world.

Procedure is a process which is adopted under specific circumstances. It is usually short and expressed in narrative form. It is used to address recurring situations, or an anticipated exceptional situation.

Production line. A permanent organization structure which is needed to coordinate people, tools and resources to handle multiple concurrent and continuously generated examples of a production process.

Project. This is a temporary organizational arrangement to achieve a set of objectives by enacting a single instance of a process. When the objectives are achieved, the arrangement is dissolved, and the resources (human and machine) may be allocated to a new project. Projects make use of plans and procedures.

Programs. Software programs are examples of the most rigorous kind of process. In general, what they have to achieve must be fixed, and precisely known before they are written. They are an example of open-loop control. Programs determine behaviour (of the machine), but computer systems do not determine the behaviour of the user organization, although they may strongly influence it.

Programmes are processes which handle multiple instances of projects or cases. In this context projects and cases are regarded as objects.

Taylorism. This is the early application of the science of management promoted by Frederick Taylor (1911). It is associated with the sub-division and routinizing of work activity, and with time-and-motion studies. It tended to view work in mechanistic rather than social terms.

Type and instance are terms of classification, one of the basic explanatory mechanisms, but the latter term, instance, has a meaning which is specific in the IT context, and is referred to below. It says 'this is one of those', i.e. it involves abstracting from the particular a set of features which may be identified as occurring in a significant number of other particulars. The object of the classification can be static (an object) or dynamic (a process). The pure scientist is mainly interested in the type, being concerned with the instance only as giving information about the type. The engineer or clinician is primarily interested in the instance, relating the instance to the type in order to achieve desired effects in the particular instance. And thus we are also interested in relating the specific instance to the general type of activity pattern, whether in order to understand what did happen, predict what will happen, or affect what will happen. For any given process type there will be numerous occurrences. They will not always be identical. They will be non-identical in marginal, non-modelled ways, but in most modelling systems processes will also diverge slightly from the model from time to time. If this were not so, the model would (a) have to be extremely complex to deal with all the variations, and (b) have to be modifiable to cope with unexpected factors. If we look at activity in, say, an insurance business, we can see instances of the insurance process. If a definition existed, it would be a type as distinct from the instances or occurrences which could be observed. In an IT context, an instance is an executing example of some code, so for discussion in the organization process context, the term occurrence is often used to describe an actual happening of a process.

3.6 Process Representation and Models

Process descriptions can take many forms, and it is possible to use straightforward narrative to describe processes. In fact this is often the medium of process description, but it can be unsatisfactory because such a description might suffer from the inherent ambiguity of natural language and it can be semantically unclear. The consequent depth of explanation needed for precision undermines the understandability of the description.

Models, either physical or graphical, provide a way of mapping and preserving a clear relationship between model and real-world subject. Different kinds of relationship are used in different ways to help explore different problems. Four things are necessary for a model to exist: that part of reality that is the subject of the model; the model itself; the relationship between them; and an observer, user, or creator of the model.

Models are representations, expressed in some modelling medium, of something of interest. A model stands in some abstraction relation with its subject. The point of creating a model is to provide a way of studying certain features of the subject. A model will thus emphasize certain properties of the subject, by including them in the model, and suppress others by omitting them.

What is present in a model and what is omitted is a decision of the modeller and is based on the model's purpose.

A model is so-called because it is used for the reasons outlined earlier rather than being, for example, a symbol. A logo can represent an organization but does not model it. A model has a structure which can be systematically related to structures in the real world. Any model entails an abstraction of certain features which are regarded by the user or modeller as being of interest in the real-world situation. Features in the real-world subject are often represented in a different form in the model according to different mappings, and the mapping can be relatively loose or constrained.

Models are found to be very useful, in fact indispensable, in many contexts. They are needed for a number of different reasons, by people with different interests and concerns. They are of great assistance in representing a part of reality such that a better understanding is achieved of the reality itself. They do this by focusing on those aspects of reality that are significant in the context. This understanding can help us to improve the shape of reality. Thus models in general can aid in the following ways:

• Simplifying complexity. Models help people to understand more complex realities than would otherwise be possible.
• Common understanding. A model representation can be semantically superior to, say, a narrative description and thus it can promote knowledge and learning.
• Study of alternatives. A model assists in evaluating alternative shapes of reality at low cost. It thus provides a framework or a relatively value-free reference point for inquiry.
• Shaping the real world. A model can be used as a part of reality to influence, control, guide or direct what happens in the real world.

In the context of organizations, processes and IS, models help us in many different ways. The most obvious is to capture process behaviour. When captured, it is possible to expose that behaviour to rational analysis and investigation for consistency, and it is possible to use the model to investigate different possible future shapes of reality. These models can act as a repository of organization knowledge, and can facilitate learning about the organization and its processes. Certain kinds of models can be used more directly as means of gathering real-time information about business activity, and furthermore to guide that process activity.

Different kinds of models are appropriate for these different uses, and these are outlined in the remainder of this section.

3.6.1 Passive Models

Models have traditionally been constructed in a passive modelling medium. That is, the model, once created, is independent of its subject. This means that it only bears a relationship to its subject at the point in time at which the modelling is undertaken. The subject modelled may or may not change, but the model will not change of its own accord if it does. The models produced to date by most IS methodologies fall into this category. An entity-relationship diagram or dataflow diagram represents the modeller's understanding at a particular point in time. If things change then the diagram can be revised but there is no automatic link between these two events. The subject of a model may currently exist, but alternatively the subject may be something which might exist in the future, and the model is then an abstract representation of part of a possible future. These alternatives are used in the context of business processes where we might use one to capture the current, as-is process and another to model a potential future, to-be process. In both of these cases the modeller deals with two domains: the domain of the business process, and the domain of the model. They are both descriptions, but one is also a template which will be used to shape future process behaviour. It can be either prescriptive, describing what can take place, or it can be proscriptive, stating what shouldn't happen. The modeller will choose the modelling medium depending on the purpose of the model, and most approaches to modelling business processes use a textual or graphical language.

Figure 3.3 shows a typical high-level passive model of an insurance business process. Its medium is a diagram made up of ellipses and lines where each line links two ellipses. It can be interpreted as an activity model: it shows a number of abstract activities which are involved in the process and connections, or dependencies, between them. Often arrows are used for the connections to indicate the output to input linking between processes.

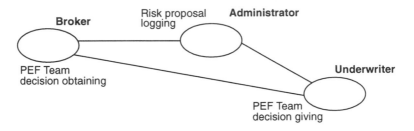

Fig. 3.3 A Simple Model of an Insurance Process

It can also be interpreted as representing a number of interacting roles. Each ellipse represents a responsibility for doing part of the process which is assigned to an individual, team, or division, or even a different organization, and the connections represent their interactions.

Most graphical process models such as this are static. Their emphasis is on the structure of the process rather than on its dynamic behaviour, but it is often possible to interpret the model to get a general view of that behaviour, for example to discover how a typical policy inquiry is handled.

3.6.2 Passive Models that are Dynamic

Business processes are a good example of subject systems that have dynamic properties that we would like to investigate or to better understand. In some situations we want a model that can represent detailed dynamic behaviour, for example in order to optimize resources or to investigate potential impacts of one process on another.

There is a large discipline of computer-based simulation which is based on developing mathematical models and then implementing these as computer programs. By changing parameters it is possible to simulate the behaviour of the subject system in varying circumstances. For example, the insurance company might be considering moving into a new area of business. To assist in planning resources, a model can be built to represent estimated resources and the proposed process, and it can be run in simulated real time with varying demands for policies. The effects of queuing can be studied, and different configurations of process and resource can be tested.

This would be a mathematical model which represented an analysis of the problem. The model's abstraction function would be based on patterns of demand being represented by a statistical distribution which matched historical data. The validity of such representations is a key part of the analysis which must be done in such models, and this might not be easy when studying the models. The value of these generalizations is that the simulation is able to compress time: in five minutes it might simulate five years. This enables a large number of different scenarios to be evaluated at a reasonable cost.

The model does not to provide an abstract representation which is synchronized with its subject system. There is no direct causal link with the subject system. These models are dynamic but they are not active.

3.6.3 Active Models

The idea of an active model is that it is constructed in a modelling medium which allows the modelling relationship to be maintained even though elements of the subject may change. Instead of simply mapping between the subject and the model, there is a causality: an event occurring in the subject causes a corresponding event to take place in the model. The active model and its subject are synchronized so that the model reflects the current state of its subject. Whether this synchronization is in terms of seconds, minutes or days, is part of the abstraction relation between the active model and its subject. Obviously this means that the medium of an active model must enable a change in reaction to some stimulus. IT systems are well suited to play the role of an active model. They can do this by sensors placed in the real world detecting certain states, and reporting them to an IS which can represent these states by means of a model displayed on a monitor. By looking at the monitor we are aware of the model's interpretation of the real world.

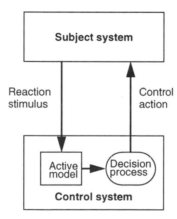

Fig. 3.4 An Active Model as Part of a Control System

An active model can be used for monitoring, that is to provide a high-level view of the current state of its subject. For example an underwriting manager might want a list of policies in preparation, or the value of insured risk at that moment in time.

Examples of active models can be found in workflow systems (Fischer, 1995) and it is interesting to note that one of the benefits accruing from such systems is the improved monitoring available. Rather than having to phone around the organization to try and find where a particular form has reached, the current status can be obtained by simply querying the system.

Active models are also often to be found in control systems, for example railway signalling, aircraft-collision avoidance, or power-station control, where the purpose of the active model is to be a means of monitoring the subject system and to warn of behaviours which breach thresholds (and therefore require attention). Such systems are modelling subjects that are changing state and it is required to understand some, but not all, of these changes.

In a control system there will be a decision process element which uses information from the active model to produce a control action which affects the subject system (see Figure 3.4). In a railway signalling system a reaction stimulus indicating the event that a train had entered a specific section of track might be followed by a control action to alter signals ensuring that no other train enters the same section. In our insurance process, a reaction stimulus from a certain risk being underwritten might cause a excess risk warning to be sent to the underwriting manager: a control action. If we are using IT to implement an active model-based control system, then the active model and decision process will often be closely interwoven. Indeed, the decision process that is required may be a prime determinant of what is modelled.

The addition of a control action through a decision process leads to the model being active in two senses:
• The model actively changes in response to changes in its subject system.
• The model actively affects the behaviour of its subject system.
The model is maintaining the quality of the modelling relationship in both of these senses. If the purpose of the model is to provide a mechanism for imposing constraints on the subject system, this not only limits the possible behaviour of the subject system but also the scope of the active model.

It is important to realize the scope and generality of these concepts. The word *control* suggests limitation which is perhaps unfortunate. A system such as that depicted in Figure 3.4 is really a feedback system. Feedback systems can be constraint systems, whose purpose is to prevent the subject system from going beyond some acceptable threshold. However, feedback systems can also be enablers of behaviour in the subject system. For example, in a retail logistics system, the model may constrain the scheduling of deliveries to ensure that no two trucks will be delivering at the same time. Alternatively, knowing that a delivery has arrived may enable some of its items to be sold before they ever reach the display shelves.

We should be clear that the active model's subject system is not necessarily external to the system that is running the active model. An underwriter would probably use a spreadsheet on a networked PC to calculate a premium, and a word-processor to phrase a clause to be included in the policy document. These are activities in the subject system of the active model, yet the underwriter may also receive signals from the active model on that same PC.

These relationships are only about ensuring correspondence, in selected areas, between the two domains. In dealing with organization processes of any complexity it is usually the case that these relationships fail to be maintained in more and more circumstances over time. When this happens, we say that inconsistencies arise – the model is no longer representative of the real world. Of course the specific inconsistency might be transient – and consistency might be regained when the process moves on. It will however recur under the same circumstances. This issue will be discussed later in the Section 3.8.

Figure 3.5 illustrates how an active model can be developed and used in an organization. We will assume that a business process exists and is ongoing, initially guided by some procedure manuals and a lot of experience. In future it is to be directly supported by an active model. We will follow the route from capture of a performing process, its use as the basis for a redesigned process, its translation into machine-executable form, and lastly the process being supported by the enacting active model.

Initially, the performing process is, say, captured and modelled in some diagrammatic way. Using this descriptive model the goals, interactions, essential behaviours, and capability of resources can be subjected to inquiry and assessment. This model can provide the basis of a process redesign, in the knowledge of what the process support technologies can offer, as a prescriptive model. This redesigned process model is then encoded in some machine-executable language, and facilities provided to integrate other software tools and applications which are going to be used to augment human resources in the new process.

This code is compiled on a machine and executed. The executing code is now a part of the performing process (but note the remarks on domains made in the following section). It is a resource of the process. The people and software tools, participating in the process, work within the IT environment supporting the coordination which allows events to be tracked and new tasks to be made available. The engine driving the model schedules certain activity to take place, and signals this to the participants in the process. As these activities are undertaken and completed, the model detects the termination events causing in turn a rescheduling of activities and corresponding new signals to participants.

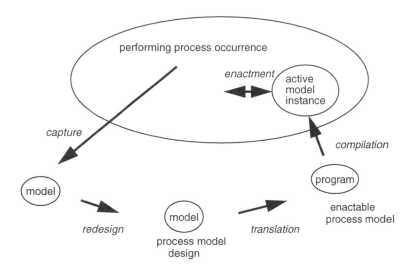

Fig. 3.5 The Relationship Between a Performing Process and its Active Model

We have three issues to resolve in the active model:
• What will the modelling relationship be?
• What will be the reactive links between the model and the business process (its subject)?
• What will be the active links between the model and the business process?

For a process describing the applying for insurance, one set of answers might be briefly:
• The model will record the current status of each inquiry (status can be new, in progress, suspended, quote, in force), and the person responsible for it.
• There will be reactive links for changes of status and of responsible person.
• There will be active links: (a) to inform the responsible person when an inquiry has been suspended for 20 days, and (b) to inform the new person responsible when an inquiry is assigned, or reassigned, to them.

An alternative set of answers might be:
• The model will record all the company's customers and the current state of all their policies and inquiries.
• There will be reactive links to update the model when an inquiry is received, a quote is refused, a policy starts, and a policy expires.
• There will be an active link to ensure that the company's total liability to one customer does not exceed some amount.

These two sets of answers will give quite different active process models. This is to be expected as the purpose of each model is quite different. The former coordinates the handling of each inquiry as it passes through the organization; the latter coordinates the organization's view of each customer.

There are two ways of looking at the kind of support provided by an active model. One, top-down, is to support the organization view of how things ought to be done. The system guides or controls the activities of individuals so that they do their work in a way which is perceived to be correct from the top of the organization. In particular, this view is concerned with coordinating activities across the organization to ensure the right things arrive or appear at the right place at the right time. The second view might be thought of as bottom-up, and this is the computerized assistance to help individuals (although in some organization cultures the word *compel* might be substituted for *help*) to do their work, or achieve their goals. This might, for example, mean that only a standardized word-processor is available for use on company documents, or it might be that all documents needed for a task are fetched automatically rather than the worker having to call them up individually, or the automating of routine work such as time-sheet collection and handling.

To some extent, *all* business software systems embody a model of behaviour and this model defines the possible interactions between the system and users that form part of the system's environment. What they fail to do is to maintain the model–subject relationship, and to explicitly model and support the coordination that is the core of an organization's function.

3.7 Process Domains

As indicated earlier, the study of organization processes (the coordination of human and software agents) is in many respects much less tractable than the study of manufacturing processes (the coordination of machine agents). The field of study is still immature, whereas the science of machine control has advanced steadily over the years. Evidence of this can be seen in the reduction in the number of human operators needed to ensure that machines work effectively. However, we are not seeking to apply the machine paradigm to business. People are individuals, and they cannot be controlled as can machines. To effect desired behaviour they can only be influenced, persuaded or trained to respond in certain ways. On the other hand they can demonstrate inspiration, intuition, imagination, and an understanding of purpose.

The outcome of human activity, with a given set of conditions, can be far from certain. What ought to transpire may not, and on the other hand that what seems impossible can in fact happen. Simple organization processes, such as expenses-claiming, can be usefully reduced to a sequence of steps which are relatively stable, over the years. This is the area of simple workflow. However, many organization processes are more concerned with intellectual activity (such as the software development process, or the insurance underwriting process) which cannot yet be routinized to the same degree. The concern here is to establish suitable work contexts for system developers or underwriters, where these contexts are tailored according to the particular phase of the process.

The advent of process technology (as represented by PSEEs, and Workflow Management Systems) has further complicated the picture as we try, through model enactment, to guide the activity of workers. In order to go some way to unravelling this complexity, Dowson and Fernström proposed the three distinct domains for studying organization processes. It is here extended to four in order to clarify their relationship to the concept of process itself. They believed it to be useful, in the context of organization processes which are supported by process technology and characterized by human non-determinism, to,

'distinguish (static) process definitions from their dynamic enactment, and to recognize that process performance... may not conform to what is specified in a process definition.'

Dowson and Fernström, 1994

The domains, including examples of each domain, and their relationships are shown graphically in Figure 3.6 and more fully described below:

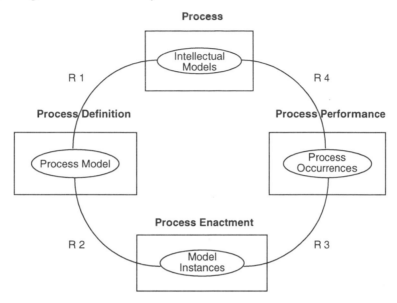

Fig. 3.6 Process Domains

- Process. This is an abstraction of the activity that is taking place in *performance*, i.e. without the fine-grained detail such as actual bindings to users, actual objects and tools. It is the template from which occurrences are derived. It may be any combination of narrative description, local rules, and the tacit knowledge and experiences of teams and individuals. Individuals may well have different understandings of the process, and the issues which were discussed in Section 3.2 are relevant to this domain.
- Process Definition. Here are concerns about defining the model. How to capture the model (as-is or to-be), how to represent it, which formalism to use, how to change the model. There are different kinds of definition model ranging from the generic model to customized. The generic model, or template, has to be refined, tailored, or specialized into a customized model in order for it to be used.
- Process Enactment. The prime concern here is about the IT support system, or process-centred environment, where the customized process model is expressed in computer code, it is bound to users in the system, to data objects and to tools and applications. There is interaction between the users and the system, with the system acting as a traffic policeman routing data objects and event signals around the network of users, machines, applications, tools, databases, and external services. Just how the enactment model interacts with a performing process depends on the architecture of the system and the nature of the model.
- Process Performance. This is the real world, where people do real work and engage in purposeful activity which is directly related to the process so that, ultimately, planned deliverables are furnished when needed and of appropriate quality. The activity of people (of course working through workstations or networked PCs) and machines is supported by the enacting model which seeks contributions from the users as and when necessary. Exactly how this is done depends on the support system and the culture of the organization.

There are many relations between these domains, the most significant of which are:
- R1. The model captures the process, and the process maps to the model. Usually the model is derived from the study of one or more occurrences. However, the process which is

modelled may not in fact be exemplified by observed occurrences, and may be based on historic information.
- R2. The enactment is an example of the model, and is bound to real users, machines, and data objects. In software terms, the enacting model is an instance of the process model type.
- R3. The enacting model influences process performance, performance responds to enactment and vice versa. It is here that the model/subject inconsistencies become apparent, e.g. if the enacting model seeks to invoke an activity for a process participant for which the latter is not ready, or knows to be redundant.
- R4. The performing process is an occurrence of an abstract process.

This view of the distinct domains in which a process has different meanings enables us to appreciate the complexity of human–machine interaction, and so attempt to deal with it in a more systematic manner. It can be applied to all kinds of model enactments.

In this book our particular interest is in the domain of Process Definition and the major content of Part 2 is in this area, but process enactment is also discussed in Chapter 10.

3.8 More about the Meta-Process

3.8.1 Introduction

The issue of evolution was first raised in this book early in Chapter 2. One thing that we know about any designed business process or information system is that it is *unlikely* to be perfectly suitable for the purpose for which it was designed. This is not because the organization is in a state of chaos, or because the designers were incompetent, or because people did not know what they wanted. The fact is that processes can be context sensitive, and the tools at our disposal are not yet (and may never be) sufficiently adequate for representing the context of human behaviour in all its subtle complexity. If we cannot represent it then we cannot design explicitly for it. It follows that our designed information system, intended to support the process, might not be correct and may well have to be changed subsequent to implementation.

In fact, even if we were able to model a process perfectly and use it to construct a support system for that selfsame process, the support system would begin to atrophy almost immediately. In following the process, people would see better ways of doing things: see short-cuts, see alternatives for tool usage, see the opportunity for concurrent working, and so on. It is desirable, and in fact even necessary, to be able to respond to these concerns.

It seems strange, therefore, to design models of operational processes and IS to support such processes without also designing the mechanism which will allow them to change, to support the co-evolution of business and technology as goals, technologies and the environment change. One way of dealing with these issues is to construct a process to guide this change, as if change itself was a routine part of the normal operation of a process.

The need to structure change in IT systems has been recognized for many years and techniques and tools have been designed, and are continuing to be designed, to address this very issue. The focus in the information systems domain has been to *design for each change* and to improve maintenance processes, rather than *design-in change*, which represents our position.

Most managerial control is concerned with regulating activity, such that outcomes are within pre-defined bounds and it focuses on the manipulation of resources and handling exceptional situations. However there is another aspect to control, which is to change the process itself. For example, changing the outcomes of the process (e.g. to produce different things), or to adapt the process to changes in the environment (e.g. to produce the same thing, but to best accommodate a change in state legislation), or to change the process to improve its performance, or to make better use of staff skills. This latter kind of control is within the domain of the meta-process. A meta-process is a process whose purpose is to manipulate another process. The most obvious reason for manipulating a process is to change it, and one of the most common reasons for wanting to change it is to improve it. This is of course can be viewed as just one way of controlling the process.

Can we have a meta-process for the meta-process? The answer is yes. There is no reason why the meta-process should not be subject to the same or similar kinds of scrutiny that are commonly applied to straightforward operational processes. As with the operational process, there may well be scope for improvement of the meta-process, and for revisiting lower-level objectives.

We focus on the meta-process rather than the more general management control process because the latter brings within its domain many issues with much wider ramifications (e.g. organizational concerns and social issues) that are outside the scope of this book. In modelling change processes, our aim is to be as culturally neutral as possible: we try not to assume what is good or bad. Rather, we propose a model which can be adapted for use in any organizational context to be in sympathy with what is perceived to be the ethos of the organization.

The approach taken in this book is generic. If we can determine such a structure for the meta-process, then this structure should be capable of being used in any number of different organizational contexts. Many of the artefacts needed by normal control can be built into an operational process: resourcing, workloads, reporting, etc. What is missing is a way of specializing this control to include the control of change.

3.8.2 Change and Evolution

Change is becoming more pervasive, a response to relentless pressure to minimize cost yet maintain or improve quality, and to the need to exploit rapidly changing technologies. The soaring costs of badly handled change are becoming apparent. We need to find ways of achieving the balance between the use of process in maintaining consistent products (if that is what is desired) whilst at the same time encouraging process innovation.

Workers in the area of software configuration management indicate that there are different aspects of change which must be addressed. There is the nature of the change itself, and what it is to be applied to. Our interest is in anticipated or planned change. Such change can be short- or long-term, tactical or strategic, incremental or radical. It involves changing a process in some general desired direction (to use different resources, produce different outputs, utilize different skills etc.), and can be:
• Improvement – making a better process.
• Maintenance – routine correction of errors as they become manifest.
• Enhancement – accomplishing more tasks in the process.
• Development – filling out the process definition.
These different kinds of change may be made to all or any of three kinds of process model: to the template or abstract model if the changes are to affect future process solutions; to its customized form in the process definition, the detailed textual or graphical plan of the process; and to the currently enacting process.

There is much literature on the subject of evolution in IT systems (ICSM, 1999), and a growing body of work referring to evolution of process models. Unfortunately there is little consistency in the use of the term. In biological terms, *evolution* refers to the phenomenon whereby each successive generation of an organism is tested against the environment within which it exists. Those that have a poor fit with the environment are less likely to survive to produce new generations, whereas those that are more suited to their environment tend to survive, and so their offspring also tend to survive. Organisms that fail the test tend to die out, those that pass tend to survive.

Any analogy with business processes and information systems is a false one; however, some interesting parallels can be drawn. We can say that a business information system is continuously tested against its environment, and this testing gives rise to many modifications which are incorporated in new versions of the system. In this context the word *environment* means the users of the system, both at a practical level and at a strategic level in an organization. These new versions can be thought of as being better suited to the environment.

As mentioned earlier, the relationship between the model and the world must be maintained if models are to remain valid. The relation has to be consistent over time. Lehman has pointed out (Lehman, 1991) that the maintenance of consistency is one of the purposes of evolution. There is a natural tendency for these inconsistencies to increase as time passes (Belady, 1985). This occurs for many reasons. It might be because assumptions held by the modeller about the real world process are wrong, or because environmental conditions have changed. Alternatively, inconsistencies may arise as staff see better ways of doing things or because the skill set of the workers changes. The process of change may itself generate further inconsistencies – changes to the model to resolve certain inconsistencies might be made in ways which are badly structured, thus propagating yet further inconsistencies.

Evolution is thus the way that inconsistencies between the model, the system, and the real world are kept to a minimum. It does this by means of constant testing and adaptation of the model from a previous form to a new one. It is change with direction, consistency, quality, and responsiveness.

In the absence of maintenance, the system will deteriorate. The activities in the real world will depart more and more from the activities modelled in the system, and the system will have to be discarded (Lehman, 1980). There is a parallel to this in the term *entropy*, used in the natural sciences as a measure of disorder in closed systems. This has been adopted analogically by systems scientists (Katz and Khan, 1978) who find it appropriate to apply this law to organic-like systems where it refers to a natural tendency to increasing chaos, i.e. where positive action is needed simply to avert degradation. It is these concerns about organization processes that underpin the need for a meta-process, a mechanism which manages process evolution in order to maintain consistency.

Changes to the generic model can be performed in isolation from the operational process ('the next time we do this, we ought to go about it *this* way, but it's not worth changing everything now'). The definition can be changed, tested, and forgotten about in the knowledge that the next time it is adapted into a process definition, the amended behaviour will be invoked. A growing body of work has addressed this kind of change, particularly in the software engineering domain as reflected by the continuing interest shown in the International Conference on the Software Process (ICSP, 1996), International Software Process Workshop (ISPW, 1998), and the European Workshop on Software Process Technology (Gruhn, 1998). A particular focus at these venues is often process improvement. A number of approaches for process improvement have been studied, mostly project-oriented systematic cycle models, proposing that the lessons from individual projects ought to be somehow packaged and used to improve the next project. Some – for example the Software Engineering Institute's CMM (Paulk et al., 1993) – are the result of many years' study. This method categorizes the software development processes of organizations according to a maturity level which is said to give an indication of predictability: the organization's ability to successfully plan a development project. CMM promotes the idea of an organization's Standard Software Process, and measures its maturity. This is the abstract process model that every software development project which is initiated in that organization has to follow. It has of course to be tailored for the particular needs of each project.

Changes to a process occurrence or instance are much more complex than changes applied to passive models. The application of the change takes a finite period of time, and during this time the state of the instance may well be changing. The way to structure the change might well be to define a transient-change process which could itself be supported.

A meta-process is not simply a special case of a production process that produces changes rather than products. In addition, it needs to have a mechanism to detect the results of change. It needs to support feedback, to assess it, to initiate corresponding change when appropriate, and to implement that change.

3.8.3 Requirements for Evolution Support

The remarks in the previous section lead us to certain specific requirements for any model of a process which purports to support the evolution of an operational process (Derniame et al., 1999). Such a model has to:

- Manage the consistency between the performing process, and the process model guiding the enactment. The purpose of this managing activity is to identify and resolve inconsistencies. Any inconsistency between the process model and the performing process will be manifest as a problem. These inconsistencies must be picked up, analysed, and some decision made as to their resolution. Some may require changes to be made to the enactable process model.
- Manage the integrity of the structure of the process model during evolution. The purpose of managing is to maintain the structural integrity of the system. There is ample evidence (Leintz and Swanson, 1980) that, as more changes are made to a system, so the order of the original system tends to be destroyed. This is because of the limited time and possibly limited understanding of those making the changes, but also because changes tend to create new problems. A model will have to address this specific concern.
- Manage the complexity of the problem. Managing the problem so that it can be solved by known means. It is most unusual for the solution processes for particular problems to be obvious. A mechanism will have to be included in the model which acknowledges the complexity of the real world, and which provides mechanisms for dealing with it.

To consolidate this explanation of the meta-process, we will describe an approach towards defining a model of such a process. It is based on the human intuitive problem-solving process.

3.8.4 The Basis for an Approach

First we can see if it might be possible to structure change activities as a process, by taking the case of a single planned change. The target of the change is a process model p which is guiding some real-world activity. It is on-going, people and machines are being guided by it, following a certain pattern. We want to change that pattern of behaviour for another, say p', preferably without interrupting the work which is being done. This is illustrated in Figure 3.7. Now we determine the pattern of activities (or change process) $cp1$ which, if applied to p, will cause it to be transformed into p'. Implementing process $cp1$ results in p being transformed to p'.

If we then want to move from p' to p'' then we will have to come up with another, different set of change activities, $cp2$. Now real-world change processes can be very complex indeed. We

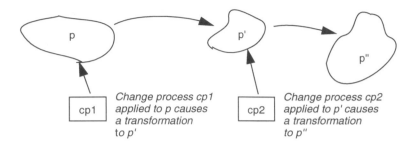

Fig. 3.7 The Transformation Process

understand that in our turbulent business environment the process *p* is likely to change quite frequently, and the labour of constructing a new change process *cp ab initio* for each and every change can be onerous. It seems highly desirable and sensible to devote some effort to understanding this change process with a view to establishing a single process which would have as one of its inputs, process *p*, and as its output, process *p'*. This is the meta-process.

We can start by asking the question *why?*. What is it that warrants the change? It may be a problem, it may be an opportunity, or what Checkland (1981) refers to as, 'expressions of concern'. It is very unlikely to be neatly encapsulated, in the way that mathematical problems can be stated.

This general question was addressed by Simon in the field of artificial intelligence for the development of a General Problem Solver. Viewing the organization as an adaptive organism, Simon believes that there is a class of problems whose solution recognises a fundamental relationship between state and process. This relationship is between the world *as sensed* and the world *as acted upon*. The *problem* is perceived as a difference between two real-world states: the way it is, and the way we would like it to be.

'Given a desired state of affairs and an existing state of affairs, the task of the adaptive organism is to find the difference between these two states and then to find the correlating process that will erase the difference.'

Simon, 1981

Thus, viewing change as a problem to be solved provides a simple structure for the change process; it is the essential link between the initial behaviour which *p* represents, and the altered behaviour represented by *p'*. This structure has three components (shown in Figure 3.8):
• Activity associated with identifying the problem.
• Activity associated with devising some course of action.
• Simply carrying out this action.
However this is not quite the whole story. We know from experience that the course of action might not be the right one, and even if it is the right one, details might have to be changed to ensure that the problem can in fact be solved. We can take advantage of the fact that following a course of action is not a blind process for we humans. As we follow it, we learn more about it and about the problem we are trying to address. In so doing we become more aware of the likelihood of success.

Thus, once we have progressed a little way along the problem-solving process, we can re-assess the situation. We can reflect on what has been accomplished and what remains to be done. This reassessment takes place in the light of the improved understanding of both the problem itself and the process which we have adopted as a means of solving it. In other words, it can be tested against its environment. As a result, we can do one of three things. First, if things appear to be going well, we can do nothing. Secondly, if the solution process is seen to be in some way deficient, the objectives which determine this process can be reviewed and a new course of action devised and acted upon. Thirdly, it may also be the case that the objectives are unattainable, in which case the problem cannot be solved, so either the definition of the problem can be changed, or the project can be abandoned.

There is thus a need for periodic review and reassessment. For this to occur there has to be some knowledge of the state of the solution activity, and this is achieved by feeding back state information to the decision-maker.

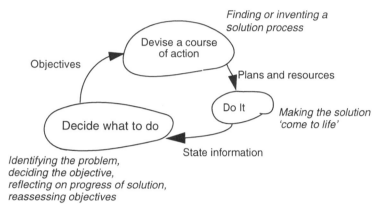

Fig. 3.8 A Problem-Solving Process

To recapitulate, we view a desired change to a process as a problem, which can be expressed as a difference between real-world states. The transformation from the problem-laden world to one that is problem-free lies in determining a pattern of actions or steps (i.e. a process) which will hopefully achieve the change, and then implementing this process. As the steps are carried out, so our knowledge of both the problem itself, and the current solution process, improves. This learning will impart a growing recognition of the likelihood of the objectives being achieved, and the situation may arise when the solution process ought to be adapted in some way to improve this likelihood of success, or indeed that the objectives themselves need to be amended in order to make them more attainable.

The process as it stands has some useful properties: it is simple, it is generic, and it provides for feedback. However it is not very useful in this form, and Chapter 5 introduces a model based on this approach and it is illustrated by example in Chapter 9.

3.9 Conclusion

This chapter has identified, explored and developed a number of fundamental concepts that we need in order to improve our understanding of the process phenomenon, and how we should model it.

In Section 3.2 we related the organization processes we observe in banks, insurance companies, hospitals etc. to the more abstract concept of process itself. In so doing we identified the characteristics of such processes that cause difficulties for us. Later we proposed a particular view of the process, the interactional view, which is a key development in our understanding of business information systems.

Our difficulties in grappling with the concept of process are reflected in the many ways available to us for representing and modelling them. No particular kind of method is suitable for all situations and viewpoints. The alternatives were discussed and a unique approach using the active model was developed which has the property of maintaining the model/subject relationship even when the shape or form of the subject changes.

The distinction between automatic, machine-like processes and the non-deterministic human activity processes was clarified by means of identifying the different domains of process modelling. In particular it provided a framework for exploring the difference between how a process might be defined, and how it might actually unfold in real life.

Lastly, the concept of the meta-process was introduced as a way of dealing with a number of problems associated with process models – the recurring problem of inconsistency between subject and model, the problem of maintaining the integrity of the model over time, and how to deal with the situation where process activity must start before the process is fully defined.

Many of these concepts are still fluid; however, they offer a promising basis on which to develop of our approach to business information systems. They provide a platform for the modelling method set out in Part 2 of this book.

4

Engineering of Processes

The previous chapters have explored the problem domain with which we are concerned – organizations and their software systems – and now in this chapter we move on to issues surrounding the way that we determine solutions. It introduces the essentials of an engineering approach to problem-solving through process modelling. It discusses the characteristics of such an approach, some relevant issues, its limitations, and how it needs to be refocused to addresss the real needs of business.

4.1 Introduction

A key phrase that emerges in Chapter 2 is that expressing the need to *design for freedom*. There is a fear among professionals that the provision of IT to support their work will inevitably lead to a more constrained, more closely monitored work environment that will be bereft of those features that make work interesting – variety, self-imposed prioritizing, the opportunity to explore alternative ways of accomplishing tasks, and so on. Such activity is difficult (if not impossible) to describe in detail and consequently information systems tend to ignore them. This is often blamed on the poor engineering of IS, however it may not be the engineering as such that is the problem, but the way that it is used.

Engineering is the application of scientific principles to the solution of real-world problems. It is not about finding the truth (although of course the truth is important), it is about intervening in the real world with artificial constructs intended to ameliorate some condition otherwise affecting people. It is about making best use of the knowledge that we have, albeit imperfect, incomplete and uncertain, and finding safe, pragmatic and economic solutions within known constraints. An engineering approach implies an objective frame of reference, a reasonably non-controversial definition of the problem, a systematic analysis of the problem domain, the development of alternative proposals for solutions, and analysis of them, to establish if they are likely to be acceptable and practicable and, if so, which is the optimum solution. Solutions have to be implementable. This approach is the opposite of an intuitive, inexperienced, high risk trial-and-error intervention (although these sometimes have their place, such as when there is thought to be no time for a more systematic approach).

The engineering of processes is a way of solving problems arising in the context of an organization, in particular those organizational problems whose solution lies in exploiting the use of coordinative and integrative technologies. As with other problems suitable for engineering-type solutions, a problem statement can make specific reference to a process, or it may only identify symptoms from which the actual problem(s) may have to be deduced, and which must in turn be addressed. The common concern has a clear starting point in the identification and definition of a problem. Simon remarks that:

'Science is concerned with understanding the natural world, and engineering with intervening in the natural world with artificial constructs for human benefit.'

Simon, 1981

The term *engineering* thus relates to a kind of problem-solving through the construction of artificial artefacts (both physical and abstract). It is used to adapt nature to suit people, but in so doing it may change people's behaviour. It produces things as opposed to experiences. It also relates to a domain of expertise, something essentially practical. It deals with real-world knowledge and has values which place importance on economy of use of materials, and has a scientific basis. The artefacts produced frequently remain in existence for a very long time, and therefore for some kinds of artefact, such as software systems, problems arise about how to adapt them as their environments change over time.

The next section will outline the historical development of the engineering approach from earliest times to the present day. In Section 4.3 the engineering approach to problem-solving is discussed, along with its merits and constraints. Following that, Section 4.4 explores issues of the application of software engineering in the area of business systems. Consideration is given in Section 4.5 to treating process engineering a professional discipline.

4.2 Historical Development

The origins of the engineering approach were in the craft solutions to everyday problems. They were based essentially on personal experiential knowledge arrived at by trial and error, learning on an individual basis from observing what solutions worked and what failed. Each solution served as a model for the next. As communication skills improved, so the dissemination of this knowledge became more widespread, and this experience, characterized as rules of thumb, became part of folklore. It had its peak of expression in the ecclesiastic structures of the Middle Ages. A craft approach is associated with the culture which Alexander (1964) refers to as *unselfconscious* design. All thinking effort is applied to solving the problem, and very little, if any, addresses the quality of the activity used for solving the problem.

The Renaissance brought about a new spirit of inquiry, so it became possible to conceptualize and start to understand why some solutions worked, and some didn't. It became possible to communicate conceptions in designs which were in fact models of proposed interventions, and which facilitated the development of ideas, enabled control of larger constructions, and allowed debate and discussion on the outcomes without very expensive experimentation. When the design is implemented in the real world, the problem which it addresses will hopefully be resolved. This kind of culture is referred to by Alexander as *self-conscious* design; explicit consideration is given to the process by which real-world problems are solved and there exists a cadre of specialist practitioners who undertake this, and who can be distinguished from practitioners who implement the solutions.

During the 19th century the view became widespread that only knowledge gained through scientific inquiry could improve the human condition. So much so, that the so-called Positivist Epistemology took root which asserted that:
• Empirical science was the only source of positive knowledge of the world.
• Mysticism and superstition had to be cleansed from mankind.
• The technology itself had to be made political and moral.
This was the basis of Technical Rationality (Schön, 1983) which became the frame of reference of the application of the results of science to the improvement of the human condition by practitioners of various disciplines (notably medicine and engineering). It is an objective reduction-

ist approach which seeks to characterize a situation in terms of identifiable objects with well-defined properties, finding which general rules apply (determined previously from observation and experience), and applying them to a current situation. This approach has been very successful and has, until recently, hardly been questioned.

In the Middle Ages, the only kind of engineering that existed was in fact military engineering. The drive of the war efforts, at that time, forced the development of engineering skills in defences, siege engines, and tunnelling. As the commercial exploitation of these skills for the benefit of society as a whole became a practicality, a new discipline was established, that of civil engineering. In other words, the more specialized discipline split from its parent when the needs of practitioners (for the sharing of experiences) were not met by their parent body. This development has continued to the present day, and if process engineering were ever to be regarded as a discipline, then it would be seen as an offshoot of software engineering.

4.3 The Engineering Approach to Solving Problems

4.3.1 Technical Rationality

The modern manifestation of Technical Rationality came about in the explosion of research work during and subsequent to the Second World War. If a great social objective could be clearly defined, if national commitment could be mustered, if unlimited resources were made available, then it could be achieved. This notion reinforced the idea of scientific research as the basis for engineering practice. But now the flaws are becoming more prominent, and there are many instances where technologically based human endeavour has brought about harmful unforeseen consequences, demonstrating a failure to live up to their norms, an inability to help society as much as promised, indeed of even degrading the human condition. Professionals are becoming increasingly aware of the phenomena of complexity, of uncertainty, of instability, and of value-conflict, which do not fit with Technical Rationality, and which they are ill-equipped to address.

The Technical Rational view of the use of natural sciences has thus been overly simplified. The emphasis on the *solving* ignores the *setting*. The latter refers to the process by which the engineer defines the decision to be made, the ends to be achieved, and the means which may be chosen. The problems which are addressed are not given, but are constructed from a description of problem situations which can be puzzling, troubling or uncertain. Problem-setting is a necessary condition of technical problem-solving, but it is not a technical problem! In problem-setting we name the things to which we will attend, and frame the context in which we will do it.

The engineering approach is frequently (and with some justification) criticized for being too mechanistic, unresponsive to human needs, lacking in vision, subservient to management pressures (e.g. time), and unawareness of or disregard for political issues. Calls are heard for a reversion to more intuitive approaches. Blockley criticises the scientific method as being simply, 'selective inattention' (Blockley, 1992). It selects from the totality of the problem only those aspects that can be dealt with, and proceeds by decomposing that problem situation until the components can be solved. These partial solutions are then reassembled into the complete solution. Critics aver that engineering knowledge is neither value-free, nor complete, and furthermore that objective rationality is in fact impossible to achieve (Simon, 1976). The methods of engineering do not take cognizance of the concept of bounded rationality, which recognises that there are constraints on the cognitive and information processing powers of the decision-making agent.

4.3.2 Design Strategies

Engineers are not so much interested in the steps needed to solve the problem as in the solution itself, the physical intervention which brings about the desired change, such that the real world plus intervention yields a better world. The interest in the steps is secondary insofar that the solution must be practicable, and capable of being implemented. The engineering intervention is conventionally looked upon as having three distinct steps: understand the problem, design a solution (the *Oxford English Dictionary* definition of which is, 'to contrive or to invent'), and implement that solution in the real world.

The development of a design is an essential preliminary to the implementation in the real world of a solution, and central to an engineering activity. Thus design can exist as both a noun (the product of the design activity) and as a verb. In this section we are concerned with design as an activity. Dasgupta (1991) has identified its principal features:

- The requirements which are the specification of the problem may initially be neither precise or complete.
- A design is an abstract description of a target artefact which serves as a blueprint, a medium of criticism and experimentation and analysis.
- Designers are faced with the problem of bounded rationality: the limited capacity of people to make full rational decisions, and limited ability to grasp the full implications of such decisions, so they are always conjectural.
- Design decisions are, more often than not, satisficing procedures (those that lead to satisfactory and sufficient solutions, as opposed to those that optimize solutions).
- Designers must treat as real the imagined future.

The distinction must be drawn between the organizational process of design and the personal process of design, the former more concerned with coordinating the sub-products of design activity, the latter concerned with the skills, techniques and tools needed to construct these sub-components. Many design activities require the concurrent effort of many people: the coordination of this activity is itself a major task and the control of team activity (project management) features largely as a domain of interest. There is no single strategy to create a design. The activity is highly context-, skill-, and cognition-dependent. Different people approach the problems in different ways yet may well arrive at the same solution. The methods adopted are different and a number of paradigms can be identified.

Certain steps, not strictly speaking sequential, can be identified in engineering problem-solving. Any activity can legitimately be called a step if it can tell the designers what they need to know, but don't know, in order to proceed towards a complete design. The existence of three broad phases of Analysis, Synthesis and Evaluation (known alternatively as divergence/transformation/convergence) have been generally accepted. What remains unclear is just how they are brought together and interact. The route does not exist in any detail before the design activity begins: the route will only be known in the abstract, but the detail must be invented and emerge for each occurrence. These phases consist of:

- Analysis of requirements. Defining the requirements of the problem that is to be addressed. This requires divergent thought, as the original problem statement (or design brief) may be erroneous. It involves a reappraisal of the problem statement with a view to drawing out the hidden assumptions on which the statement is based, and the assessing of the validity of these assumptions.
- Synthesizing solutions. Decomposing the problem into component problems until such a point that these components can be solved, and the solutions synthesized together to construct the total solution. Establishing a pattern that is precise enough to allow convergence of more abstract solutions on to a single design which can be refined in detail.

- Evaluating alternatives, and selecting the one most suitable for implementation (criteria can be simple, such as cost, or quite complex, such as user-friendliness) and verifying by analysis that it is in fact correct. There is generally only limited optimizing of solutions. Not all the design may be done at this point: well-understood components can be left till later, knowing that whatever solution is adopted for them, they will have no unforeseen affect on the grand design.

The Analysis–Synthesis–Evaluation (ASE) paradigm assumes that the requirements are known before synthesis takes place, and that the design activity and design artefact can be compartmentalized. It is a highly ideal situation, and although this state of affairs is very much the exception rather than the rule, this is the model of the design process which is most commonly accepted and has in fact been reasonably successful in 'hard' engineering. Notwithstanding these reservations, this approach can be useful for some components of the overall design activity.

In recent years a number of workers have realized that part of the problem of ASE is that whereas Technical Rationalism might be an appropriate paradigm to adopt for certain parts of the development process, other components might be more successfully treated by taking other viewpoints. For example: the development process can be viewed as one of mutual learning, where, over the duration of a development project, the expert learns more about the business environment, and the users learn more about the potentials of the technical systems. It is clear from this viewpoint that the requirements will never be fully and correctly known, and the development process must somehow take cognizance of this.

Hirscheim and Klein (1989), referring to information systems methodologies, point out that the kind of solution which is adopted can be heavily influenced by the viewpoint from which the problem is approached, for example in the way that the requirements are elicited, developed and analyzed. There is, as yet, no appreciation of which is best, but they can be discussed in order that the values associated with different viewpoints are appreciated. The authors have characterized approaches in terms of subjectivity/objectivity, and order/conflict, and indicate four typical viewpoints, which they refer to as functional, neo-humanist, social relativistic, and social relativist. The conventional engineering approach can be seen to be that of functionalist, with the engineer playing the role of expert, and the problem definition is insulated from human concerns. Approaches characterized by other viewpoints may well lead to a better solution. The practical outcome of this is that although it might not be possible yet to prescribe an optimum problem-solving route, the issues can be presented, stakeholders can be made aware of them, and borne in mind as the search for a solution takes place.

Dasgupta describes other paradigms appropriate for the design activity itself:

- AI. A kind of automated problem-solving approach with its most successful application in the so-called *expert systems*. It takes relatively ill-structured problems, and searches for a solution by applying rules to a a knowledge base of domain information. It needs much domain-specific knowledge and, so far, has been unsuccessful in eliciting what Schön refers to as *tacit knowledge*. It is not yet a useful general paradigm for process engineering, although Decision Support components based on AI paradigms play useful roles.
- Algorithmic. Appropriate for well-structured problems, i.e. the requirements are all empirical in the sense that it is possible to determine exactly if the design meets the requirements. This views design as the execution of a domain-specific algorithm. Its use is in problems that are well-structured. In the field of process engineering this approach is not useful in-the-large but might have application in smaller components of the overall problem.
- Formal Design. The requirements can be represented in a mathematical system, and the design process is one of mathematical modelling, and thence reasoning and proof. A method of overcoming the problem that the testing can show the presence of errors but never their

absence. It is particularly important for safety-critical systems, but cost difficulties inhibit widespread use even in that domain.

• Evolutionary Design (also known as Theory of Plausible Designs). A view of the design process where each elaboration of the design is tested against the requirements, and the result of this test determines the form of the next cycle. It recognizes that the requirements for the design may need to be changed, so, over the period of design activity, there is continuous testing and mutual adaptation of both design and requirements and they converge to ultimately be consistent. It takes an empirical scientific view of the design activity. This is of particular interest where the criteria for correctness and usefulness lie in the domain of business values, organizational consensus, fashion and prejudice, and is the paradigm promoted later in Part 2 of this book.

Of course as well as the design strategy being evolutionary, the artefact made manifest from the design must itself evolve. This evolution, however, takes place in a different environment from that of the design. It is an environment of users, users in the wider sense of those who make use of the system in their work and also those who have a responsibility for the overall performance of the system. It is this view of evolution that is modelled in the Process for Process Evolution which is introduced in Chapter 5.

Part of the design activity is the preparation of the specification for implementation. This is a narrative to support the graphical designs, generally giving overall guidance on how the design is to be interpreted. Once the design is complete, it has to be implemented in the real world. The detail logistics of translating the conceptual model, typically on paper, into its manifestation as a real physical object that in fact will solve the original problem are not the concern of the designers. They are the concern of the implementer.

4.4 The Engineering of Software in Organizations

In Chapter 2 it was noted that an important reference point for the process approach developed in this book is software engineering. This discipline arose from the seeming inability of the software development community to provide what the wider community expected of it, which was cheap, dependable and trouble-free software. It was not spawned from another discipline, but it emerged as a tangible response of academics and developers to these problems. The Institute of Electrical and Electronics Engineers provides a useful, but limited, definition of software engineering:

'The application of systematic, disciplined, quantifiable approach to the development, operation and maintenance of software; that is the application of engineering to software.'

IEEE, 1990

The engineering of software thus implies the application of rigorous methods and quality-control techniques to resolve highly complex design problems. The same principles of rigour should apply whatever the problem domain (e.g. the cockpit of a jet fighter, an insurance company, a hydroelectric plant). Notwithstanding the many notable advances in the field of software engineering, many of the problems which the discipline has sought to confront have proved intractable. It is arguable that this is especially true in the context of organizational software (e.g. banks, sales teams and, for that matter, ambulance services and stock markets). Information-systems research has been able to explain this failure by reference to the objectivist assumptions underlying engineering approaches. An assumption of objectivity in many software engineering projects is inherently unsustainable. Faced with divergent thoughts and opinions about the need for some IT implementation, the engineer is forced to ask, 'Whose problem am I addressing?', or, 'Whose solution am I creating?'. It is in trying to deal with such questions that the engineer reaches the limits of the engineering paradigm of technical rationality, and the need for a more holistic view of the problem domain becomes apparent. This implies a dialogue between the software engineer, social scientist and management scientist.

It has already been mentioned in Section 4.3.1 that there are intrinsically two facets to an engineering approach: the problem itself and the techniques which the engineer has available to address such problems. As has also been mentioned, it is often the case that the engineer cannot address all aspects of a problem, but will address that part of it that is capable of being addressed. The fact that solutions cannot be found for some aspects of the problem does not mean that they are unimportant.

The availability of techniques is dependent on the exploitation of technologies, and the demand by users for better solutions. When an engineer cannot address an aspect of a problem, it is either because it is too difficult for technologies, or because technology developers have not considered it important enough to address.

The issue of change was first raised in Chapter 2. A problem of technologies is that, far from assisting organizations to develop, they can be seen in some cases to be inhibiting that change. Now software engineers are becoming aware of these issues, especially as their own businesses are typical of those which seem to be in a state of unremitting flux.

Many issues relating to system evolution have emerged in the software engineering domain (Robertson, 1998). However, the aspect which is pre-eminent is the fact that owners of systems have in the past been obliged to set down a set of requirements for their systems without much regard for potential problems. The missing requirement is for the system itself to support the management of inconsistencies, a requirement that would result in systems that could support their own adaptation. There is a need to keep the system in synchronization with its environment and this implies the need for an active model which will maintain this relationship over time. An important aspect of this synchronization is its degree, i.e. what constraints are applied or what autonomy is acceptable over a number of dimensions. These dimensions include the freedom to modify business gaols, the freedom of users to undertake tasks in certain ways, and the freedom to adapt behaviour over time.

It is this need that has led to the development of the active model which has already been referred to, and the Process for Process Evolution which is introduced in Chapter 5.

4.5 Process Engineering as a Discipline

Professional disciplines in general seem to have certain identified characteristics (Shaw, 1990): practitioners in general serving a kind of apprenticeship for about 10 years after obtaining the relevant academic qualification; possessing about 50,000 items of domain knowledge (items that have to be recalled by the practitioner and which cannot be deduced); having tacit knowledge, which is the ability to solve domain problems without knowing exactly *how*; possessing a repertoire of standard solutions to recurring problems and having a distinct vocabulary which allows them to address concerns in their domain in a precise and succinct manner. Thus it is appropriate to characterize engineering and its offshoots as professional disciplines.

Interest in process modelling as a field of inquiry arose initially from the concern of the software engineering community about how to address the so-called software crisis. The insight that quality products needed a quality process, led in the mid'80s to work both in the modelling of processes, specifically the software development process, and also in the development of process-support technologies. These technologies themselves were initially environments for software developers which coordinated the use of tools but later became environments to coordinate both tools and developers. The technical problems which had to be overcome were so vast that little attention was paid by computer scientists to the true nature of the organization process which the technologies were intended to support. Now that these hurdles have been largely overcome, the software process technology community is becoming much more interested in the true nature of these processes in order that they may design technologies which offer more intimate, flexible and acceptable process support.

Thus, over a period of time, similar concerns were identified in the wider business community and a special vocabulary developed, not shared by all software engineers but becoming a bridge between the communities of computer science and management science.

The field of process engineering has been recognised in literature only recently (Lehman, 1991; Madhavji, 1991). It has emerged from the domain of software engineering by virtue of the fact that workers found themselves studying organization processes from the perspective of software engineers in order to better represent such processes in suitable technologies.

Inconclusive comparisons can be made between soft engineering approaches (i.e. those dealing with information systems or economic models) and those of physical (traditional) engineering, especially when trying to understand why soft engineering has been relatively unsuccessful. Some say that the rules of physical engineering just cannot be applied to 'soft' disciplines.

An engineering approach has traditionally been tied to Technical Rationality, and many problems in the domain can best be addressed in this way – apparently successfully providing cost-effective solutions with, generally, low risk of failure. However, the discipline of software engineering, the parent of process engineering, has not been characterized by such success.

However, engineers are learning from some spectacular failures, and recognize that for too long they have been associated with a single objective viewpoint of the problem, and a rather narrow scope for the solution. This is slowly changing. The existence of other viewpoints are recognized by some workers, accepted and welcomed. The expert alone cannot properly find the best solution. This view has to some extent been recognized in the number of varied design paradigms which have developed, and which will be discussed in the following section.

Engineering is not an exact science. Outcomes may not be totally assured, but it is now recognised that requirements can and *must* change in response to external events, and also in response to features of an emerging design. This instability is recognized in certain new design paradigms which try to keep the best features of Technical Rationality but seek to accommodate the non-deterministic features of human behaviour, the uncertainty and learning by making use of an evolutionary approach, which is outlined later.

A discipline of process engineering would naturally have much in common with that of software engineering, yet the latter is still trying to establish its identity after 30 years. Jackson (1994), on discussing software engineering, asserts that, 'the design space is, as yet, very narrow, there are no "standard" designs'. It is the same with process engineering. We are at an early stage in development and need to build up a library of such standards (as accepted by practitioners rather than defined by committee). The absence of such standards means that our frame of reference is ill-defined and the results of the engineering of processes are not very predictable. However, as a means of going some way to addressing this, we have identified the concerns which, we believe, shape the way that we should approach problems and thus in turn shape the solutions that emerge. However it must be said that we have yet to, 'characterize the problem for which our expertise provides a solution'.

As a first step towards achieving this mature discipline, a frame of reference can established from which to view problems (or problem states), and which might form a basis for valuing solutions (i.e. to raise awareness of those values which can result in a good solution, and what properties are sought). A solution which is elegant when viewed from a traditional engineering viewpoint may be a poor solution when viewed from a sociological viewpoint. The concerns of importance to the process approach are as follows:

- Our domain of interest is a socio-technical system. IT cannot be considered in isolation from its users, and vice versa.
- People are important. The most brilliant technical solution will be unsuccessful in implementation if users remain unconvinced.
- Study of process can often bring about improvement. However, it must be remembered that the structure of organization activities is only one facet of a process.
- It is essential to improve our understanding of what processes *are* if they are to be consistently successfully supported.
- Problem-solving is evolutionary: requirements and design evolve jointly to attain a state of mutual adaptation, and the implemented solution itself must also subsequently evolve in relation to its environment of users and other influences.
- A *satisficing* solution (one that is considered satisfactory and sufficient) is usually considered to be adequate as there is as yet inadequate knowledge of means of optimizing.
- Active models may have a key role to play in supporting process evolution, so improving organizational efficiency and effectiveness.
- There is no single right way to go about designing business systems which encompass organizational processes and their support, but using an engineering approach to frame the design activities will improve the likelihood of success.

With this in mind it seems appropriate to use an engineering-based framework in order to address the issues arising in the exploitation of the organizational phenomenon known as process. A number of threads are beginning to come together, their common theme being the growth of IT and the move towards integrating IT with the business workforce, management, and their goals. There is a growing awareness that IT as a mediator could be one of the prime influences which determines the shape and effectiveness of organizations. This being the case, it seems sensible to establish a framework in which to consider the issues.

Unfortunately, unlike traditional engineering, no approach can, as yet, guarantee a perfectly good solution. The most obvious drawback in our context being the lack of robust and structured sociological input, which must remain so until results from studies in sociology are more repeatable. In the meantime, the advocacy of an evolutionary strategy will result in adaptable solutions. Undesirable inconsistencies uncovered in practice will be addressed by local tailoring and thus go some way to ensuring that process support can provide a long-term service to users.

4.6 Conclusion

In this chapter we have sought to set the art and science of engineering in its historical context, and to explain and to justify the use of an engineering approach to the kind of problems addressed by business systems. It has focused on issues around designs and design activity, and advocates an evolutionary approach to the solutions. Such an approach would allow organizations to tailor their systems to their needs much more effectively than can be done at present. This is reflected in subsequent chapters.

This concludes Part 1. In Chapter 2, the organizational context of the problem and the process approach have been positioned with respect to the nature of the domain, and to other initiatives in the field of Information Systems and Software Engineering. Some basic concepts been described that help understand the kind of things that we are trying to deal with and the kind of techniques that help provide a solution. Our approach to the issues has an engineering basis.

Jackson reminds us that problems come with two parts: the context and the issue. So far we've had a look at the context, and the next part describes the core of our approach: the method, guidance and techniques which will enable a practitioner to capture a process and then design the kinds of model that are at the heart of any Information System intended to truly support business process activity.

Part Two

Practice

5

The Nature of the Method

This section of the book seeks to illustrate how thinking about organizational systems can be utilized in the design of software support systems. This chapter functions as a bridge between the earlier theoretical part of the book and the distillation of a process approach which follows. It starts by presenting a case study of a fictional insurance team. This case study is used extensively in the following chapters. Three important implementation concepts are introduced. These are the Organizational Process Modelling (OPM) method, the architectural concept of the coordination layer and the P2E meta-process model. Each of these can be understood to be a pillar upon which the particular process approach espoused in this book is founded.

5.1 Introduction

A disillusioned analyst writes: 'It can be very hard to satisfy a specification for a software system. It can be heartbreaking to find that this specification was never or is no longer valid. If it helps to apportion blame, who should be labelled the culprit? Perhaps we can blame the users who express their intentions rather imprecisely as hopes and aspirations or, if we're really lucky, as operational goals. Is there not some corrective action we could take? Maybe if we force the users to live with the consequences (as, actually, we tend to do), they'll be a little more conscientious next time they specify their needs. Maybe we could drag them away from their business meetings and teach them all formal specification. But then again, to be fair, maybe it is the management of the organization who are at fault. They clearly failed to anticipate changes that would affect the organization and undermine the value of our system at the same time. It is not as though we analysts are asking much. We do not require that they anticipate every business change, *just those that affect the specification*. Then again, looking at it from their point of view, how could they do this? How can you tell when legislation is going to change, or when a competitor will introduce a new product? How can you tell what your own manager's intentions are, let alone the intentions of those above him. All those management information systems we build are not much use in these situations. So, it looks as if it might simply be the intrinsic nature of the organization that is to blame. It just keeps on changing. It changes so quickly and so unpredictably that our software development process might not even get a chance to complete its execution. In the meantime, what happens? As if to rub salt in the wounds of the professional analyst, the users get impatient and start to create their own applications and databases. Havoc reigns. We tell them not to do this, that they are creating as many problems as they solve, but they just shrug and say they must. "Business pressures," they say. It seems that we are *all* on a nonsensical treadmill which goes faster for some than it does for others...Thus, it can only be the fault of the nature of the organization itself. The cause of the problem is beyond the wit of all of us...but wait...maybe we have a way...We must make the domain *stand still* long enough for us to validate all requirements and correct all bugs.'

Rather than trying to make the world stand still, a more fruitful strategy might be to find ways of managing change. If organizations are understood to be dynamic systems, then it is necessary to understand how software systems contribute to the dynamism, and through this to be able to comprehend and manage their relationship with other parts of the system.

The intention of this section of the book is to illustrate how thinking about systems can be realized in a process approach to developing software systems. It is *a* process method, not *the* process method. The motivation in presenting it is to demonstrate the feasibility of incorporating systems thinking in the design of software systems, to try and come to grips with the nature of organizations, and to illustrate the kinds of process method and technology that may result. Hence, two definitions can be proposed:

• Process modelling is a discipline for analyzing and designing the behaviour of systems.
• The method in this book is a process-modelling approach to analyzing and designing the behaviour of the software component of human organizational systems.

The presentation focuses upon the *Organizational Process Modelling (OPM)* Method. OPM starts by conceptualizing the organization as a system of interacting and dynamic elements. It describes coordinative actions between users, between users and tools and between tools. In doing this it is concerned with the description of operational goals of users and their mapping to technical capabilities. Thus, it seeks to describe *why* people collaborate and *how* their goals are fulfilled. Then, where it is appropriate, the models thus created are embedded into software so as to serve as an active framework for the behaviour of people and disparate applications and databases. Throughout, it is emphasized that an intervention of this sort is not isolated from other, wider organizational issues, and that the method is essentially seeking to mediate between organizational need and technical capability.

OPM is only one part of a jigsaw through which it is intended to develop a meaningful and fruitful approach to the problem of designing information systems. Another important concept is that a process-based system can usefully function as a coordination layer in a broader system architecture. This architectural role for process modelling is implicit in OPM. Once again, it is *a* system architecture and not *the* system architecture. A third part of the jigsaw is provided by P2E, a generic model of process change which is used to address system evolution. The P2E model is used to describe and support the process of change. The technological realization of these concepts though the Process*Web* system is described later in Chapter 10.

The remainder of this chapter starts with a brief presentation of the case study that is used for illustration throughout the remainder of this book. Then, equally briefly, the case study is examined and redescribed using some of the theory presented earlier in the book. Thus, picking up on the themes presented in Chapter 2, this chapter is concerned with:

• An Introduction to the Case Study.
• Some Systems Thinking about the Nature of the Intervention.
• The Interactional Basis of Organizational Process.
• The Evolution of Organizational Process.

5.2 An Introduction to the Case Study

Although the issues raised in this case study are derived from actual situations in a number of different organizations, the case study itself is fictional.

The case study concerns the a specialist team within Parker, Ellington and Fitzgerald Insurance Ltd (the PEF Corporate Team).

5.2.1 The PEF Corporate Team: a Tale of Administrators, Underwriters and Several Databases

The following description is extracted from a report made on an insurance company who were the subject of a process modelling case study. The purpose of the study was:
• To model the existing process activity.
• To model a target process vision.
• To develop the IT support of this company.
The modelling work was only a part of a broader organizational change and there was regular contact with two other teams. The first of these was called the Business Strategy and Human Resource team. They were given the task of developing strategies for realizing corporate objectives and also had responsibility for human-resource issues. The second team were called the IT Enhancements team. They were concerned with technical implementation issues associated with the company's main databases.

5.2.2 Description

'The PEF company as a whole are enjoying a gradually increasing market share within the UK and world insurance markets. This is largely due to the expansion of their corporate risks operation which is based in London, Glasgow, Dublin, Barcelona, Tokyo, Nairobi and their new offices in Budapest and Cracow. The focus of this study is the London corporate risks team.

Twenty users took part in the process modelling case study. Twelve of these are administrators. Six are underwriters (i.e. risk assessment experts) of various levels of seniority. Two are IT specialists. In addition, four of the company's senior managers joined in the workshops which concluded the initial phase.

The company has invested heavily in two worldwide databases based upon mainframe computer systems. The first is known as *In Progress*. It stores details of all the risk proposals that the company is currently considering. The second, known as *Business*, stores details of the risks that have been underwritten by the company. However, despite the importance of these databases to the operations of the team, currently the team's business processes are characteristically manual. Most work is done using bulky paper files which contain the policy submissions received from brokers.

These submissions arrive by post or are brought into the office by the brokers themselves. The files are used by underwriters who scour the details of the submission as part of their risk assessment. They add handwritten notes to the files which describe the reasoning which underpins their decisions about premium quotes and so forth. Administrators use paper forms upon which they handwrite summary details of each submission. These are attached to the files. At specified points in the process the information contained in these forms is transferred to a database. Cases which progress to the successful negotiation of a premium will be entered into both databases, thereby requiring duplication of effort. Locally, in order to remedy perceived information shortages, initiatives have resulted in the development of new databases (e.g. containing brokers' names) using local systems. Although these do act as a remedy to the information shortages, they also add to the problem of repeated data entries. They require that additional actions are carried out by users so as to keep the databases up to date and in accord with other databases. Certain items of information are entered in triplicate to databases and at least once to paper forms. This is an example of where IT design has succeeded with analysis but failed with synthesis. That is, although these databases might of themselves be well designed and able to satisfy some requirement, when we consider how the IT system as a whole serves the company's staff it is apparent that the relationship is not satisfactory. The desire to be served by a system which requires data items to be entered once and once only was a something of a leit-motif for the modelling exercise.

The work of the underwriters has been shaped by the traditions and practices of the insurance industry in the City of London. Brokers, who act on behalf of a client, will visit the company's offices by prior arrangement or sometimes on spec. They will present a submission to the underwriter and may require an initial assessment as to the likelihood of the company issuing a quote. The personal relationships between brokers and underwriters can be of critical importance. An important part of an underwriter's job is to develop and maintain relationships with brokers who can bring valuable business into the company. There are several benefits to this from the broker's point of view. For example, a good relationship with an underwriter means that he/she can be more confident of the terms that can be obtained for a client. Thus, the work of the underwriters can be characterized as being concerned with the professional assessment and management of submissions and with the development of links with brokers.

The administration work is concerned with recording and distributing files and maintaining database records. Corporate and legal standards have to be adhered to. For example, the company requires that a completed policy document be mailed to each client within a specified length of time after the acceptance of a quote. To help maintain these standards a quality tracking system is used through which administrators record the completion of various work actions.

The potential for process redesign increasingly became the major topic of concern as the study progressed. In considering process redesign the participants were concerned jointly with how they might want to work, how IT might serve them and the additional possibilities IT might afford them. A whole range of issues were discussed. For example, issues raised included the repeated data entries into different databases, ambiguous field names, and the possibility of radically reinventing the process around electronic submissions from brokers. The users involved in the redesign exercise had many ideas about how changes might be made. In every case care was taken to correctly attribute new ideas to the meetings or people who first generated them.

The users were not required to express explicitly the motivation for their ideas but often they did so voluntarily. In many cases their motivation concurred with those expressed by the senior management of the company (e.g. greater efficiency, improved job satisfaction) but there were also personal motivations (e.g. a better c.v. through experience of working with advanced IT systems). The focus on processes as well as the qualitative analysis of sets of interviews, gave insight into both official methods of doing work for different goals, and the less obvious hidden agendas and ways work was achieved. The matching of activities to objectives was significant. It was possible to identify a hierarchy of objectives from the corporate and strategic to the tactical. We recommend that more work is done in this area but for now, at least, it seems we have a view of a set of operational goals.'

Yours, P. Modelling Team.

5.3 Some Systems Thinking about the Nature of the Intervention

In order to better comprehend the contribution of process modelling to a broader systems intervention, reference can be made to the socio-technical systems model of organization. This tells of the organization being made up of a social system (people) and a technical system (e.g. tools, method, knowledge). The implication of this model is that successful change is concerned with the integration of the needs of both these systems through joint optimization (Emery, 1959). How can the process modelling intervention be positioned amidst the assembly of other specialized interventions that are likely to be needed if the social and technical systems of the insurance team are to be jointly optimized? The following diagram (Figure 5.1) seeks to answer this.

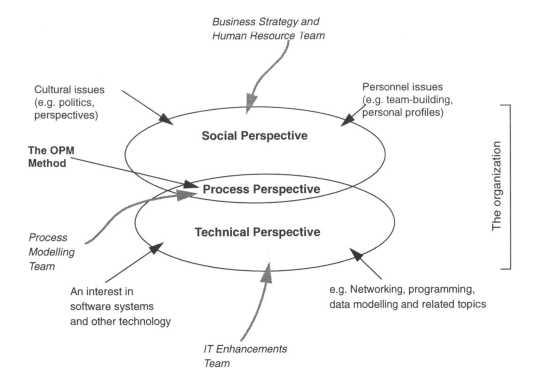

Fig. 5.1 A Socio-Technical Representation of the Organization

Figure 5.1 represents the organization as a socio-technical system. It shows how a concern for the social system will embrace issues such as culture and personnel. These are shown in the diagram with straight arrows connecting them to the "Social Perspective." Correspondingly a concern for the technical system will embrace issues such as software technology and programming. Examples of these issues are also shown with straight arrows connecting them to the "Technical Perspective." Process issues stand at the interface of the two systems, i.e. how they interact with each other. This follows from the definition given earlier wherein process modelling is understood to be a discipline for analyzing and designing the behaviour of systems. Mediation is a useful word to use in this context because there is not a one-way relationship between the two subsystems. Sometimes, people will organize their behaviour around perceived technological capability (e.g. BPR). More typically we think of technological capability being created in response to a perceived social need (e.g. conventional software lifecycle). Ultimately however, as the goals of the relationship are always cast in the social system, the technology is always the serving system whilst the social system is the served system.

The realization of this model in the case of the PEF Corporate team is indicated by the italicized labels and curving arrows. Remember that the process modelling activity interfaced to the work of two other teams: *Business Strategy and Human Resources*, and *IT Enhancements*. Through this we rather simplify the fact that in the real world organizational change can be a multi-disciplinary endeavour involving managers, operational staff, personnel officers, systems analysts, accountants, psychologists and others.

5.3.1 Organizational Process Modelling (OPM)

In the following chapters it will be shown how a process perspective upon the problems encountered by the PEF team can be developed using the OPM method. OPM starts with a simple description of people interacting with each other before identifying the goals that they seek to achieve and the activities that they carry out. The identification of these activities leads to the identification of the software support services that they require to carry out them out. Thus, in essence, it allows a description of social system behaviour (i.e. people, goals) to be mapped against technical systems (i.e. the software support systems). OPM is set out in Chapters 6, 7 and 8.

5.4 The Interactional Basis of Organizational Process

This section seeks to take this systems thinking a little further by focusing upon the interaction theme that was introduced earlier in this book. It starts by highlighting how organizations are composed of interacting elements, and that the focus of the modelling exercise are people and their software tools.

The following sub-sections are presented:

• A system of interactions and goals. This describes how the modeller can codify interactive behaviour through the goals given to them. A simple customer–supplier model is developed as an example.

• The social aspect of technical integration. This extends the consideration of interaction to address the integration of software tools. It illustrates how a software support system might be utilized as a coordination layer in order to facilitate interaction between tools, between tools and people and between people.

5.4.1 A System of Interactions and Goals

A process approach is concerned with developing a behavioural view of the system expressed in Figure 5.1. Therefore if we think of the organization is as a kind of box, and then imagine lifting the lid off it, what do we see? The modeller will see many different, interacting components. Some of these components will be human and some will be technological. The interactions between the components may appear to be random or even chaotic. However, the modeller will learn that they are all related to invisible and sometimes ephemeral phenomena called goals. These induce a certain amount of regularity, the degree of which is variable.

Figure 5.2 repeats the diagram shown earlier in Chapter 3. It can be taken to describe an organization. In the figure it is possible to identify the usual pattern of people interacting with other people, people interacting with software tools and software tools interacting with other software tools. It could be one of any number of kinds of organization (a bank, a government department, a software team etc.) For the purposes of this chapter it can be taken to represent the PEF corporate team.

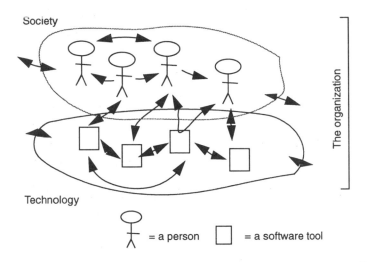

Fig. 5.2 Organization, Interactions and Organized Interactions

The interactions that take place between people will always be subject to a degree of negotiation. Their usefulness, meaning and procedure will be defined by those taking part in them, in accordance with the context which they find themselves in. It is worth again emphasizing that interactions are always significant. It can be argued that in the most fundamental sense *organizational* goals are achieved by the *interaction* of people with each other. This might be illustrated through a customer–supplier (or transactional) relationship. In Chapter 3 we discussed this through two examples, those of a travel agent and a secretary. It is worth briefly revisiting this second example and thinking again about a manager in the PEF Corporate Team interacting with a secretary in order to send a letter. The manager asks the secretary to create the letter. The secretary carries out certain activities (e.g. word-process letter, print letter) in order that the goal is fulfilled.

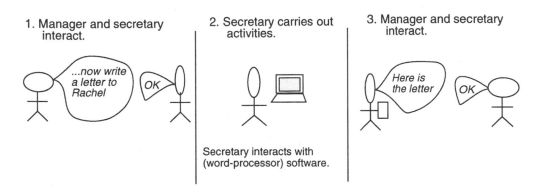

Fig. 5.3 An Example of Interaction as the Basis of an Organizational Behaviour.

The example gives us a picture of human interactions (i.e. manager and secretary) spawning dependent actions which satisfy a goal. However, it is useful to develop this a little further and by considering interactions in a broader sense. In the technological, software-rich environment of today it is vital to consider the interaction of humans with software packages, and the interaction of these software packages with other software packages. Thus, it may be observed that the secretary interacts with a word-processor in order to create the letter. The word-processor may, in turn, interact with a database in order to read the address fields for entry on to the letter. Thus the notion of interaction gives us a basis for the exploration of a broader range of coordinative issues in a complex organization. In so doing it is possible to distinguish collaborative interactions (i.e. between people) from integrative interactions (i.e. involving software applications).

5.4.2 The Social Aspect of Integration

The term *integration* is often associated with the technical issues arising where it is deemed that one technological device should communicate with or share the features of another technological device. At its most simple the issue of integration can be understood to be concerned with interworking between technological components so that they, once integrated, have a more satisfactory relationship with people than they did previously, when non-integrated. So, in fact, from this it can be argued that integration is as much concerned with the relationship between the social system and the technical system as it is between parts of the technical. An integration issue, viewed from the social system, is likely to manifest itself as an inability to carry out a desired activity or a difficulty in achieving some objective. For example, in the report of the case of the PEF Corporate Team it was noted that staff found that the requirement placed upon them to duplicate data entries to two or more different databases was boring and onerous. It was also judged by the users to be ineffective use of their time.

The following picture expresses the problem of integration as a socio-technical problem.

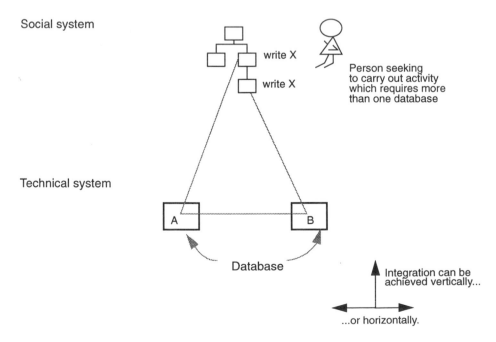

Fig. 5.4 Data Duplication Due to Non-Integrated Databases.

We can explore this issue further by considering the coordinative moves that take place within this simple scenario. Database A is the one which is used to store details of work in progress (i.e. the In-Progress database). Database B is used to store details of business that is already *on the books* (i.e. the Business database). Both are large mainframe computer-based databases. A is newer than B having been introduced when the company's operation began to expand. There needed to be some way of keeping track of work *in the pipeline* and so Database A was created. We can think of the process as being like one of tendering for business. All new work is entered into database A. That work for which the tender is accepted is also entered into database B. This involves duplication (of data fields X).

It would be nice, say the users, if they only had to enter X once. If a software system is dedicated to the task of coordination then this wish can be fulfilled. The users input X to this coordinative system (it might be called an interaction layer or, more typically, a coordination layer), and it updates A and B as and when they need it. This is represented at Figure 5.5.

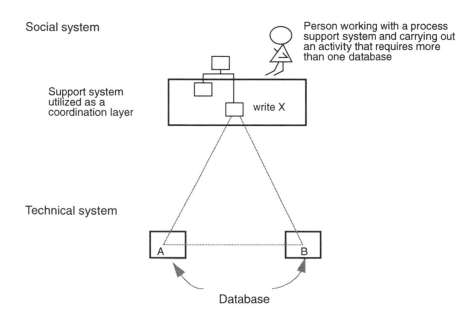

Fig. 5.5 A Software System Coordinating Two Databases

In a typical scenario, the user may interact with the support system which accepts the input, opens database one, opens database two, writes to database one and writes to database two. The implementation detail, and there are several alternative scenarios, is not the concern of the book. The point is simply that the support system contains a model which, when the activity, 'Write X' is carried out, causes it to write to the two databases.

If this thinking is developed further, albeit in a rather wilfully simplistic way, it is possible to see that the problems of data sharing, passing documents, prompting and synchronizing can be regarded as the same whether the agents concerned are people or components of an IT system. Eventually, all that matters is that the behaviour of the software system should be designed to serve the needs of the people involved in the process. Thus, a software system of this kind is able to play a key coordinative role between people, between people and tools and between tools. This is expressed in Figure 5.6.

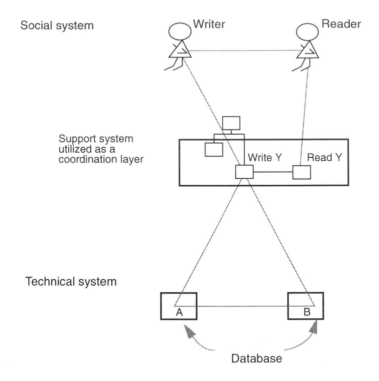

Social system

Support system
utilized as a
coordination layer

Technical system

Database

Fig. 5.6 A Coordination Layer Supporting both Human and Software Interaction

What is represented here is a simple situation where the writer interacts with the software system which implements a process model as a coordinative component. When activity, 'Write Y' is carried out it causes the coordination layer to write to the two databases and to pass the same data to the reader. The implementation details and alternative model scenarios are not of issue here.

The point is that the software support system is being used to manage interactions. In so doing it is able to make the socio-technical relationship more harmonious. What constitutes *harmony* is something that the process modeller will have to reflect upon, not just in the case of the PEF Corporate Team but in every project with every different team.

5.4.3 The Coordination Layer

This brings us to the architectural concept of the coordination layer. This is a simple idea which underpins the process approach developed in this book. The process models and process modelling activities are deployed so as to create an active model which serves as a coordination layer in a greater architecture. It supports the coordination of people and other software tools. Thus, a simple system architecture is presented at Figure 5.7 (see also White and Kawalek, 1993; Greenwood et al., 1995).

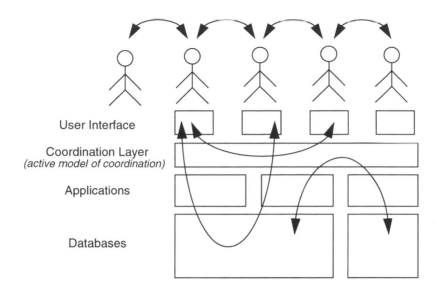

Fig. 5.7 An Abstract Representation of a System Architecture

We can conceive of the greater IT system as being made up of databases, applications, user interfaces and a coordination layer. The coordination layer provides coordination services to the broader organization directly (e.g. workflow type behaviour) or indirectly (e.g. by coordinating applications). Therefore it can be thought of as being able to bring the services a person needs to that person when they are needed. In this way it is able to define the working context for a person.

The representation shows four coordination examples. These are:
- Interpersonal (not mediated by IT).
- Interpersonal mediated by the coordination layer.
- Interpersonal mediated by a shared database.
- Between databases (or alternatively between applications) mediated by the coordination layer.

There are other possibilities also, but these are sufficient to show directly that the coordination layer is only one of several means by which the organization can coordinate.

It is useful to reflect upon the issues in the PEF insurance team and to consider the potential value of the coordination layer in that light. It gives us a way of overcoming the problems of data replication (and thence, integrity). It allows data to be entered once, to the coordination layer and then shared amongst different databases as and when it is useful to enter it to them (i.e. as in Figure 5.5 and Figure 5.6). Furthermore, looking beyond the immediate needs of the PEF team towards new methods of remote working, whereby users might be physically isolated from the office, the coordination layer may potentially be a fundamental binding which helps to hold the organization together.

In classical mainframe systems a role akin to that of the coordination layer was provided by a Transaction Process (TP) monitor. More recently, data warehousing implements an integration layer for queries across databases. The distinguishing characteristics of the coordination layer derive from the use of a process model to fulfil this integrative role and the design philosophy which underpins its application.

5.5 The Evolution of Organizational Process

This section explores the second of the themes introduced in the Positioning chapter of this book. Thus, the concern is evolution and how, by thinking about organizations and their software systems, we can see why our process approach must address change issues.

The following sub-sections are presented:

- The modern domain. In this section it is described how software systems can both induce and stifle change.
- The nature of software systems. Lehman (1992) describes the uncertainty of software system application arguing, 'With the real world forever changing, an increasing number of assumptions embedded in the system will, unless corrected, become invalid.' It is then noted how this message stands in contrast to industrial practice wherein the *product* is installed and then maintained much like a central-heating system or an air-conditioning system.
- The implications for the OPM Method. This section again draws upon the concept of a socio-technical system, and proposes that it is necessary to be able to distinguish logically between the operational system and *the system which changes the operational system* (i.e. the meta-system). The implication for a process approach to business information systems is that it must consider both an operational process and a meta-process.
- A process approach: metaphorically speaking, the machine versus the organism. This section develops the preceding arguments through metaphor. It suggests that systems thinking encourages a view of organizations as being like dynamic organisms. Thinking this way about the application domain has the potential to affect the form and capabilities of the software system which is produced as a result.

5.5.1 The Modern Domain

Remember the fable of the disillusioned analyst who hoped that he might stop the world whilst he prepared himself for it. Of course his plea was precipitated by his observation that it is in the nature of organizations to change. We might recognize the sense of this by observing how we describe organizations (and whole societies) through a history of innovation and change (e.g. the rise of share ownership, the introduction of the production line, the move to bureaucracy, the rise of federation). Moreover, this situation is not only facilitated by technology but actually encouraged (*inflamed!*) by it. IT systems in particular have induced tremendous change potential to organizations (e.g. new services, new products, new networks, new processes). Of course there is nothing intrinsic to change that means it will always do good; change can cause harm as readily. Intuitively therefore, the aim would seem to be to control the rate and direction of change, to innovate in order to secure advantage and, in a commercial setting, to replicate in order to nullify the advantage of others.

Today, both private and public sector organizations are required to assess and reassess their performance and goals. At conception, every software system is ostensibly a servant of human goals. Despite their capacity to induce organizational change at design and implementation, a software system is liable to become unfit for purpose if it cannot be changed as the organizational goals change further. Its net effect alters from the furtherance to the stifling of change. The ramifications of being unable to change software systems can be far-reaching. Organizations that are dependent upon unfit software may themselves, as a whole, become unfit. This metaphorical ecosystem of people and software technology may become entropic. It may become ill-adapted to its environment and vulnerable to predators.

5.5.2 The Nature of Software Systems

It can be concluded that if it is important for organizations as a whole to be adaptable and flexible then it follows that the software that constitutes the serving system must be adaptable and flexible. It is paradoxical for the serving system to be an obstacle to wilful innovation. Lehman writes:

'A computer program or software system is a model of a domain and of an application or problem in that domain. For *real* applications in *real* domains, that is for *real world* applications, the domain is essentially continuous, unbounded and dynamic whereas the software model is essentially discrete, bounded and, unless changed by human decision and action, static. Moreover, there will always be a time delay between a decision to change the software and satisfactory completion of the change. The software model is, therefore, an approximation, essentially incomplete and with embedded assumptions...With the real world forever changing, an increasing number of assumptions embedded in the system will, unless corrected, become invalid. Even if by some miracle there are none, this can never be known. The system becomes progressively less satisfactory and unpredictable. Uncertainty of behaviour follows.'

Lehman, 1992

This account runs in countervoice to conventional industrial practice whereby software 'machines' are built to transform their environment by solving problems and which once installed will require only maintenance. Current industrial practice does not emphasize the uncertainty and time-specificity of large software systems. What commercial consultancy would want to admit to designing a system that is, '...an approximation, essentially incomplete and with embedded assumptions...'?

This is reflected in current methodology. Intensive requirements, design and implementation activity is followed by a much longer maintenance phase. This phase is given far less attention in the literature and yet into it are subsumed the concerns of product updates, minor enhancements, error correction and substantial requirement changes (hence rewrites). Upon entry to this maintenance phase, software systems become known as legacy systems. The use of the term legacy suggests an historical event over which no control can subsequently be exerted. A pattern of repeatedly replacing legacy with legacy develops, presumably to the advantage of software suppliers. It follows from this that a fascinating software engineering challenge is to provide the means of breaking the pattern. Software engineering should be able to provide useful solutions in an environment of uncertainty: to design reliable systems which retain their usefulness through a process of adaptation.

5.5.3 The Implications for the OPM Method

For an organization to adapt in an ordered way implies that it must be able to *reflect* upon itself. Working with bounded rationality, it must be able to observe its own state to some degree of accuracy and detail, and to contrast this with some other alternative state. Adaptation is then the process of implementing changes to itself which will diminish the difference between a perceived current state and a perceived preferential state (see again Simon, 1981).

Using the socio-technical model to interpret the implications of this it can be said that the arrangement of the socio-technical system *as is*, must be logically separable from the socio-technical system *to be*. Therefore the model presented earlier at Figure 5.1 must logically apply at two levels, an operational level (*a system for doing*) and a meta-systemic level (*a system for change*). This idea is illustrated in Figure 5.8. It follows that if process modelling is to contribute to the management of organizational change it must embrace operational process (*a process for doing*) and meta-process (*a process for change*).

The OPM Method is thus not just concerned with process modelling *as is*, but also with making *to be* possible. It is concerned with the process of change. Effectively this means that it seeks to design change capability into processes and, by implication, into the software systems which are part of these processes. In doing this it may be necessary to make software systems *reflexive* (i.e. they contain the means of their own evolution).

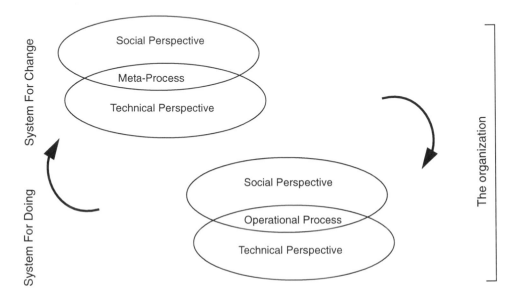

Fig. 5.8 Systems for Doing and Systems for Change: a Socio-Technical Representation

5.5.4 A Process Approach: Metaphorically Speaking, the Machine Versus the Organism

This thinking can be summarized through a metaphorical exploration. Morgan (1986, p. 33) recounts how thinking about organizations as machines has traditionally been associated with the drive for efficiency and rationalization. He reports that a machine metaphor potently exhorts us to:

'Set goals and objectives and go for them. Organize rationally, efficiently, and clearly. Specify every detail so that everyone will be sure of the jobs that they have to perform. Plan, organize, and control, control, control.'

Morgan, 1986

The difficulty with thinking about organizations as machines arises from the need to acknowledge the limits of rationality; as it can be impossible to comprehend the full complexity of the organization from any one perspective, so too the organization cannot fully comprehend its environment nor can it anticipate changes in its relations with that environment.

By accepting that the organization is inherently uncertain, we are accepting that there are limits to its rationality. An alternative metaphor becomes useful: the organization is like an organism or species seeking to adapt and thrive in a changing and often hostile environment. It is an adaptive whole. Thinking about organizations in this way reinvokes the systems concepts of *open system* and *autopoiesis*.

As an open system, the organization depends upon a life-sustaining interaction with its environment. Organizations need custom, money and new ideas. They need tools and components that are created elsewhere. They engage in a continuous cycle of input, internal transformation, output and feedback (whereby one element of experience influences the next). A change to the environment of an organization represents a challenge to which the organization must adapt.

This open system metaphor leaves open the question of how the organization adapts to its environment. That is, as organizations are man-made, then surely it follows that at some level, changes to its interactions with its environment must be *designed*. A further metaphorical exploration of the organization as a closed, autopoietic system makes this clear. The PEF Corporate Team will serve as an example. The team can be described as being engaged in a continuous pattern of interactions that are self-referential. For example, it interacts with brokers, clients, reinsurance companies and so forth. Self-referentiality dictates that the organization cannot enter into a pattern of interactions that are not prescribed in the pattern of relations that define it as an organization. In practical terms this forces us to consider how the interactions which an organization engages in are determined by the pattern of relations that is the organizational structure. The consequence is that as the environment changes the organization may also have to change. It may have to redefine its identity. This can be a painful process of socio-technical reinvention whereby existing structures are adapted, dispensed with or supplanted by new ones.

From this metaphorical exploration it can be seen that the OPM Method tends to adopt a view of software systems as being like a component of an organism. This thinking is summarized in Figure 5.9.

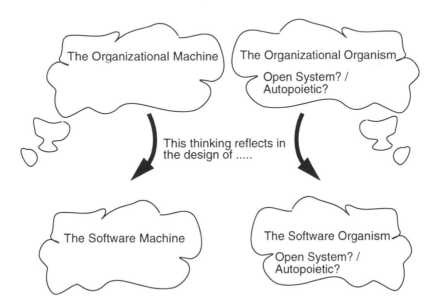

Fig. 5.9 The Machine and the Organism

5.5.5 The Process for Process Evolution (P2E)

That change is intrinsic to organizations leads us to seek a model for describing and managing the process of change itself. In order to meet this need a general problem solving paradigm is adopted (see Chapter 3) through the Process for Process Evolution (P2E). This is a generic meta-process model which describes how the formation of goals in the social sub-system is related to the identification, implementation and carrying-out of methods through the technical subsystem. It has been derived from the Promoter Reference Model (Derniame et al., 1999). The model is illustrated below in Figure 5.10.

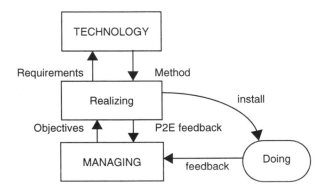

Fig. 5.10 The Process for Process Evolution (P2E)

The model consists of four components. Each of these can be thought of as a set of activities which are carried out in an organization. Note that in the diagram a component labelled in upper case is generic and can be specialized. A component shown in mixed case is specific. Each of the components is described below:

• Managing – this is concerned with perceiving the state of the process, deciding upon desired goals ('Objectives'), assessing progress towards the achievement of these objectives, and then reassessing progress and objectives according to feedback.
• Realization – this is concerned with moving towards the fulfilment of the objectives by the provision of a process model. This process model is specialized both for these objectives and for the organizational context, and the implementation of this model in the environment.
• Technology – this is concerned with furnishing the method for achieving the set goal. In other words, it acts as a library so that existing methods can be reused in different contexts. Where no suitable method is available, a new one is created and then specialized by Realization.
• Doing – this represents the real-world performance of the methods (i.e. the real-world process). It constitutes both the activities themselves and the feedback from the activities to Managing.

It follows that by moving through the P2E, from Managing through to Doing, the organization is navigating towards the set of objectives which it has defined for itself. The organization's identity becomes embodied in the set of behaviours which it can carry out through the P2E structure. Hence, it is autopoietic. The maintenance of this identity is then preserved through feedback. The loop from Doing to Managing enables the organization to keep this navigation on course towards these objectives, or else to set new objectives.

The use of P2E is discussed in more depth in Chapter 9.

5.6 Conclusion

This chapter has acted as a bridge between the theory and thinking introduced in Part One of this book and the realization of our process approach that dominates throughout the rest of Part Two. Three different components of the process approach have been introduced, viz:
• The Organizational Process Modelling (OPM) method.
• The coordination layer architecture.
• The Process for Process Evolution (P2E) meta-process model.
Along the way it has again been useful to pick up upon the themes of interaction and evolution. This process approach to the development of business information systems perceives the organization as a network of interacting components. Change is intrinsic to this network: patterns of interactions between these components change, new components are introduced, existing ones are removed.

The Parker, Ellington and Fitzgerald (PEF) Corporate Team is used to illustrate the process approach throughout the following chapters. The report of the process modelling team upon this case study should serve as a reminder about the application domain as the case study is progressed.

THE FOLLOWING CHAPTERS

In Chapter 6 the concern is to define the scope of the study in which we take part. Chapter 7 describes the way in which models can be created which describe interactive behaviour patterns. Both of these chapters are concerned with setting out the OPM method. Chapter 8 develops these models to provide a definition of the behaviour of a support system. This chapter develops OPM further and shows how it relates to the architectural concept of the coordination layer. Chapter 9 shows how P2E can be used to guide the development of the active model.

THINGS TO DO

• Coordination is not a new issue. We have seen how different solutions have been proposed at different times and in different contexts. As the presentation unfolds in the following chapters consider how an approach based upon an active process model differs from other approaches (e.g. TP monitors, data warehousing).
• Sometime later, the analyst featured at the start of this chapter reflected upon what he said... Given that organizations have to change, he mused, and that they depend upon software systems, it must follow that these software systems have to change. This can be done in two

ways. The first possibility is to incorporate new software tools which serve new goals into the organization. This might be done in conjunction with the discarding of existing software tools. The second possibility is that the software systems themselves can be changed.

'I can see now,' the analyst says, 'how the coordination layer will help me do the former whilst, if I understand it right, P2E will help me do the latter.'

Describe some change scenarios which affect both organizational processes and IT. When might the coordination layer be useful? When might P2E be useful?

• A related strategy is to design for resilience. In other words, if systems are initially designed to accommodate flexible working, then they are less likely to need to be changed in the first place.

Design resilience will have to be achieved through the design process. As the description of OPM progresses over the next chapters, think about how the designer could promote design resilience.

• Thinking about it again, the analyst concedes, 'I can see that I was trying to control the organization by controlling the IT system. By developing a rigid and detailed specification I was, in effect, seeking to constrain the ways in which the organization worked. It was as though I was trying to run a centralist economy – it gets difficult after a while!'

The coordination layer makes it possible to allow differentiation whilst retaining a variable degree of integration. It is as though we have adopted a regulated market economy – the system is much more flexible.

How might the necessary degrees of control differ between the control room of a nuclear plant and the office of a sales team?

• It is easy to depict P2E as a hierarchic model. 'Managing' might be understood to be the boss of an organization setting goals and handing them down to the hard workers in 'Doing.' In fact, the model need not be seen like this at all. It is derived from a general problem-solving process and is recursive. This means that it can be applied at many levels. To illustrate this point: think about how you apply a process for process evolution in your own life: e.g. managing your career.

6

Process Contexts

This chapter commences the description of the Organizational Process Modelling Method (OPM). Here, the concern of the method is to develop an analysis of the problem domain in which it is applied. This is done to try to encourage critical thinking about the modelling exercise. It also serves to highlight changes, conflicts, contradictions and obfuscations that serve to inhibit comprehension of the problem space. This is done by focusing on two specific views. The first is the context of the intervention which aims to solve some problem, or at least to illuminate it. The second is the context of the problem process itself.

6.1 Introduction

The purpose of this chapter is to identify the features, concerns, and constraints that influence the direction and success of the modelling intervention. It is based on practical experience and is not intended to be prescriptive. Its primary concern is to encourage a useful level of reflection, of *critical thinking*, about what is being done as the Organizational Process Modelling (OPM) method is utilized. Returning to some of the concerns put forward in Chapter 2, here we will discuss the environment of the system, and the interactions between the environment and the system.

The system in which we are interested can be thought of as comprising the process to be supported, engineered or appraised, its human agents, and its IT support. It exists in an environment which might be thought of as two layers of an onion skin. The immediate environment of this process is comprised of the problem space, organization space, temporal space, and informational space. These all relate to a perceived problem and its potential solutions. The outermost layer of the onion is the process modelling environment, wherein the issues surrounding the intervention itself are discussed, the nature of the problem and the problem space, and the nature of the approach to be adopted. The boundaries between the two are not strictly delineated.

If the intervention is conducted as a project, then the issues become manifest as those commonly associated with projects: time, cost, quality, planning and coordinating the intervention, monitoring its efficiency and effectiveness, setting targets for the results of the intervention, etc. However, whenever processes are developed in an evolutionary way, then these same issues have to be addressed as part of normal business activity.

An understanding of the environment helps place process issues in context and, sometimes, provides explanations which do not emerge at the process level. This chapter does not address the issues surrounding the identification of which process to study, nor how to choose between competing processes to determine in which order they ought to be investigated. Of course the focus of any study might be expected to align with the area where the biggest problem/opportunity is seen to exist, but just how this might be determined is outside the scope of this book.

6.2 The Context for Process Modelling

Problems in the real world are rarely well-defined. Usually the awareness is only partial; there is confusion between malaise and symptoms of malaise, and indeed the significance of the problem can vary depending on professional viewpoint and the passage of time. Solving these kinds of problem needs an intervention of some kind. Checkland and Scholes report that for SSM:

> '... it was found useful to think of an intervention in a problem situation as itself being problematical'
>
> Checkland and Scholes, 1990

The implication of this is that process modellers need to understand the structure that underpins their involvement in a work environment, and that one of the earliest concerns will be to ascertain exactly what it is that the intervention is intended to achieve. By considering such questions at the outset, we hope to arrive at a statement which might provide a reference point to ascertain by just how much the perception of the project changes from its inception. Experience has shown that, for many of those involved, this purpose is often only understood in very general terms at the outset of the work. It may be expressed as a desire to improve a process or to see if there is scope for improvement. However, the experience and learning of all participants during the course of the work allows the context to be revisited and revised if appropriate.

By establishing a context, or at least starting to establish it, all parties should be more clear as to the aims of the intervention, the plan for their achievement, the identification of the players of the major roles, and their responsibilities in the intervention. It ought to explain why process modellers are involved at all. What it is about the nature of the problem situation that suggests that a solution might be uncovered through process modelling?

The context statements thus created need to be revisited during the course of the intervention, as many aspects of the definition may change, both as the organization undergoes long-term translation (they are never static, much as it might seem) and as the parties to the intervention interact, learn and understand what they are trying to do. In particular the objectives may change as the intervention proceeds. It may, for instance, be impossible to tell at the start whether the process being studied will only need optimizing, or whether a complete redesign will be required.

Establishing the context encourages communication and, at least in part, is a consensus-forming activity. Typically it will be performed through meetings, with a preponderance of effort at the outset, tailing off but possibly never quite completing! The different issues which ought to be visited in context discussions include the following.

Purpose

The problem owner frequently has an idea of the solution – hence the search for a process modelling solution. However this position has itself to be examined, and possibly corrected if the true nature of the problem is such that its solution is more likely to be accessible through some other means. We have to be more confident of the kinds of problem to which the process modeller can make a positive contribution. Typical reasons for interventions are:
- Perceived inefficiency – such as observed wasted effort, documents apparently not ready when needed thus causing delay, activities that appear to be duplicated unnecessarily.
- Confusion over seemingly complex activity, giving rise to questions about what it is doing or achieving.
- Inability to relate means to ends.

• Problems in managing the complexity of different systems.
• Desire to set up a framework to carry through process evolution.
• Need to cut costs.
• Need to adopt different skills.
• As a kind of insurance to confirm existing approaches.
• The need for a second, possibly independent, opinion on an issue of concern.

The OPM approach is not one of problem-solving in isolation. In today's rapidly changing world it is clear that organizations must be much more adaptable than in the past. The fact that their current primary Information System has given 20 years' service doesn't mean that the next one will also last 20 years; it might be 10 or just 5. So we tend to view the context for OPM as one of problem managing. We may be able to address a problem by introducing a new system, but we also want a mechanism to be in place to identify issues and to handle change as they are needed without excessive disruption. The aim is not to seek to set up a project to produce a system to solve the problem, but rather introduce a way of working so that the organization is better equipped to deal with problems as they arise.

Deliverables

This comprises the items that are needed to model and understand the process, and will constitute evidence of the modelling activity having been undertaken. If the modelling is carried out as a project, they will form part of the conditions for financial settlement. If the modelling is being done as ongoing activity integral to the operational process, such as a support process, then deliverables might take the form of periodic reports. It is appropriate to agree among parties just what form they will take, when they will be required, and who is responsible for approval. It is helpful to know to what uses deliverables will be put.

Scope

This sets out to establish the boundary of the study. It may be clear or diffuse. If the process is confined to a single organization unit, then the boundaries might be clear; if, however they penetrate a number of units, then it will probably be an inexact boundary. If the latter, it will have to be revisited during the currency of the project. It may only be possible to determine the scope after some preliminary work establishing both the depth and breadth of intervention. Another aspect of scoping is to position it relative to corporate history, and to place the intervention in the organizational context of other ongoing activities which may impact on the work.

Approach

By describing the approach, the modeller seeks to give an account of how the investigation will proceed towards its objectives. It is akin to the way in which a professional therapist or medical practitioner describes the perspective from which a programme of care shall be developed. For example, in addressing a particular situation a psychologist may select from different approaches such as cognitive, behavioural and developmental. A doctor may select from approaches such as medical, alternative medical and social.

Of course, in the case of OPM the account will focus upon the modeller's understanding of the process approach, and the relationship it holds with other approaches. The process approach focuses upon interaction between agents, between agents and tools, and between agents and tools. A process view of organization activity will have a relationship with other views, particularly the data view, and cannot be treated in isolation. Processes make reference to data but are not concerned with the structuring of this data. In setting out the approach the modeller should try to account for how different perspectives can be brought together.

The problem of preconceived solutions has already been mentioned. It is useful to question if the problem is in fact what it seems to be, and whether it should be addressed by the techniques of process modelling. Problem situations may continue to be poorly defined and therefore might have to be revisited during development, in fact until the problem statement and solution are compatible – a classic example of evolutionary development!

At this juncture it is important to appreciate what are of greater or lesser importance. There will almost inevitably be conflicts; hidden agendas which have to be teased out and resolved if possible. However it is also the case that sometimes conflicts cannot be resolved. Under those circumstances the approach of the process modeller will usually be the way acceptable to the process owner. If this is not possible the modeller will need to confront the political challenge of changing the process in a way that may be at variance with the will of its owner.

As the process approach is described so it is necessary to describe how it will operate, and what its scope shall be. A particular issue is the utility of process capture. Some may take the view that they are only interested in the future, i.e. taking a blank canvas to shape their processes of the future. This may be well and good, but there are two arguments for having some existing process capture. First, if the project aims to evolve an existing process, it is essential to know the starting point of the evolution. Secondly, it might be necessary to determine *why* the process is the shape that it is, to explore intentions and concerns, to help ensure mistakes made in the past are not replicated in the future.

The issue of values has already been mentioned in Chapter 2, where differences in interpretation have been briefly discussed in the context of information systems developments. It is necessary, if a reasonable evaluation of a process is to be carried out, to establish what are the values of the organization. These can be of profound effect. For example if it is preoccupied with what are seen to be efficient utilization of resources then a more Taylorist (Taylor, 1911) emphasis might be developed by the organization. Alternatively, if there is concern for communication and control, if it is felt that there has to be a shift in the power balance in the process such as the promotion of empowerment, then a cybernetic viewpoint using a viable system model (Beer, 1974, 1979; Espejo and Harnden, 1989) might be fruitful.

The important matter is that the values of the process modeller do not become imposed on the solution in an unwarranted manner. The aim of the process modeller is to facilitate modelling of the process, together with the wherewithal for users to adapt it as they seem fit in the light of their subsequent operating experience.

Stakeholders

The term *role* has been introduced in Chapter 3. Here we use the term to identify different stakeholders and their responsibilities in the intervention. There may be different parties involved in the intervention, all with their own interests, their own agendas, and their own ideas about what would constitute a solution. Interventionists may be software engineers, modellers, information-systems designers and so forth. Clients may be accountants, or owners and participants. These must be identified at the outset to allow communication channels to be established.

The following stakeholder roles, corresponding roughly to job descriptions, have been identified as occurring in many interventions:
• Process modellers – those undertaking and facilitating the intervention.
• Clients – those who commissioned the intervention – very likely the problem owners.
• Process owners – those with the power to implement changes to the process.
• Participants/users – those whose work contributes to the process.

• Process managers – those who supervise the process activity on a day-to-day basis.

Of course a single individual may represent different interests: the manager may also participate in the operation of the process. It is important for the establishment of the objectives of the intervention, and for the smooth running of the intervention, to identify who is responsible for each role, their organizational relationships, and, if possible, where their interests lie. The same people may play several (or indeed all) of the roles. Indeed the clients are commonly the process owners. However, all groups involved will have their own interests, and these need to be reconciled as far as possible. Where they cannot be reconciled then the differences need to be known so that their effects on the intervention are understood.

It should be noted that roles may be played by groups rather than individuals. The only role where there is likely to be a problem identifying clear responsibility is that of process owner. This may be distributed to some extent, as often in hierarchical organisations a manager at one level may be allowed to make certain changes to the process, but more radical changes need to be referred upwards.

Stability

It is likely that in the contemporary business environment, the subject area will change during the course of the study. This can be difficult to capture but an overall strategy for ongoing change may be available from managers in the organization. It should be taken into account. The issue is important, if only to be aware that a time-limited process capture may pick up only a snapshot of a transient situation.

Budget and Resources

Budget is important: what funds are available; how will they be used; where will they be used? Key people have to be identified, in particular those who are going to have responsibility for actually contributing to the process modelling. It may or may not be undertaken as a project. It may be ongoing activity, developing and implementing models, extending and evolving these models as an adjunct to normal business activity.

6.3 The Context of the PEF Corporate Team Case Study

The utility of describing the process context is illustrated here by reference to the PEF corporate team, introduced in Chapter 5. It is a statement of process context that was created early on in the PEF study by the modelling team. The statement was found in the project file. It represents the view of the study that was held at that early stage.

'Context Analysis: Version 1.1, created by P. Modelling Team

Purpose

This is a) to model existing process activity, b) to model a target process vision, and c) to develop the Information System for this company.

Deliverables

These are to comprise two models (each being a set of diagrams together with explanatory notes) and a specification for the IS, together with intermediate bimonthly status reports.

Scope

Although PEF is an international business, this work will be restricted to the UK operation. Initial conversations suggest that the broker and underwriter relationship will be a focus. There is a clear distinction between the brokering and underwriting organizations. The scope is to be restricted to underwriting. There is a possibility that in the future, broker activity should be studied more fully in order to come to a conclusion about the possibility of integrating the two businesses much more closely.

Approach

Justifications for process modelling include the need to understand behaviour within the organization and its relationship with its business partners (brokers mainly). Managers have repeatedly emphasized their wish to work with team members, for there to be a *team push* to the innovations as well as a *management pull*. At the last meeting, one manager said, 'a process focus will help us do this, won't it?'

It is apparent that existing IT infrastructure will be a big issue. There are expensive legacy systems. The team is characterized by a strong will to improve but a strong fear of losing the value inherent in these systems. Process modelling will have to interface to data modelling at some point. Object approaches may be applicable for new designs.

There is a strong emphasis upon learning, developing tools and techniques to keep the business moving forward. Process capture will be very highly valued. One manager at initial meeting: 'Relationships are vital, but they are very hard to understand.' An administrator at the same meeting: 'It's very hard to learn what is going on. I have been here three years and am only just beginning to feel comfortable.' Speculation: the organization will gain much from understanding themselves as a network amongst networks!

Culture of common ownership of problems and solutions in the PEF organization. Staff were keen to promote the interests of the business over their own. Little sign of defensiveness. Strong evidence of cohesiveness, job security.

Stakeholders:

There is a wide range of stakeholders in the insurance process:
• Administrators,
• Brokers,
• Underwriters,
• Other PEF teams,
• Policy administration agency,
• Insureds,
• Prospects.
Ownership of problem and solutions is not entirely clear at this stage. Administrators and underwriters are participants. The process owner is the head of operations for UK and Europe. Problem ownership seems to be shared amongst participants, management (especially process owner) and IT management.

Stability

The mantra in PEF is expansion but lower unit costs. This seems to stem from a marketing assessment. Profitability in the corporate sector is likely to decline longer term. PEF corporate to look for lower-risk business in a wider business area. 'We've had our easy wins', said one manager.

Budget and resources

Final budget and resources are to be agreed. Management were responsive to our idea of a pilot study. Current assumption is that the modelling work is to be facilitated by two full time workers over a three-month period. Longer term, there is some support for the view that modelling will be undertaken by PEF corporate themselves. Then the process modellers will place more emphasis on IS development.'

6.4 Context of the Process

As the context of the process modelling intervention needs to be investigated, so too must the context of the process itself. The aim here is to provide a foundation for the modelling of a process and a common understanding of the issues to be addressed. Identifying the goals of a process, its inputs and outputs, may contribute substantially to its understanding. These may not be easy to identify. Think about it this way: what is the process there for; what does it transform?

The establishment of a definition can proceed by examination of documents, unstructured discussions with participants or workshops. A definition based solely on an inspection of documents will be of limited usefulness. Many important, if not crucial, aspects of the process often only emerge through discussions with participants either in discussions or workshops. Examples of such aspects include alternative views of the purpose of the process, or hidden dependencies whose existence is known only to participants.

A more comprehensive and useful definition of a process is based on the idea of a root definition (Checkland and Scholes, 1990) and endeavours to define the organization activity which is relevant to the study, by:
• Stating the objectives of the process.
• Stating the boundaries and interfaces of the subject process. The boundary resides at the activity whose inputs or outputs cease to concern us. At that point, we are interested in defining an interface, i.e. what is provided by the process, and what is received into the process (or what is used by the process) and under what conditions.
• Categorizing the subject process.
• Illuminating what feeds the process, and what is fed by it.
• Determining performance criteria to be used in any evaluation, thus what is important and what is unimportant in the context.
• Identifying those who are going to carry out the study in the organization.
    The process definition thus helps us:
• To determine what is required of the process.
• To scope the investigation.
• To perform an evaluation of the process.
• To minimize risk of failure.
This should also illuminate environmental conditions which have an impact upon the process. As the investigation progresses it will be able to consider whether such impact is perceived to

be adverse or positive. Even when a clear definition exists, it can be viewed in radically different ways by different participants.

Goals

It may be that a clear and coherent statement of the process objectives can be quite readily obtained from the client or process owner. However, it is still important to check this with the other parties (clients, owners, and participants) as it is not uncommon for there to be disagreement about the significance and details of objectives. There may also be occasion to revise the statement as the intervention progresses.

Objectives obtained from documents must be merged with objectives emerging from discussions with participants. All would be very neat and simple if organizational objectives formed a hierarchy, such that objective A would met by achieving B and C, which would be met by achieving D, E, F, and G, etc. However, in practice the situation is always more complicated. Objectives may conflict, or they may interleave, such that a sub-objective contributes to the achievement of more than one higher-level objective. The significance of objectives can vary with time and also with transient conditions in the organization fuelled by relatively short-term pressures.

Nonetheless, objectives might be usefully analyzed through decomposition in order to try to establish a relationship between the objective and the process which is purportedly satisfying that objective. A useful technique for this is Eden's Strategic Options Development Analysis (SODA) (Eden, 1989) which aims to set out problems in terms of a directed mapping of issues and dependencies.

However, not all objectives are realized by a top-down imposition. Objectives may emerge from the process in a bottom-up manner, where others have made use of some of the outputs of the process, and these have to be integrated (if they are acceptable) into overall objectives.

A useful way of identifying the significance of objectives is to identify and assess the feedback loop. Is there any attempt within the organization to ascertain if progress is actually made and if it contributes toward that objective? An absence probably implies a lack of commitment to the objective.

At the same time, as this general investigation of objectives proceeds, the modeller may want to start to think about the operational goals of the process. The modeller may ask, 'When X and Y get together, what are the goals they each seek to achieve?' This is important, as it will become clear later on that to think about interactions between people and the goals achieved through them is a very useful way of investigating organizational processes.

Boundaries

We have to define an interface between the area in which we are interested, and the rest of the world. What is provided by the process and what is received into the process? The boundary can be sketched in whenever we are not interested in what happens to a product of the process or how a data resource came about.

Boundaries may be initially sketched out along organizational lines, i.e. the subject process might be constituted by the work done by the staff answerable to a particular manager. However this is at best a rough and ready guide and not in itself sufficient. By starting to think about patterns of interaction and goals, the modeller will begin to challenge the assumptions underpinning organizational structures and hierarchies.

It can be very useful to seek to categorize the process. By this, we mean to identify from clues the kind of generic process that it represents. This is useful in that it prompts us to think about a pattern of activity. For example the PEF insurance risk-assessment underwriting process can be viewed as a bidding process. In such a process, organizations detect work or proposals which might be potentially profitable. Enquiries are elicited. These enquiries go through a review process. Those of no obvious interest are discarded immediately. Remaining ones merit application of resources to find out more about the proposal, and about potential solutions and potential success and profit. A firm bid will be made for the work, some negotiation follows, and the right to undertake the work (or cover the risk) is won and a contractual relationship is entered into. Identification of an activity which might constitute part of such a generic process will encourage a search for other activities of that process. When doing this, care has to be taken not to prejudge the outcome and, if a process is seen to not fit any category then this has to be recognised. The context makes the process.

Maturity

It might be useful to supplement a contextual investigation with a *maturity* assessment. The maturity of a process is an indication of the predictability of its outcomes. An immature process is one which is very unpredictable. Few performance measures are taken during its execution and no one really knows the reasons for its success (or, more often, failure). If it is successful, it is usually as a result of heroic efforts by participants, and is not something that can be repeated very often. Unfortunately, the usual solution to the repeatability problem is not to improve the process but to replace the participants!

The concept of maturity gained prominence through the SEI's Capability Maturity Model (CMM) (Paulk et al., 1993). This is a conceptual structure which is used by software-development organizations to improve their project capability. It has been adopted by the U.S. Department of Defense (DoD) as a means of improving software quality through improvement of process quality. All organizations providing software to the DoD are subject to assessment through the CMM. This is a process-focused approach; no measures are actually taken of product quality. It can be contrasted with the alternative Spacelab approach (Basili et al., 1992) which attempts to relate product quality to process improvement more directly.

The essence of the CMM method is that an assessment is made of the maturity level of the organization. This consists of an investigation of features which, it is argued, higher maturity processes must possess (e.g. project tracking). Based on this further activities are proposed which will bring about an incremental process improvement. It follows that a maturity assessment supports an evolutionary improvement path. It is based on an appreciation that radical changes are fraught with risk which might be unjustified. There are studies underway to extend CMM to a more general form suitable for business in general such as by Halé (Halé, 1995).

6.5 Route Map

The modeller needs to consider the procedures and skills of systems investigation that will be useful as the work progresses. Later, it shall be seen that OPM is built around the idea of dialectics wherein the need to reconcile variance between different models is used to encourage a sharing of viewpoints amongst stakeholders. OPM exploits the amenity of process modelling as a technology for user participation. Now, in this contextual investigation, the concern is to decide upon and describe some basic techniques that might support the investigation.

It has been seen already that a study of documentation is a useful approach. The merit is that documentation can constitute a rich history of organizational learning, it can describe formal procedure in great depth and helps the modeller to understand the assumptions and context of the participants. The drawbacks include the danger of relying upon outdated sources and the onerous effort that may be required.

Ideally then the modeller will set out a route map which deploys a study of documents as a supplement to one-to-one discussions and group workshops. The process will be one of mutual learning. The process modellers have to learn about the process and domain. The participants will learn about new perspectives upon the domain as well as learning about techniques of process modelling. Process capture (Chapter 7) can be a particularly valuable learning experience. An existing organizational process will have been forged out of contextual relationships in which the organization participates. It will be the result of many years of organization learning and experience. If it is to be ignored, the lessons will be lost.

Granularity is an issue which should be commented upon at this stage. The modeller has many options. It can be the easiest thing in the world to become immersed in process capture whilst forgetting why it is being done. By thinking about an appropriate granularity for the model, the modeller is forced to consider what the model is being used for. The amount of detail must be justified.

6.6 Evaluation

Any process modelling intervention will rely upon suitable evaluation techniques to help to describe its usefulness. Evaluation can be qualitative and, if possible, quantitative. It should take place in terms which are relevant to the organization. Consideration has to be given to identifying the outcomes that are of value to the organization. Some primary criteria were indicated by Feiler and Humphrey (1993):

• Efficiency: a measure of dead or idle time, and of the existence of redundant activities.
• Effectiveness: answering the question: 'does the process thoroughly address its goals?'
• Efficacy: seeking to assess if the process goals really relate to the problem ostensibly being addressed.

In addition to these rather limited criteria, the model will have to measured with reference to the values of the organization. These values may not be overt, and may only emerge as the inquiry proceeds, and may be in terms of capability, facility for evolution, affect on work environment, and so on.

6.7 The Broader Dialectic

There are three primary concerns of our process approach: Context, Capture and Design. These are explored further in subsequent chapters, but the relationship between these three concerns can be thought of as forming a broader series of dialectics. According to the *Collins English Dictionary* (1991), the term *dialectic* refers to a debate, '...intended to resolve differences between two views rather than to establish one of them as true'. OPM operates through a series of dialectics in which design decisions taken in one step are questioned and then validated or revised at different steps.

Thus, as we undertake dialectics within the concerns of the context of a process, so too we undertake dialectics between the concerns of context, capture and design. In other words, we seek to reconcile the viewpoints developed through these separate concerns by mutual adjustment of them. The series of dialectics is represented in Figure .

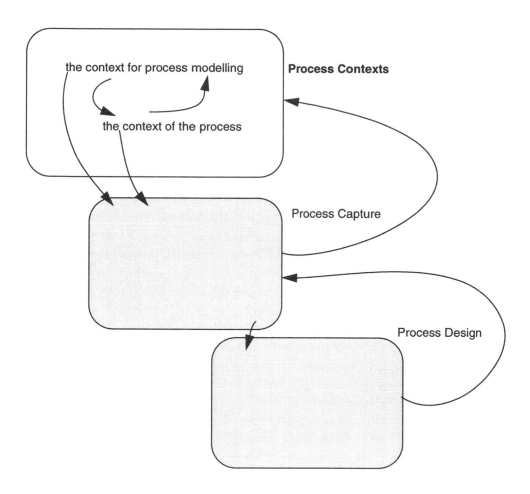

Fig. 6.1 The First in a Series of Dialectics: Process Contexts

6.8 Conclusion

This chapter has sketched issues which may have significant impact on the success of the process modelling study. The result of the intervention can depend on the way in which the intervention is grounded, and on an understanding of what is critical and what is optional. The better the context can be established, then the better the chances that the intervention will be a success. Describing the context is a relatively cheap activity but can contribute a great deal as the study progresses.

It is important to remember that the context is not fixed. It is a frame of reference, but this frame itself may well shift as learning and understanding develop. It needs to be revisited from time to time in order to ensure it reflects what has been uncovered in the inquiry.

Two contexts were described. One for the intervention in the organization, and one for the modelling of the particular process. These provide the essential background to approach the process domain using techniques described in the following chapters.

Starting an OPM study with these analyses of the context means that the whole exercise begins in a reflective mode. The modeller thinks about what is being done in a critical way. This reflective thinking does not cease but continues throughout the capture (Chapter 7) and design (Chapter 8) activities.

THE FOLLOWING CHAPTERS

The next chapter describes the way in which models can be created which describe interactive behaviour patterns. Chapter 8 moves on to developing these models to provide a definition of the behaviour of a support system. It takes OPM further and shows how it relates to the architectural concept of the coordination layer. Chapter 9 shows how P2E can be used to guide the development of the active model.

7

Process Capture

This chapter describes how OPM is used to describe organizational processes. The basis of the approach is to identify interacting agents and then to describe their goals and how they achieve these goals. The three simple descriptions that result are known as the model of the system, the model of goals and the model of method. The creation of these models requires a high level of dialogue with the users: the people whose work it is that we are seeking to represent. As progress is made the modeller operates by revisiting earlier design decisions through *dialectics*. The end result is a modularization of the problem domain and useful descriptions of organizational behaviour. This makes it possible to go beyond the concerns of Process Capture by making a design intervention in the organization through the creation of an executable process support system.

7.1 Introduction

The previous chapter looked at how to define the study scope. This is important, for it is never easy to draw the boundary around the system under investigation. It is important to be open-minded, to be *critically minded*, so as to be prepared to constructively assess and reassess the validity of the problem domain that has been defined. If you go about setting the process context in this critically minded way then there is not a lot more to learn in this chapter; all that is involved here is to try and understand, in a little more depth, the behaviour of the system that is being investigated.

In this chapter, simple process modelling techniques are used to describe the problem domain and in so doing to describe the study context again. Thus, as the problem domain is defined in Chapter 6 it is subdivided again and again in this chapter. The most important thing to remember whilst doing so, is to try to break up the problem space into modules that are meaningful to the agents who take part in the process and, additionally, give a well formed set of modules that can be used in designing software support. These modules we will call *roles*.

So, the focus of this chapter is to create a detailed description of the system that we are investigating. What is it? What are the parts that interact? What purpose do these interactions serve?

The following sections are presented in this chapter:
- **The What, the Why and the How.** This describes how the model of the system, the model of goals and the model of method respectively represent *what*, *why* and *how* descriptions. The vocabulary used in creating these descriptions is then presented.
- **The Modelling Notations.** This section introduces the two notations that are used by this version of OPM. These are Conceptual Models and Role Activity Diagrams.
- Managing the Modelling Exercise. The concern of this section is to address a number of questions that arise in undertaking the modelling exercise. Amongst its concerns are the

goals that we hope to achieve in modelling, the relationship between *as is* and *to be* models and labelling conventions.

• The Participation of Users. This section presents the rationale for establishing a high level of user involvement in the modelling exercise. It suggests how this can be facilitated and how it relates to the creation of the models through a series of dialectics.

• Creating the Model. The logic of the stages in the OPM modelling process is presented in this section. It is noted that this can stand in general terms only. It also shows how the creation of the different models leads to the development of decisions about the modularity of the models.

• Modelling the System. This section sets out the means by which a simple description of interacting agents is developed. It includes advice about the creation of a further context model.

• Modelling the Goals. The concern of this section is to take the model of the system and to create a simple description of the goals of the agents. The section considers different ways in which the modeller might divide up the organizational behaviour and how dependency might be denoted.

• Modelling the Method. The simple description of goals is developed into a model of how these goals are achieved. This is known as a model of method. This section describes how the model of method is created. It describes various ways in which the model can be developed, for example by defining sub-roles and utilizing certain concepts. It concludes by showing how the model can be used to identify and represent the structure of tool integration that is implicit in the models developed from an understanding of the interaction of agents.

• Conclusion. The conclusion shows that the concerns of this chapter are part of a broader investigation. The next step in this broader investigation is to design an intervention in the organization by creating a process support system. This is the concern of the next chapter; Process Design.

7.2 The What, the Why and the How

Right from the start of this book it has been observed that organizations such as the PEF Corporate Team are composed of people interacting with people, people interacting with software and software interacting with software. This gives us three kinds of interaction which are expressed in Figure 7.1.

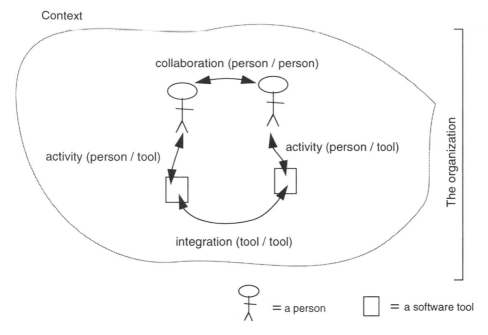

Fig. 7.1 Collaboration, Activity and Integration

To paraphrase the concerns expressed in the opening of Chapter 2, our focus is upon the software support of organizations but our concerns are necessarily dual: the software support and the organizational context. Ultimately, looking at the PEF corporate team problem domain, everything that is most interesting to this study can be described as an interaction. This means that a few human pastimes are beyond the scope of this intervention (e.g. 'Reflect upon your schooldays', a purely mental process!), but even then you are welcome to describe such occupations in the models if you think that they are relevant contextual detail.

An interaction is a behaviour involving two or more *element*s in the process. By elements in this context is meant both agents and tools. The term *agent* is used to describe and classify people. Tools are tools, and those of most interest in this study are software.

The model built in this chapter will give a *what, why and how* view of the process we are studying. By this is meant the following:

- A high level, structural view of the agents that interact is developed. This is a context model of the system which is explored in more depth in the other models. It tells *what* interacts. Human interaction sets the context for interaction involving tools, so we start by considering the people in the process. It is in this sense a model of *who* interacts.
- Having identified the interactive behaviours in a simple way, they can then be specialized by declaring the operational goals that they seek to achieve. This goal model is thus a *why* representation of the behaviour we are interested in.
- Given a description of what interacts and why, a description can be developed of the way in which the goals are achieved. This is done by creating a model of the method which is used to show *how* the goals are achieved.

Each of the *what, why* and *how* models is described in a graphical model. There are rules which determine how one model maps on to another, although, as shall be shown, the modeller has a large degree of freedom. It is not simply a matter of proceeding in a top-down manner. Furthermore, although there is a declared sequence of creation for the models, this is not something which is necessary to prescribe. Different people work in different ways.

7.2.1 Vocabulary

Imagine that we are in some modern organization. Like so many others this organization seems to be perpetually reinventing itself. This process of invention and reinvention is actually fundamental to its nature. If an opportunity is identified, the organization wants to take it. If a deficiency becomes apparent, it wants to rectify it. It is not stability but change that is the natural state of many healthy, vital organizations like this one. The motivations are many: competition, service, adaption and innovation. The challenge is to manage the state of change, to direct it and to synthesize the concerned parts. The danger is that change can begin to control the organization, rather than the organization managing the change. It can become too much, like a drugs overdose, causing oscillations, indirection, uncertainty of behaviour and seizure.

Among this organization's most valued assets are its software systems. These systems are vital to the carrying out of many tasks. What is more, many of the new ideas and initiatives cannot be supported other than by the introduction of some new system (e.g. introducing a new database) or the modifying of an existing system (e.g. defining new tables in an existing database).

Although it is obvious that software systems are *vital* to modern organizations, this does not mean that they always do good. Nor does it mean that any particular system will not do more harm than good. These things need not be contradictory: it is possible for something to be vital and yet to be harmful in other ways. Back in this ever-changing organization this becomes clear: time and time again some application or database is introduced to support some urgent operational need, it satisfies this need, but some other problems arise as a direct result. It is difficult to maintain the integrity, usability and manageability of all of these separate tools.

A process approach to this organizational problem domain is to try and understand the relationship between the various parts of the broader organizational system. It is to try and understand how people and software systems contribute to the fulfillment of goals and how they interact with each other. It is to try and equate the capability of the software system as a whole with the variety of activities it is required to support over time.

The following vocabulary is used to express the different *what, why* and *how* views of organizational behaviour:

• Agents. The concept of agent is used to describe and classify a position in the organizational system being studied (e.g. 'Underwriter', 'Clerical Assistant'). An agent can also be the organization itself (e.g. 'PEF Insurance Corporate Team'). Thus, agents are people or groups who take part in the interactive behaviour described in the model. This concept makes it possible to describe behaviour that is of interest, both by reference to the agent who carries it out and to the instance of that agent. For example, the assessment of a risk proposal is done by an Underwriter; 'Anna' is an Underwriter.

• Interaction. Interactions are behaviours that are shared by different agents, agents and software tools and by different software tools. Interaction is modelled in two ways. Initially it is understood to be a relationship, *interacts with*. Later, this is developed to describe lower level interactions which are *part of* the relationship. Thus, initially the method will state that an *interacts with* relationship exists between agents (e.g. Underwriter interacts with Clerical Assistant). This means that it is known that two components in the system interact but that the interactive behaviours are not or cannot be described in detail. Later, the model is developed by describing the interactions by reference to the states in which they take place.

- Cardinality of Agents. It is useful to express the cardinality of agents. It is likely that in most cases there will be many people instances of particular agents (e.g. 'Anna', 'Shaun' and 'Jessica' are all Underwriters). Sometimes, however, there may be only one instance of an agent (e.g. 'Joshua' is the Chief Architect). We can distinguish between these two cases by declaring a multiple cardinality for the former and a singular cardinality for the latter. To do so is useful, for the model will express logical behaviours which are carried out by agents (for example, 'Submission Assessing is carried out by Underwriters'). There is potentially a multiple cardinality of both the work package and the agent and it is therefore necessary to consider which agent carries out which case or work package. To take an example, *Firm X* is a company which seeks insurance from a commercial insurance team. For the insurer to underwrite the risk, they need to assess it. This means that 'Submission Assessing' will have to be carried out by an Underwriter. As Underwriter has a multiple cardinality it is necessary to ask 'Which Underwriter will assess the submission from Firm X?'. The Firm X work-package in this sense represents an instance of a generic behaviour. When stipulating a multiple cardinality the OPM method does not give an exact figure. All it means that there is potentially more than one. A singular cardinality means one and only one.
- Goals. A goal is an expression of people's intent. It is possible to conceive of many different kinds of goals (long term/short term, realistic/unrealistic). The method is restricted to considering the *operational* goals, i.e. the functional goals of interactive behaviour expressed in the models. Therefore, in this context a goal is understood to be a state which it is intended to achieve by entering into an interactional behaviour.
- Non-functional goals. An additional non-functional qualifier can be placed upon operational goals. For example, to the goal 'Process new order', the qualifier 'within fifteen minutes' may be added.
- Dependency. Goals can be dependent upon other goals. It might be necessary to state explicitly what these dependencies are. For example, it might be inferred that *goal Y* (to give a present) is dependent upon *goal X* (to purchase a present).
- States. A state is an externally observable and identifiable mode of behaviour within the system that is investigated.
- Activities. The simplest interpretation of activities is that they are that which agents do. Hence, in insurance company *X* 'log proposal', 'assess proposal', and 'fill in movements form' are all activities. The verb is an essential part of their label. In the state-based models which are used in this method, an activity is that which causes a change of state.This is an adequate definition but it is also useful to develop a more fundamental understanding by relation to the concept of a complex system made up of many people and many software tools. What then, are activities in this context? Clearly they are *interactions* between agents and tools. To take the most obvious case: an activity undertaken by someone at work can be understood as an interaction between that person and the tool they use. Thus, if the person happens to be an administrator and the activity is 'log proposal', then this denotes an interaction with the technology used at that point in the process (in this case, a database for logging proposals).
- Roles. In the broadest sense, roles can be understood to be modules of behaviour which interact with each other and which contain activities. A role can then be defined as a set of activities which are undertaken by an agent towards the achievement of a common goal. The mapping of role to goal gives a logical relation between all the behaviours within it. It also describes how it is intrinsic to roles that they are assigned to agents who possess goals.
- The Basic Constitution of the Role. To make the modelling of behaviour simpler, certain capabilities can be thought of as being common to all roles. These capabilities are known

as the basic constitution of the role. As a starting point it is regarded that all roles have two basic capabilities. These are the power of reassignment and the right of exit. First, any particular role that is assigned to an agent with a multiple cardinality, can be reassigned to another instance of the same agent type (e.g. Anna and Shaun are both underwriters; Anna can reassign a role she possesses to Shaun). Secondly, a role can fail to complete the behaviour defined for it. This means that a role can be exited at any point (e.g. any underwriter can decide not to continue with the assessment of a submission before it is completed).

Having a basic constitution for roles means that there is no need to model these intrinsic capabilities. However, if it is necessary that these basic powers are waived, then this will have to be stated explicitly in the model (e.g. if underwriters cannot reassign roles to other underwriters).

• Sub-roles. Sub-roles are sets of activities which are potentially common to many roles. They do not interact with other roles.

7.3 The Modelling Notations

Two modelling notations are used. These are Conceptual Models (CMs) and Role Activity Diagrams (RADs). They are simple and useful techniques.

Modelling techniques are the means to an end and not the end in itself. As the circumstances of different projects dictate, there may or may not be better ways of creating the *what*, *why* and *how* views. To debate which modelling notation is best in some absolute sense is always fruitless. It is like debating which is the best tool wrench, car, kind of bridge or programming language. Clearly, the exigencies of the project being undertaken dictate which notation you (as an experienced modeller) are likely to find most helpful. The best way to proceed is to consider examples of the use of different notations, to use them yourself and to describe those features which were important to you when you used the notation. To us, the particular advantages of Conceptual Models and RADs have been, respectively, their simplicity and their expression of modularity.

7.3.1 Conceptual Models

Conceptual Models (CMs) provide a very simple set of symbols. Their creation was motivated by many process modelling projects in which there was a need for a largely semantic free, flexible notation. In this they follow the simple representations used in Soft Systems Methodology (Checkland, 1981). Here, CMs are used simply to say 'this interacts with that'. Thus, this use of CMs is only one interpretation of the possibilities they present to the modeller.

7.3.2 Role Activity Diagrams

The basic form of the Role Activity Diagram (RAD) was introduced by Holt (e.g. Holt et al., 1983) as a way of representing coordinative behaviour. RADs are used here in a distinct way but are developed from the original template of Holt and the expansion of the syntax and semantics by Ould (1995).

RADs are intuitively simple and easy to read. They allow behaviour to be subdivided into a number of modules. This modularization allows the description of complex behaviour in a highly legible way. The unit of modularization in a RAD is a *role*. The relationship between roles is very significant because OPM relates the structure of roles to the structure of goals recorded in the operational domain. This is discussed and described later. Thus, RADs are used to allow the rationalization of some complex problem space into a number of well-defined and understood modules.

It might be useful to think of roles as a little like modules in a computer program. As a module executes a specified package of behaviour in a machine, so too a role can be understood to execute a specified package of behaviour. As with program modules, the way in which the modular structure is defined is all-important and should seek to promote decoupling and cohesion. A module loses identity when it is too highly coupled to other modules. In other ways, there are differences between roles and modules. In the normal case, roles will be used to depict behaviour that is undertaken by a person. The executed behaviour is likely to be context-sensitive, to involve judgement and may be to some degree extemporaneous. Moreover, to satisfy its various contingencies, a role is likely to call on different machines or different functions within a machine. In this a role is on a meta level to a program module.

A key to the primitives of RADs is given later in Figure 7.16.

7.4 Managing the Modelling Exercise

7.4.1 What Are Models For?

It is important to be very careful about the validity of process models as representations of the behaviour of people. A process model cannot, except perhaps in the most extreme case, be taken to be a valid, *detailed prescription* of the behaviour of people. There are many studies which have shown this; for example, studies by Wynne (1979) and Suchman (1983) have shown that even routine work, which appears superficially to be mundane and procedural, involves extemporization and problem-solving. Thus Wastell et al. (1994) suggest that formal representations be treated as 'normative idealizations'.

Modelling can be easy or difficult. It can be detailed or abstract. It is always imprecise because models are not reality, they are just models.

7.4.2 The Goals We Hope to Achieve

In creating the process model it is hoped to achieve the following:
• A description of the collaboration of agents.
• A description of activities carried out by agents.
• A description of the integrative behaviours of tools.
• A traceable mapping of organizational behaviour between models used for analysis and design and, ultimately, through to the executable software support (see also Chapter 8).
The following aims are supplementary to those listed above:
• A high-level and appropriate capture of non-functional business rules (e.g. underwriter must respond within 10 days).
• To support reuse in modelling.
• For the models to be simple and rapidly assembled.

7.4.3 'As Is' and 'To Be' Modelling

The modelling techniques presented can be useful for *as is* and *to be* modelling. They are useful whenever there is an issue which can be usefully expressed in a *what*, *why* or *how* model. These *what, why* and *how* views of the behaviour under investigation can be used to feed an *executable or active* design step within which the software support is developed. This is the subject of the next chapter.

7.4.4 A Solution as a State in an Evolution

Consider again two factors raised earlier in this work:
• It is in the interests of organizations to change. They seek to adapt to changing circumstances and to change their environment to their advantage. They innovate, rationalize, extemporize and replicate.
• Organizations are immensely complex as well as dynamic. Their overall purpose is ambiguous. A software designer cannot be certain of how a system will contribute to an organization. This is more especially the case because a software system of consequence will change its environment.

This leads to the conclusion that software systems should evolve in a way which is consistent with the evolution of the organization as a whole or, taking the argument further, should even provide a *means* for the evolution of the organization. It follows that design is not a one-off process. Moreover, it is characterized by uncertainty. In this light the malleability of software, which is in some senses problematic as it undermines the management of its form, becomes not only an advantage but provides the basis for a design approach.

This is discussed again, later on, when process capture is presented as part of a larger process spanning context and design issues (see Figure).

7.4.5 Labelling Conventions

A labelling convention is necessary to ensure the accessibility of the models. The following conventions are proposed:
• The *what* models are 'models of the system'. They show what agents interact with each other. They can be labelled by the interactions that they show or in any other meaningful way.
• The *why* models are 'models of goals'. They can be given a label which describes the general intent of the goals depicted within them. In addition, they can be assigned a number which relates to the model of the system from which they are developed. The first goal model relating to a particular model of a system will be 'goal 1'.
• The *how* models are 'models of the method'. These are given the same general title as the model of goals that they develop. They too are described by a number which relates them to the goal model that they develop. The first model for a particular goal model will be 'method 1'.

For fuller descriptions a table can be used. An example is given below.

Model	No.	Description
System (*what*)		Broker interacts with Underwriter *(any meaningful and unique label)*
Goal (*why*)	*n*	Obtaining and giving decisions *(any meaningful and unique label)*
Method (*how*)	*n*	Obtaining and giving decisions *(label of relevant model of goals)*

Table 7.1 Label Examples

In this example the label 'Obtaining and giving decisions' is chosen to summarize the goals represented within the model of goals in a helpful way. The label is retained in the model of method. The goal and method models both relate to the system model 'Broker interacts with Underwriter'.

7.4.6 The Underscore

Within the models themselves the underscore is sometimes used. This is done where, because of space restrictions, it is useful to denote which words form part of the same statement.

7.5 The Participation of Users

7.5.1 Dialogue

The participation of end users (*process participants*) is fundamental. The process of information-gathering that underpins the modelling activity is essentially one of dialogue. The users inform and suggest ideas to the modeller. The modeller informs and suggests ideas to the users. The users also inform and suggest ideas to other users.

Two very important aspects can be emphasized here. The first relates to the utility of software systems. The software systems that are used in an organization should be meaningful to the users in the sense that it should be possible to discuss the capabilities and contributions of software in relation to the tasks the users want to carry out. The easier it is to relate the structure of the users' tasks to the structure of the software systems, the easier it will be to identify deficits, to spot opportunities and to make changes. Secondly, there is the more general need for comprehension of the organization and its relationships. It is important to know, to an appropriate level of detail, who contributes to what and what are the opportunities for interaction. Modelling is fundamental to the understanding of complexity and thus fundamental to the development of this knowledge.

Taking these two aspects together leads to the requirement that the models created by this method be developed in a close collaborative dialogue between users and modeller. Even better, users might actually want to create them. Users should also be the means by which models are validated. Critically, this validation is needed whenever a change of any substance is made. This need for validation leads to the concept of the dialectic.

7.5.2 A Series of Dialectics

Taking the idea of dialogue further, it is possible to see the operation of OPM as a series of dialectics. Design decisions taken in one step are questioned and then validated or revised at different steps. Different users may take part in different dialectics. The most obvious example of this is that the description of goals might require participants from each affected group (e.g. brokers, underwriters) but that the way in which the goals are fulfilled will be confined to participants from each individual group (e.g. underwriters decide how to fulfil their goals).

The process of dialectics is illustrated below in Figure 7.2, addressing both the domain of intervention ('the real world') and the domain of design ('the design environment'). The creation of the executable (active) model straddles both, for it encompasses design and the feedback from implementation.

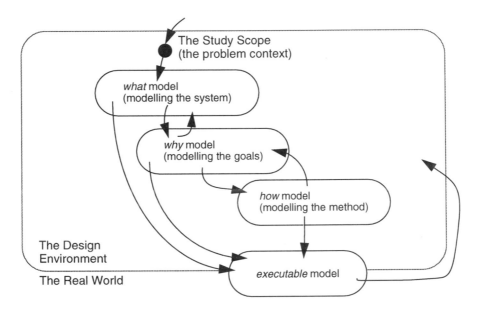

Fig. 7.2 A Series of Dialectics: From Study Scope Through to Executable

The arrows depict the conversations which seek to reconcile different views. The dialectics are used to consider all design decisions and to root out as many as possible of the assumptions which are made in the course of the modelling route. Their focus is upon the development of a sustainable modularity, for each modelling step shapes the modularity of the next. Therefore the modelling route can be characterized through its concern for modularity from the initial model of the system context right through to the executable itself. For example, in creating a model of method it will be necessary to question whether the model of goals on which it is based is a sustainable representation. Many different considerations may be raised. The following are examples of the likely concerns:
• To consider whether the labels of the goals are a valid description of the behaviour expressed in the goal model.
• To ask whether the goals so depicted describe roles that are decoupled from each other.
• To consider whether the goals so depicted describe roles that are internally cohesive.
It will become clear later that the model of method differs from the others in that it is only used to inform and enrich the debate undertaken through the series of dialectics. The decisions about system modularity are not directly affected by it. For this reason it is known as an *off-line*

modelling step.

7.5.3 Finding Subjects

A key concern is to decide who should participate at each different step. It is important that domain experts are able to shape the development of the model in appropriate ways. This may work in various ways, for example:

• In the establishment of the system context, those who 'own' the study will have input, as might those who set operational goals (managers etc.) and operational users (i.e. those who actually fulfil the goals).
• The development of other models of the system and the models of goals are also likely to involve managers and operational users.
• The creation of the models of method will be focused upon those operational users who participate in the work described.
• The executable will be created by a modeller/programmer but its validation comes through exposure to the participants in the study.

The user interview is the bedrock of information gathering. Workshops are useful as a means of sharing ideas, giving feedback and reconciling inconsistencies. Generally, workshops can usefully follow a series of interviews. In the course of an investigation there is always more to relate than can be described in process models. One might fear that some of the most interesting messages are actually being lost! It can be useful to develop simple interview summaries which are given back to the interviewees. These describe the important topics which were discussed in an interview but which are contextual to the model itself. For example, the interviewee may describe valuable ideas for the future. Interview summaries are created in order to check that these ideas are understood correctly, and to allow the interviewee to retain ownership of his or her input. It is a form of etiquette to create them and to allow these summaries to be approved by the interviewee before they are to be stored in a project database.

Interviews usually give a low-level study focus. They focus upon the *as is* and the *to be* work activities of the interviewee and the goals served by these activities. This enables the modeller to appreciate fairly quickly how the various components that make up a system (the people, databases etc.) interact. The weakness of this low level (i.e. role level) is that it may not give due weight to the corporate, branch and personal goals that may also impact upon the behaviour in the organization. This amounts to a requirement that the modeller is able, whenever necessary, to relate a role-level analysis of goals to goal analysis at higher levels. It might be useful to use established techniques such as Soft Systems Methodology (SSM) (Checkland, 1981) in this regard.

7.5.4 Competing Design Schemas

Part and parcel of people working together is the sharing of ideas and the drawing up of implicit or explicit agendas. Recently, much research has come to focus on the immeasurable difficulty of ensuring that some system (e.g. an Information System) satisfies the needs of many different users (see Chapter 2). This is a political problem.

Users may not agree on what actions they should seek to carry out. There may be dispute over objectives. In moving from an understanding of what happens now to developing a target design, there is likely to be disagreement amongst those concerned. There are questions over who should be involved in decision making. The net result is that debate about alternatives may become a prime concern as the process of dialectics unfolds. Much depends upon the ethos of the organization being investigated. It may be that alternative models are created as competing design schemas.

Wilson (1990) expands upon related themes. He describes a concept of a 'human activity system' as 'human beings undertaking purposeful activity', and 'an interacting set of subsystems or an interacting set of activities'. He uses the example of the aeroplane Concorde to show how it is possible to create complete and unambiguous descriptions of designed physical systems. However, turning to the use of Concorde as a human activity system he suggests that it is only possible to define it from a particular point of view. Is it, for example, a transportation system for the carriage of passengers between continents at speeds greater than that of sound? Or is it a system which reduces the desirability of the environment by producing noise and fumes? The answer depends upon the point of view.

7.5.5 The Multi-Disciplinary Character of the Intervention

This leaves us with a broad problem which may imply a need for some sort of design process through which alternative schemas can be presented and evaluated. Moreover, as has been already stated, the problem is multi-disciplinary in its nature. Thus OPM does not attempt to deal with all aspects of the problem of developing software in organizations but *continually interfaces* to those aspects just beyond its remit.

7.6 Creating the Model

In general, logic will dictate the ordering of the stages in the modelling process. Thus, modelling starts with the description of the problem domain and then, through a description of interaction moves towards the design of the executable. However, it follows from Figure 7.2 that the detail of the sequence of the modelling stages will also be dictated by the exigencies of the series of dialectics. Therefore the following sequence may hold in general terms only:

• Getting started. The need to understand the problem context is an initial concern. This is a general exploration of problem and domain. Techniques such as the rich picture (Checkland, 1981) can be useful. In the spirit of the method as a whole, an earlier exploration of problem and domain might be revised by a later one as the needs of the investigation dictate.

• Identify the interacting agents in a model of the system (*what*). A high level, structural view of the system is given by describing the interacting agents. This is a context model which helps in setting the scope for the investigation. It describes the agents that interact with each other. The system described in the context model is explored in more depth by developing other models. These represent segments of the overall scope. They too describe the agents that interact. These models of the system are given the mnemonic '*what*' models.

• Create a model of goals (*why*). The purpose for the interaction is added to the description of the agents. Throughout, the focus is upon the coordination that takes place in the system being investigated. Thus, having identified the interactive behaviours, they can then be specialized by declaring the operational goals that they seek to achieve. This model of goals is thus a *why* representation of the behaviour under investigation.

• Create models of method (*how*). The way in which the agents achieve these goals is described. Upon the description of what interacts and why, a model of the method by which the goals are achieved can be created. This model describes *how* the goals are achieved. It requires the unbundling of the interactive relationship thus far depicted, so that a more complex mosaic of interactive behaviours between people and people, people and tools and tools and tools can be created. The data input to these tools is described so that it is possible to identify which data is shared by activities within or between roles.

• Creation of the active model. Later on, when attention turns to making an intervention in the organization (Chapter 8), the executable is created. The creation of the *active* model considers which of these interactive behaviours are to be supported in a coordination layer, and the logical dependencies between the behaviours thus supported. Throughout, as each of these models (system, goals, method and executable) are created, decisions are made about the modularity of the model. These decisions are made, in the first instance, by the model of scope described in the contextual model of the system, and are then developed by the model of goals. A key feature is the way in which the modules described in the models are created through some very simple mapping rules and then examined through a series of dialectics. These dialectics are critical, for the creation of the model is not simply a matter of proceeding in a top-down manner. Decisions are revisited and revised as the dialectics question their validity.

7.7 Modelling the System

This model tells *what* interacts. It is in some ways akin to drawing a simplified ER diagram but there is only one kind of relationship ('interacts with'). Conceptual Models are used for the description of the following:

• Agents.
• A single type of relationship between these entities which is *interacts with*.
• Cardinality (*one*, or *one or many*).

The simplest representation of interacting agents is shown below.

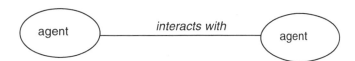

Fig. 7.3 Interacting Agents

7.7.1 Agents

Agents take part in the interactive behaviour described. The agents might be people or groups. The basic idea is to define the domain of interest (the interacting agents) and to identify them.

7.7.2 Relationship

There is only one kind of relationship between agents. This is *interacts with*. This relationship is identified between named agents (e.g. Administrator interacts with Underwriter).

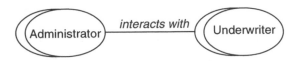

Fig. 7.4 The *interacts with* Relationship

7.7.3 Cardinality

A cardinality is denoted for agents in a simple way. It can be shown that there is *only one* agent or that there are *one or many* agents. A single ellipse from the CM is used to represent *only one*, and a double ellipse is used to represent *one or many* (see Figure 7.4). To depict cardinality in this way is useful, for it alerts the designer of the software executable, which is created later on, to the need to support the coordination of many agents of the same type.

Where there may be a many cardinality, it is also possible that similar agents interact with each other. This is shown in the following way.

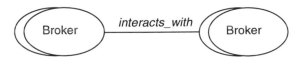

We might prefer to represent this in the following way:

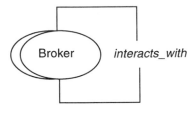

Fig. 7.5 Interaction Between Similar Agents

7.7.4 Context

In every study, one model of the system will describe the context for the study as a whole. It is used to orient the investigation. An example for the PEF team is depicted below in Figure 7.6. Between each of the linked ellipses we understand there to be an *interacts with* relationship.

This context model describes those interactive relationships of concern to the study. For example, although we can be confident that a broker interacts with a prospect (i.e. a potential client), it is not shown because it has been decided that this is beyond the domain of concern.

Sometimes the way in which the modeller divides up the subject domain will seem to be quite arbitrary, like the cutting of a cake. This is one reason why the description of the scope is important (Chapter 6). Ultimately, defining a model of interest is a matter of judgement. That

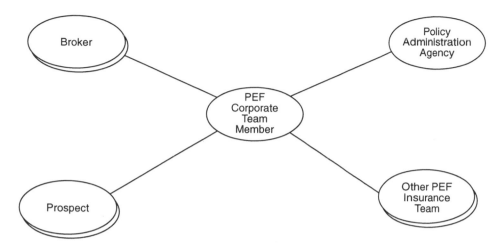

Fig. 7.6 An Example of a Context Model

judgement is going to be led by the intentions of the project, the stage of the project, the agents that are of interest and other issues. For example, if the modeller is interested in the way in which underwriters contribute to a process, then he or she will want to look at the interactions they are involved in. Alternatively, if the modeller is interested in the contribution of the whole insurance team then he or she will model the interactions of the whole team. Most likely, the modeller will have some interest in both as one sets the context for the other. The key then is to describe the models at the level of interest and to understand how that level relates to other levels.

In this light it can be useful to denote the modelling relationship between different descriptions of the system. For example, consider two descriptions for the PEF insurance company. The first states that a broker interacts with a member of the PEF team, and the second that a broker interacts with an underwriter. Given that an underwriter *is a* member of the PEF team, the modelling relationship can be described as one of specialization.

7.7.5 Marking the Study Domain

The study context is segmented into what may be quite small sub-components each of which is investigated through a series of models. Whenever it is useful to make things clearer for the reader and to show which part of the model is the focus of the study, a hashed line and a label is used. An example of this convention is shown below in Figure 7.7.

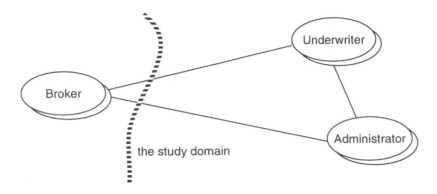

Fig. 7.7 The Study Domain Notation

This simple convention might be useful in any of the system, goal or method models.

7.8 Modelling the Goals

In developing the model of the system, the modeller has probably already been thinking about goals. In describing agents that interact he or she will, to some extent, consider the goals that are served by the interactions. By modelling the goals explicitly the modeller has the opportunity to develop a logical modularity of the system under investigation; a modularity that may later be mapped through to the software support that is developed.

In this context a goal is understood to be a state which it is intended to achieve by entering into an interactional behaviour. For any *interacts with* relationship between agents we must be able to declare a goal which each seeks to attain. The complete fulfilment of the relationship will be the achievement of both these goals.

The way in which goals are interpreted, as outcomes of interactional behaviour, is a rather simple, low-level interpretation. Goals are understood, in an operational or functional sense, as the intended product of some behaviour. This is consistent with our interest in purposeful action. We are not referring to the phenomena of hopes, motivation and ambitions which may also be described as goals (e.g. career goals, personal goals).

7.8.1 Mapping the Model of the System to a Model of Goals

The interactive relationships described in outline in the model of the system are specialized by adding the concept of a goal. A simple approach is to develop the CM to focus upon the goals with the title of the agents as an appendage. In this way the mapping to a goal model is achieved simply by moving the description of the agents and their cardinality to outside the ellipse. Thereby the system (*what*) to goal (*why*) mapping takes the following form:

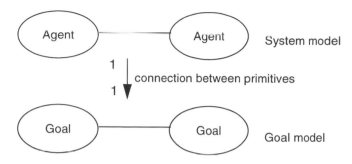

Fig. 7.8 System Model to Goal Model Mappings

7.8.2 Goals and State

The states depicted as goals are achieved through the carrying-out of activities within a pattern of interactive behaviour in a system. To help to express this clearly a convention is to use the past transitive form of the verb (e.g. Company Z's decision *obtained*). It is useful to maintain this so as to make the mapping between the *why* model and the state-based *how* model transparent. This mitigates the fact that this form of the verb makes the expression of goals a little less natural to users.

7.8.3 Failure to Achieve Goals

It is taken as a default position that an agent in an interactive behaviour can fail to achieve a goal. This means that if an Underwriter possesses a goal, 'PEF team's decision given' he or she can fail to achieve this. This means that we accept that in the normal case an agent is able to exit from the undertaking of a role at any point within it. There will be exceptions but these need to be stated explicitly. Therefore, if it is imperative that the underwriter gives a decision on a risk proposal come what may, this will have to be appended to the goal description.

7.8.4 Non-Functional Goals

The goals of the interactions are given in functional terms. It can also be necessary to express non-functional goals through business rules (e.g. success criteria). For example, in Figure 7.9 it can be seen that there is a non-functional goal that the decision of the underwriter be given 'within 10 days'.

7.8.5 The Resolution of Goals

Consider agents X and Y which interact. The goal of the interaction for X is x which is fulfilled by Y achieving its goal y. For example, X might be a broker who seeks to obtain the decision of PEF insurance on a submission. He or she may wish to know on what terms the PEF team would be willing to underwrite the property risks of a major high street store chain. Therefore the broker interacts with an underwriter. The underwriter wants to appraise the submission so that a decision is given back to the broker. In this case the resolution of goal *y* (the underwriter's goal) resolves *x* (the broker's goal). This is shown below.

Fig. 7.9 An Example of a Goal Model

This is like a customer–supplier model. *X* wants something, so does *Y*; there follows an interactional exchange wherein their goals are mutually resolved.

There are also cases where *x* and *y* are not mutually resolved. Consider the following case:

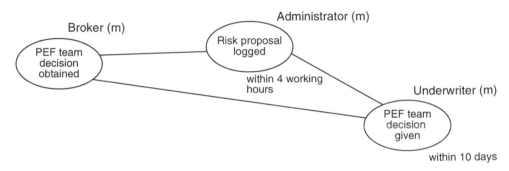

Fig. 7.10 An Example of an Interactive Thread

The resolution of goals in Figure 7.10 is not straightforward because of the existence of a goal, 'Risk proposal logged' which does not of itself resolve either of the other two. There are many patterns like this. They arise as a result of the way that the modeller segments the problem domain to look at different combinations of agents and their interactions. As was stated at the outset, there may be any number of agents or tools involved in an interactive relationship although the minimum is obviously two. The modeller will define and redefine the models of interest according to the issues arising in the study.

The term *thread* is used to describe a situation where there are *more than two*. It is just a more complex model than the simple customer–supplier type exchanges. When it comes to the agents carrying out the behaviours for real, in the organization, there will be some pattern of interactions which will unravel as though a thread were being pulled betwixt and between them. The execution of a thread of behaviour may be bureaucratic and predictable or it may involve some dynamic and complex sequence of synchronization. We just do not know yet. It is therefore important to think a little more about interactions and goals.

When two agents interact for some purpose, they might share the same goal, or have different but mutually resolving goals, or non-resolving goals whereby further related action is carried out. Remember that the goals are understood to be states that each agent seeks to attain through interacting with some other agent. Thus, assuming that incompatible goals do not occur, there are the following possibilities:

Shared goals

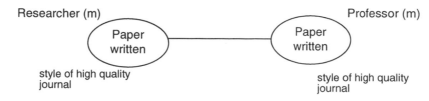

Mutually resolving goals

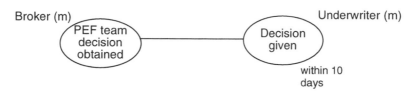

Thread goals

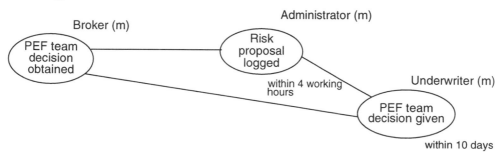

Fig. 7.11 Simple Goal Model Examples

The first example shows an interactive behaviour between agents (a researcher and a professor) with a shared goal (to write a paper and to complete this in a style suited to a high-quality journal). The second example shows a broker interacting with an underwriter. The broker seeks a decision upon a risk proposal. The underwriter wishes to evaluate this risk and give the decision. For example, after consideration, the underwriter might say, 'No, we will not underwrite this risk', or she might say, 'We will underwrite the risk according to standard conditions at a premium of X pounds'. The third example shows a very similar interactive behaviour. However, in this an administrator is involved. The administrator seeks to achieve the state 'Risk proposal logged'. This refers to the function whereby the PEF Corporate Team logs details of the proposals under consideration in a database. The achievement of this goal does not of itself resolve either of the other two goals.

7.8.6 Dependency

In some circumstances the modeller might consider it useful to note a logical dependency between goals. This can be done through the concept of initiating agent and responding agent. That is, we can ask which agent initiates the interactive behaviour and which has a responding role as a result. This can be understood through the possession of goals. Thus, in the case of the broker and the underwriter in Figure 7.11, we can regard the broker as the initiator and the underwriter as the responder. This is denoted by an arrow that points from initiator to responder:

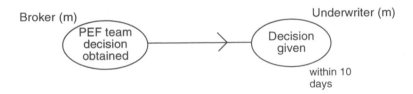

Fig. 7.12 Initiation and Response

This is quite straightforward; most initiation/response relationships are. There are innumerable examples of this model of interactive behaviour that occur in daily life. For example, when items are purchased from a store, the purchaser (as initiator) has a goal which is resolved by the store assistant (who has a goal) undertaking some activities (e.g. order items from warehouse, prepare invoice). The customer–supplier model fits well with this description of initiator and responder.

Note, however, that whenever an initiation/response relationship is shown, it constrains further development of the model. In other words, in developing a model of method, or indeed an executable, based upon Figure 7.12, it is necessary to ensure that the broker and only the broker initiates the *interacts with* relationship. This is a practical rule which arises to try and ensure consistency in the model. It means that there are actually many reasons why the modeller may not want to denote dependency: can the modeller be sure that the pattern is correct? Is it true that the underwriter never (as initiator) proactively seeks the responsibility for evaluating a submission held by a broker? Does the modeller really want to restrict the model to this? The modeller should note that the following two models are not the same (see Figure 7.13).

A cursory understanding of the commercial insurance business reveals that brokers act as agents for clients (e.g. major store chains, manufacturing companies) and take a submission to underwriters in a number of companies. The goal model 'B' in Figure 7.13 can be used to describe this. It states that the broker is the initiator. Perhaps he arranges an appointment to meet the underwriter and takes the submission to the meeting. The goal model 'A' also describes this but is more general. It can also be used to describe a circumstance where the underwriter is the initiator of the interaction and the broker is the responder. This is because it says nothing about the initiation/response relationship. The more generic model 'A' is therefore more resilient and so might be exactly what the modeller wants. For example, in the insurance company there may be an important minority of cases where the underwriter is the initiator and the broker agrees to have his or her client's submission evaluated. This may occur where the underwriter knows that the broker represents a particularly attractive client (perhaps a large and reputable chain of restaurants) and so wishes to proactively seek the business. It follows that a simple heuristic is applicable here: generic is best.

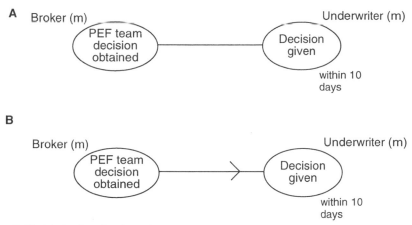

Fig. 7.13 Dissimilar Goal Models

7.8.7 Cardinality

In building a model of the system the modeller made a statement about the cardinality of the agents that take place in the process being studied. For example, the modeller said, 'We know that there may be many brokers and that there may be many underwriters'. In the modelling of the goals this was simply re-stated, outside of the ellipse.

In the model of the system created earlier, an expression of cardinality is a very simple statement. If there are many underwriters and many administrators, the most obvious inference is that any one instance of an underwriter may interact with any one instance of an administrator (e.g. underwriter 'Joseph' may interact with underwriter 'Thomas'). It might also be useful to say a little more than this. For example, take the expression of goals in the example below:

Fig. 7.14 Cardinality Inferred By Goals

The goals have been phrased in a way which tries to suggest that the fulfilment of the registrar's goal will depend upon interaction with many students. They also try to express that the converse is not true. Each student need interact with only one registrar to achieve the goal 'Registration Completed'.

This example can be used to contrast what is stated clearly by the model and what is inferred by it. It *states* that, 'We know there may be many registrars and there may be many students'. From our reading of the goals *we may infer* that, 'A single registrar will interact with all students in order to achieve his goal. A single student will interact with a single registrar in order to achieve her goal.'

So that it is not necessary to leave so much to inference, the model can be developed to state the cardinality explicitly.

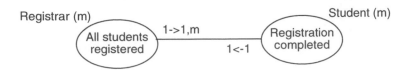

Fig. 7.15 The Cardinality of Agents and the Cardinality of Goals

The figures annotating this diagram state that the achievement of the goal, 'All students registered' will require interaction with at least one, and possibly many, students. The achievement of the goal, 'Registration completed' will require interaction with one registrar. This is a useful convention which works just as well when the modeller creates a model of *how* goals are achieved.

7.9 Modelling the Method

This section describes how a more detailed description of behaviour can be developed from the simple models created so far. In constructing models of method the concern moves from the collaborative structure to learning about the coordination of people and tools and thence tools and tools.

The focus is the development of what is known as a model of method which describes *how* the goals of interactive behaviours are achieved. For this the Role Activity Diagram (RAD) is used. In so doing the modeller starts to use a more extensive and powerful set of modelling symbols. Note for example, that with particular regard to the coordination of different agents, instead of simply being concerned for interactive relationships (e.g. X 'interacts with' Y), the modeller will consider the state in which synchronous interactions take place (e.g. X in state SX.1 has a *synchronous interaction* with Y in state SY.1).

The basic primitives of the RAD are set out below in Figure 7.16.

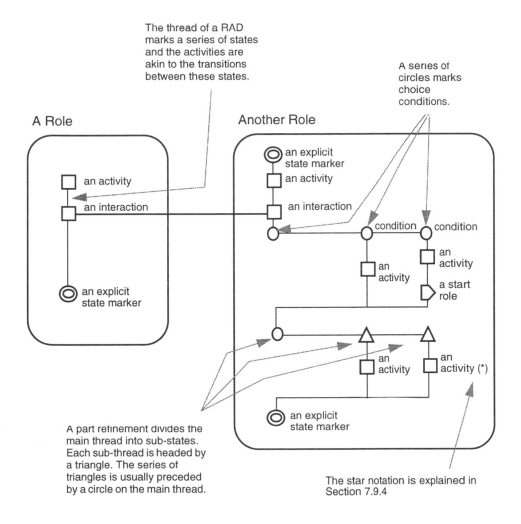

Fig. 7.16 The Primitives of the Role Activity Diagram

Overall, the modeller begins to see the domain as a complex and dynamic arrangement of people and software tools. This idea is illustrated below in Figure 7.17 which shows how, at this level, the coordination of agents can be depicted by the RAD interaction notation (a horizontal line between roles), whilst the interaction of people and tools is described through activities (boxes within the role boundary).

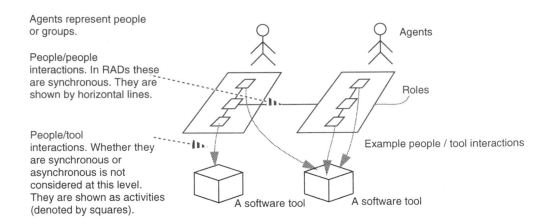

Agents represent people or groups.

People/people interactions. In RADs these are synchronous. They are shown by horizontal lines.

People/tool interactions. Whether they are synchronous or asynchronous is not considered at this level. They are shown as activities (denoted by squares).

Agents

Roles

Example people / tool interactions

A software tool   A software tool

Fig. 7.17 People to People and People to Tool Interaction Depicted in a RAD

The development of a model of method is thereby used to deepen the understanding of the complex interactive system under investigation. The modeller seeks to validate and revise the models of *why* the interactive behaviours occur and tries to shed new light on the models of *what* interacts. Moreover, the development of the model of method is concerned with moving towards the development of the executable and learning about the behaviours it might constructively support. This will become evident as the description progresses and especially in regard to the modelling of coordinative structures of tool integration.

Overall, the following aims are especially important:

• The validation of the *why* models. This is done by considering whether it is possible to develop a useful model of method for the specified goal, whether the goal is a useful description of the behaviour thus represented and whether the activities are reasonably cohesive and decoupled from other roles.

• Informing the active model design by giving the creator of the executable a model of how users work to achieve a goal. This model describes the tools they use, the order in which they use these tools and what they use them for.

In essence, what is being said is that the model of method is used to inform design decisions made elsewhere, in the model of goals and the executable. It is not used to make decisions about the detail of program behaviour; this is *not* a graphical programming method but is concerned with the shaping of an executable program through the action of a modelling route. The model of method plays a special role in this route in that, as the most detailed graphical model that is created, it is used to question the other models and assist the programming of the executable. In particular, the model will be used to assess whether the models of goals are a valid breakdown of system behaviour for the users, whether these goals can be developed as cohesive and decoupled modular descriptions and thence, following this, to describe the behaviour that must be supported in the executable. In this way the model of method can be described as an *off-line* modelling step as its purpose is to inform the development of the executable rather than to shape it directly, and to review the model of goals rather than to amend it directly.

7.9.1 Mapping from Goals to Roles

The model of the system and the model of goals are very similar. It is easy to proceed, perhaps almost simultaneously, between a description of agents interacting and a description of the goals they achieve by interacting. The mapping from the goals to roles is a little more complicated.

Within the method model the modeller specifies a set of activities which fulfil the goal. These activities are thereby logically related and it follows that they be described as a role. Thus, for each goal there is a role. This is a very clean and simple view. It is already known that the roles interact. Precisely how they interact has not been specified. The modeller can conclude that points of synchronization exist between the roles although he or she cannot be specific about the role state at which they occur. Initially, to make the mapping clear, this can be represented as a line between the role bodies but not depicting an internal state to the role. Thus, in a RAD, the line just touches the role boundary and does not penetrate through it. Finally, the goal was expressed as a state and it is known that each role will at some point achieve the state described in the goal model. Initially, the modeller cannot be more specific than this. It might be anticipated that this state is the culmination of a role, although it is presumptuous of real-world behaviour to say that this will always be the case.

This gives a simple mapping between the goal model and the method model. In effect it describes a RAD in a sketch format.

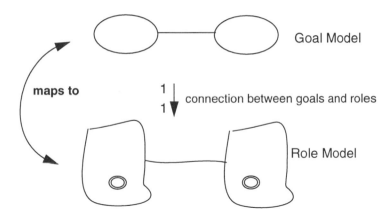

We know that the roles interact.

We know that they each achieve a certain state.

Fig. 7.18 A Simple Mapping Between the Goal Model and the Method Model

From this, the modeller can proceed to describe the detail of the activities in the role. The modeller's knowledge of activities will be gained from interviews with users. How much the modeller wants to show is again a matter of judgement although the use of RADs tends to encourage some quite detailed thinking about activities and logic which makes them more useful later on in the design of the executable.

7.9.2 Idealizations, Ideals and Exceptions

The following are examples of more detailed RAD method models. The first example below in Figure 7.19 describes the activities which achieve the goals of the interactive thread previously described in Figure 7.11.

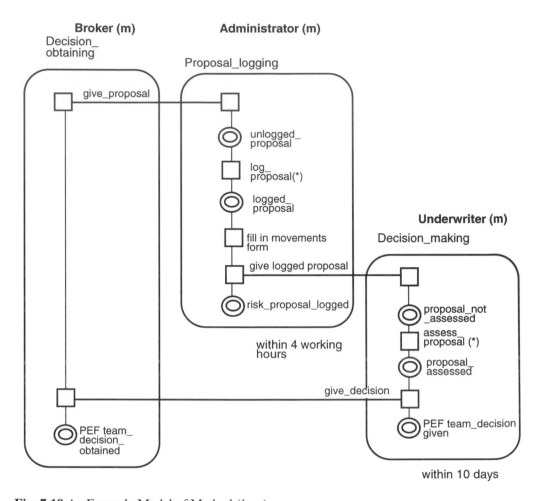

Fig. 7.19 An Example Model of Method (*how*)

The model given in Figure 7.19 is not *the* method for achieving the goals expressed in Figure 7.10. It is a representation of *one possible way* of attaining these goals. Many models can be constructed which describe the method of attainment of a single goal model. Therefore this diagram can be called Method 1. If others are drawn, for example if we wish to show the Underwriter initiating the interaction with the Administrator, the second diagram would be called Method 2.

Remember also that such models may be best understood to be 'normative idealizations' (Wastell et al., 1994). This is a pertinent reminder when we consider the detail of these RAD method models. Each is an idealization and not a detailed description of the ways in which things are really done. This in turn invites us to consider another problem with which the modeller may be confronted. Very often people will describe their behaviour in an ideal, simplified way. They might say:

• 'I do *A*, and then *B*, and then *C*. When I have finished *C*, I do *D*.'

The modeller, constrained by the difficulty of cramming boxes and labels on to the page, might be glad that they do so. Therefore it becomes tempting to ignore the fact that to do, '*A* then B then C then D' is an ideal which occurs when all goes to plan. More often than not the execution of the plan might be fraught with difficulty and, in fact, this ideal case is a rarity. The logic of it is rather more convoluted:

- 'I do A if x is available, if not I do B first and return to A when I can. C is not always essential so I leave it if this is a rush case. D must be done, but I have to do A first, therefore if I haven't done A, I do it now.'

Whilst this emphasizes the usefulness of the RAD method model in informing decisions, aiding learning and questioning the validity of earlier decisions, it also reveals limitations. It reveals the need for flexible modelling formalisms which allow the creation of models which are useful when confronted by the exigencies and complications of everyday work. Here, as well as the standard RAD primitives this model of method has the sub-role (see Section 7.9.4), the RAD ellipse (see Section 7.9.6), and the opportunity to create Method 2, 3, or n diagrams. All of these help the modeller to accommodate uncertainty, change and flexible working but, also, none can guarantee the thoroughness of the model. The modeller must retain a critical perspective and should always question the validity of the models. Ultimately, when the modeller starts to consider software support, there are no such things as ideals and exceptions, only behaviours that might be usefully supported.

7.9.3 Logical and Physical Modelling

The distinction between logical and physical models is widely recognized. A physical process model describes mechanisms that are to do with implementation. A logical process model describes only intentions and not the means of their achievement. For example, the following are descriptions of what is essentially the same process. The first is physical and the second logical.

- 'receive submission file from broker', 'log to In_Progress database', 'pass submission file by hand to underwriter for assessment'.
- 'receive proposal', 'register proposal', 'assess proposal'.

Of course there are many shades of grey between these two descriptions.

The examples in these chapters are, for the most part, physical models which portray varying degrees of implementation-dependence. It is also possible to make the description still richer, and more implementation specific, with annotations. The following is a development of the method model in Figure 7.19. It is annotated so as to describe in more detail the media through which activities are carried out. Later it will be shown how annotations are useful in recording data which is used to develop an understanding of the required tool-to-tool integration within the system.

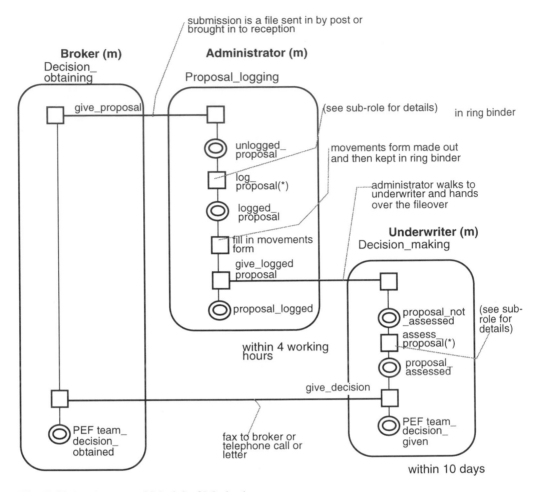

Fig. 7.20 An Annotated Model of Method

7.9.4 Sub-Roles

Sub-roles are sets of activities which are potentially common to many roles. For example, in Figure 7.19 there is the activity 'log proposal' which is within the role 'proposal logging'. The star annotation (*) indicates that this is shown as a sub-role. Following the convention established by Ould (1995) for the related notion of a black-box activity, the states in the role are explicitly marked and shown again in the sub-role. Hence, the sub-role 'log proposal' is expressed below:

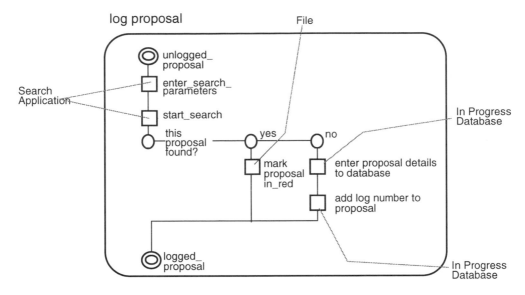

Fig. 7.21 Sub-Role 'Log Proposal'

In this particular case the sub-role has additional annotations which describe the tools used in each activity (refer back to Figure 7.17 for the logic of this). For example, in the above example the 'In Progress' database is used in the activities 'enter proposal details to database' and 'add log number to proposal'.

Sub-roles are useful for the description of tools that are used in a process. This is a consequence of the place of the sub-role in the model architecture. A sub-role is restricted to a definition of logically related activities. It cannot contain collaborative interactions (i.e. agent to agent). This restriction enables a cleaner architecture to the model. It allows a way of achieving some separation of the coordination of agents with agents and the coordination of agents with tools, whilst retaining and understanding of the relationship of these two dimensions. The structure of roles and sub-roles is expressed in Figure 7.22.

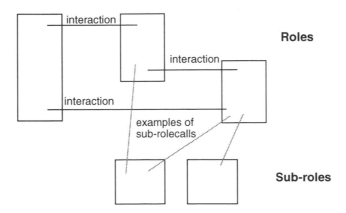

Fig. 7.22 The Structure of Roles and Sub-Roles

This idea of a reusable, invocable sub-role is consistent with software engineering practice.

Ould warns of the danger of taking such an approach, arguing that '... the world is rarely so clean'. In particular he warns of the danger of forcing the definition of sub-routines which complete before control passes back to the role above. Therefore, although there is clearly nothing intrinsically wrong with defining sub-roles in the manner of sub-routines, to do so is only akin to putting activities on a state thread, OPM must allow for sub-roles which do not behave in this fashion. For example, if there were activities after the 'logged proposal' state marker in Figure 7.21, it would still be valid as a sub-role, as long as the rule about having no collaborative interactions was not breached.

7.9.5 Start Roles

A role can start another. This is depicted using a pentagon (see Figure 7.16). By using state markers it is possible to stipulate whether or not there is a complete/return relationship between a role that is started and its starter.

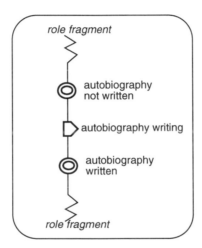

Fig. 7.23 A Start Role with State Markers

7.9.6 The RAD Ellipse

Although the development of the model started with very simple depictions of agents and goals, it seems that little by little the issues have become more complex. In practice we rarely model in a uniform way, either top-down or bottom-up, and rarely draw a steadfast system boundary. It is useful therefore to be able to declare explicitly that there is an area of activity which is beyond the immediate scope of the model. For such circumstances there is the facility of the RAD ellipse.

The RAD ellipse is used where there is cause to breach the system boundary that is currently being investigated. This boundary is given by (1) a description of the agents (2) a description of the goals held by these agents. Thus, it is a description of a purposeful network of people (i.e. the collaborative structure) that defines the system or part that is currently being investigated. In describing *how* the behaviours in this system are undertaken, it might be useful to reach out beyond this system boundary to another agent or goal that has not been described already.

For example, a description of a system involving brokers and underwriters interacting for the purposes of obtaining and giving decisions has already been developed. The *what* and *why* models of this are shown below in Figure 7.24.

The system model

The goal model

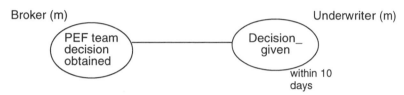

Fig. 7.24 The System Under Investigation

A model of how this system behaves is given in Figure 7.25.

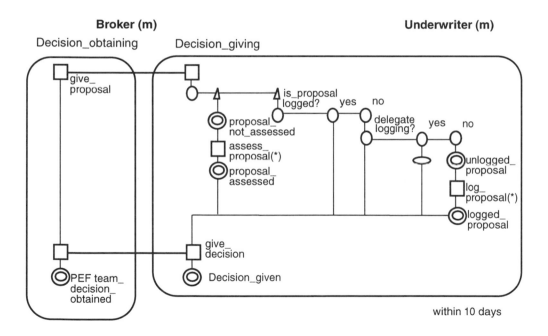

Fig. 7.25 Obtaining and Giving Decisions (Method 1)

In this model the system boundary has been breached and an ellipse inserted on the conditional thread marked 'Delegate logging?', 'Yes'. For purposes of illustration this has been left unlabelled. The ellipse is used here to denote an interactional behaviour which is not described in the goal model from which the method model was developed. It means that the modeller must consider the existing description of the system under investigation to be insufficient and that it is necessary to supplement it with a new model of the system and/or a new model of goals.

Referring to the role 'Decision giving', it can be seen that the underwriter to whom the role is bound considers whether a proposal has been logged. If it has not been logged then the underwriter can either log it or delegate the logging activity to someone else. To delegate, the underwriter needs to interact with the person to whom the activity is delegated, hence the ellipse. The ellipse can be described by stating any of the following:

• The agent that the underwriter will interact with.

• The goals of the interactive behaviour.

As a protocol to promote consistency in the model, the ellipse is labelled when the corresponding models are available. This is done in the following way. First, the modeller needs a system model (*what*) to describe the interactive behaviour. In this case, the task can be delegated to an administrator and so the modeller has the system model already which is shown in Figure 7.4. Therefore the ellipse can be labelled to state 'Interact with administrator'. The abbreviation 'i_w' is used in this example.

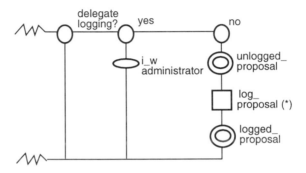

Fig. 7.26 Labelling the RAD Ellipse (1)

A description of goals to describe this particular interactive behaviour can be developed anew. It looks as follows:

Fig. 7.27 Getting the Proposal Logged

The creation of this model allows the description of the goal as a label on the RAD ellipse. We can use the model number (i.e. goal 1, see Section 7.4.5) or the full description of the goal ('risk proposal logged'). An ellipse need never be labelled with the name of a model of the method because this can be inferred directly from the model of goals.

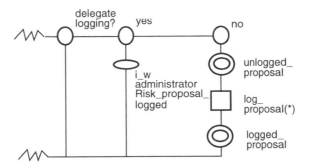

Fig. 7.28 Labelling the RAD Ellipse (2)

Finally, a new method model for the interactive behaviour denoted on the ellipse can be created. This is shown below:

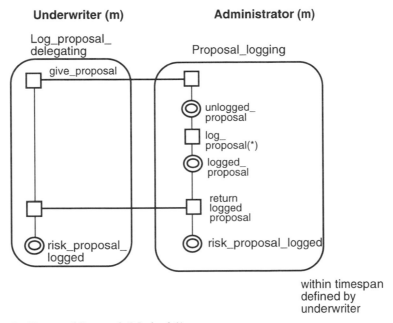

Fig. 7.29 Getting the Proposal Logged (Method 1)

Therefore, what has happened in this example is that where a breach of the boundary of the system was described in Figure 7.24, it was possible to develop a description of another system to which it interfaces. This actually involved the same two agents but it might not have been so. It showed them working to different goals which were not previously described and hence constituted a different collaborative structure (given by agents and goals).

7.9.7 The Structure of Tool Integration

Thus far the model of method (*what*) has described how people interact with other people and how people interact with tools. The model can be developed to show how tools interact with tools, i.e. integration. The annotations to the models (see Figure 7.20 and Figure 7.21) can be used to analyze and present the data dependencies of different tools. The key is to identify data that is common to these different tools and thereby presents an integration issue. For this to be successful formal reference to the names of data fields is essential. The data structure itself can be described elsewhere in any data modelling style.

Broadly speaking, the way the model has been developed up to this point presents two alternate categories of integration issues to the modeller. These are issues that arise in pursuit of a common goal (i.e. within a given role) and between the pursuit of different goals (i.e. between roles). The first category is simpler to identify and is described first.

At Figure a description is given of a tool integration issue which arises within a role. This example concerns another part of the operation of the PEF corporate team. It describes how risk officers carry out assessments of properties which are already insured by PEF and to which special insurance provisions apply. Risk officers assign points based upon the characteristics of the property and the equipment contained within it. A higher number of points will lead to more expensive insurance.

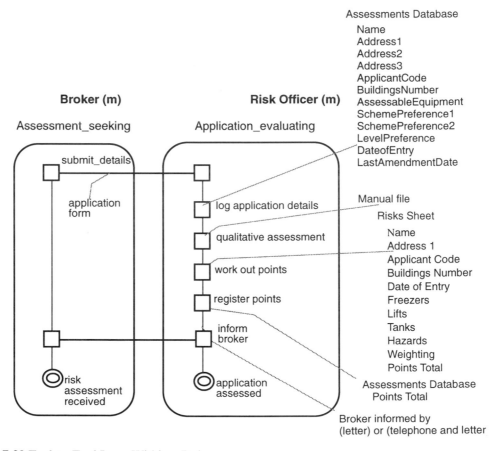

Fig. 7.30 Tool-to-Tool Issue Within a Role

The diagram describes how the risk officer seeks to assess the application. It can be seen that upon receipt of an application form, the risk officer logs some of the applicant's details in what is known as the *Assessments Database*. Amongst the details logged by the officer are the name, address, code and number of buildings to be assessed. Following this an assessment is made of the risks. This is known as the 'qualitative assessment'. The officer carries it out using the application form and other items in a manual file (such as guides to industrial equipment). The aim is to develop his or her opinion of the circumstances of the applicant (e.g. what risks are likely to be especially pernicious). This qualitative assessment is used to guide the attribution of points to the application in the next activity. A simple spreadsheet known as the *Risks Sheet* is used to add up the number of points associated with each insurance application. This is done according to scales which are frequently revised by the underwriters. An additional variable weighting factor is used to accommodate other extraneous factors (such as whether the application relates to another insurance application). Once this figure has been input the tool can produce a total. The risk officer then inputs this total to the Assessments Database before informing the broker of the risk assessment.

In this little sketch there are tool-to-tool coordination issues involving the Assessments Database and the Risks Sheet. That they occur within a role (i.e. to the pursuit of a common goal, 'application assessed') helps the modeller to identify them and proceed towards a definition of the implicit integrative behaviour. This involves the identification of the data dependencies between the tools and the definition of interactions whereby each tool is able to share data with the other.

The behaviour of the tools can be expressed as interacting roles. The model presented in Figure 7.31 shows a RAD description of the same behaviour as Figure , but is inverted to show it from the 'viewpoint' of the tools. In so doing a number of conventions are observed:
• The labels attached to each role are chosen to reflect the behaviour within the roles in a meaningful way.
• Descriptions of tools are set outside the role bodies in the place of agents.
• The model denotes agent activities where the tool is used to support some activity carried out by a human agent.
• Interactions depict tool -to-tool coordination with the shared data shown as annotations.
• There are no state markers used at the culmination of roles as they are not derived from models of goals in the same way as other RAD models of method.
Note also that such models have to be taken to be definitive statements of behaviour rather than a possible way of doing things as other models of method are taken to be (e.g. Method 1).

The implications of facilitating tool integration in this way can be understood by recasting the diagram previously shown in Figure to describe from the perspective of the human agents how the behaviour is changed. This is done below in Figure 7.32. Comparing it with the earlier diagram shows how the risk officer's data-entry task is simplified, the number of activities reduced and the risks to integrity lessened. There is no need to duplicate data between the various tools and the activity 'register points' are now not needed at all.

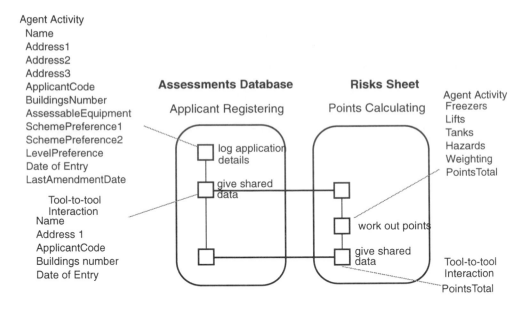

Agent Activity
  Name
  Address1
  Address2
  Address3
  ApplicantCode
  BuildingsNumber
  AssessableEquipment
  SchemePreference1
  SchemePreference2
  LevelPreference
  Date of Entry
  LastAmendmentDate

    Tool-to-tool
    Interaction
  Name
    Address 1
    ApplicantCode
    Buildings number
    Date of Entry

Assessments Database

Applicant Registering

log application details

give shared data

Risks Sheet

Points Calculating

work out points

give shared data

Agent Activity
Freezers
Lifts
Tanks
Hazards
Weighting
PointsTotal

Tool-to-tool
Interaction
PointsTotal

Fig. 7.31 An Example of Tool Roles

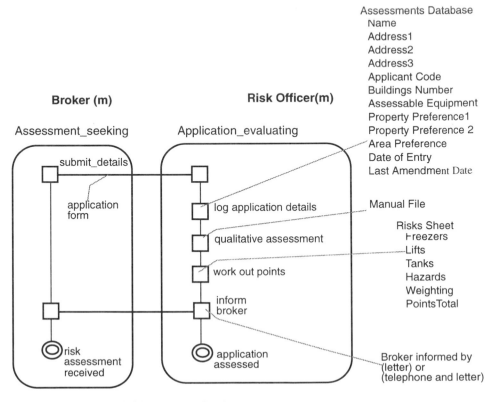

Broker (m)

Assessment_seeking

submit_details

application form

risk assessment received

Risk Officer(m)

Application_evaluating

log application details

qualitative assessment

work out points

inform broker

application assessed

Assessments Database
  Name
  Address1
  Address2
  Address3
  Applicant Code
  Buildings Number
  Assessable Equipment
  Property Preference1
  Property Preference 2
  Area Preference
  Date of Entry
  Last Amendment Date

Manual File

Risks Sheet
Freezers
Lifts
Tanks
Hazards
Weighting
PointsTotal

Broker informed by
(letter) or
(telephone and letter)

Fig. 7.32 The Agents' Activities Redescribed

Integration issues can also occur between roles. This can be shown by considering another area of the operation of risk officers. They supply a guidance service to certain clients. At the request of a broker they will visit a client's property and issue a special-risks report. This helps the client to make decisions about how best to minimize risks on site. It is part of the added-value service that PEF try to provide. Brokers value it because it allows them to work with clients to bring the premiums down.

At Figure 7.33 two models of goals are depicted. The first relates to the behaviour described above. The second depicts the goals of the interactive behaviour wherein a broker seeks risks guidance and a risk officer supplies it.

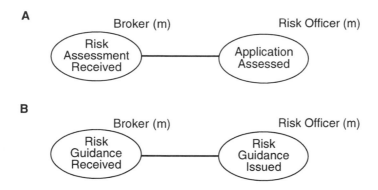

Fig. 7.33 Example Models of Goals

The uppermost goal model relates to the previous Role Activity Diagrams (models of method). Below, in Figure 7.34 a model of method for the second set of goals is given.

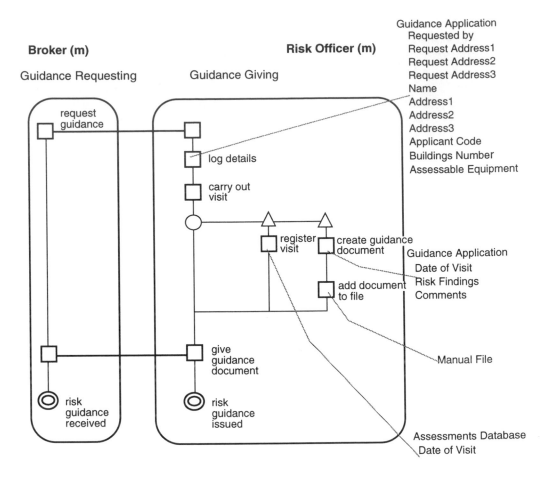

Fig. 7.34 An Example of an Inter-Role Tool Integration Issue

The risk officer uses a special application to create guidance documents. It is called the *Guidance Application (GA)*. By examining the model above it is possible to identify a field that is shared by the GA and the Assessments database. It is 'Date of Visit'. However, the situation is more complex than this. There are other shared fields which can be identified by comparing this model with the earlier one in Figure . They also share the fields 'Name', 'Address1', 'Address2', 'Address3', 'Applicant Code', 'Buildings Number', and 'Assessable Equipment'.

The guidance service is only available to existing clients of PEF and relates only to properties that have already been assessed by a risk officer. Thus it is implicit in the models of goals shown in Figure 7.33 that risk assessments will be generated before risk guidance. It follows that one model of goals is dependent upon the other and that this has implications for the updating of the various tools involved in the achievement of these goals. This is expressed below in Figure 7.35.

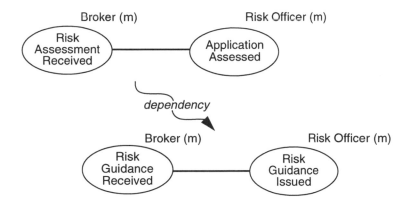

Fig. 7.35 An Illustration of Dependencies Between Goals

A tool view can be developed in the same way as before (at Figure 7.31). This time, however, it is necessary to work across the models of goals. The result is shown below in Figure 7.36.

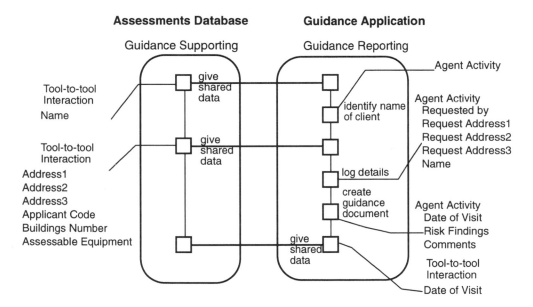

Fig. 7.36 Tool Roles Describing Interaction Across Different Goals

In this example, data is initially shared in two stages. First, values of the Name field are made available for the risks officer to select the client he is giving guidance to. When this has been done, associated values are made available from the Assessments Database to the GA.

The impact of this design upon the activities of the risks officer are significant. Contrasting Figure 7.34 with Figure 7.37 (below), it can be seen that the data-entry requirements are simplified.

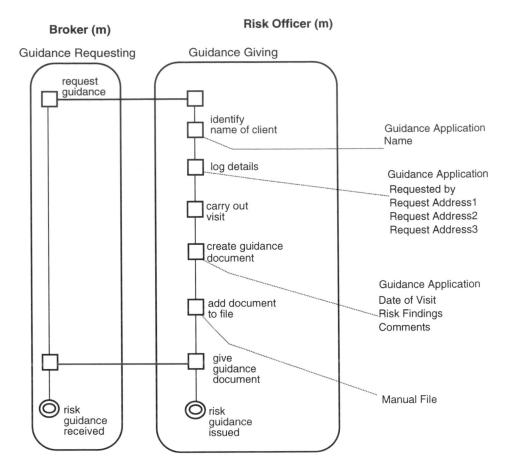

Broker (m)

Guidance Requesting

request guidance

risk guidance received

Risk Officer (m)

Guidance Giving

identify name of client

log details

carry out visit

create guidance document

add document to file

give guidance document

risk guidance issued

Guidance Application
Name

Guidance Application
Requested by
Request Address1
Request Address2
Request Address3

Guidance Application
Date of Visit
Risk Findings
Comments

Manual File

Fig. 7.37 A Redescription of Guidance Requesting and Giving Roles

In all of these cases we have started to make design decisions about sequential behaviour in the coordination layer. For example, in the earlier example shown in Figure 7.31 it is stated that the common data shared by the Assessments Database and the Risks Sheet will be input to the Assessments Database first. The circumstances of the organization under investigation will determine whether this design is sustainable. It may not be, and there may be a requirement for a different or more flexible design.

7.10 The Broader Dialectic

Process capture fits within a broader investigation. The challenge of defining a context for the OPM Method has already been addressed (Chapter 6). Now, having considered process capture, it is possible to address a further challenge: that of process design. By this is meant the development of process support for the organization. The relationship between these three concerns (i.e. context, capture and design), can itself be considered as forming a greater series of dialectics. This is represented in Figure .

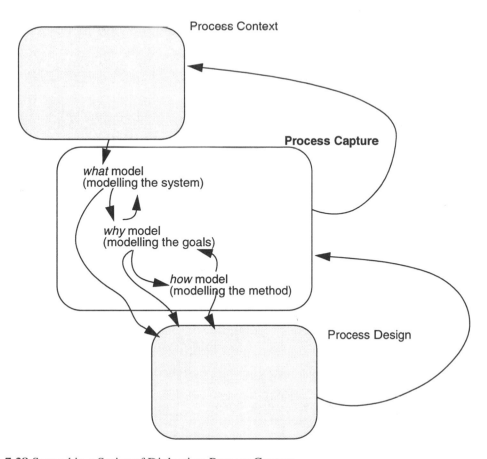

Fig. 7.38 Second in a Series of Dialectics: Process Capture

Thus, as we undertake dialectics within the concerns of process capture, so too we undertake dialectics between the concerns of context, capture and design. In other words, we seek to reconcile the viewpoints developed through these separate concerns by mutual adjustment of them.

7.11 Conclusion

What have we done? Why (*plaintively*) have we done it?

Starting with concerns about managing the modelling and dialogue with users, this chapter has proceeded to consider the development of models of the system, models of goals and models of method. It is actually quite intriguing to look at the model building up. In this chapter, little by little, we have travelled quite a long way. In a sentence, we can say that we have been able to move from an expression of relationships between agents, through a representation of the goals of these relationships to a model of how these goals are achieved. Imagine that this model represents how a business operates or how it wishes it to operate (we can express either), then perhaps the greatest value of the modelling process thus far is that it has been possible to develop your own mental understanding of the (existing or proposed) behaviour in the business. In other words, the model drawn on paper or on the UI, is food for the mental model in your head. What's more, in various ways, we might imagine that the understanding of the whole operational team (the underwriters, administrators, managers etc.) has been developed. This is not only because they have taken part individually in the building of models (through interviews etc.) but also because this particular organization wisely set up workshops to consider the processes they express. So it has not been a fruitless exercise. On the contrary, the whole team is better informed.

THE FOLLOWING CHAPTERS

The next concern of OPM is to make an intervention in the organization by developing executable process support. In so doing we move from the domain of the passive model to the domain of the active model.

In building the models in Process Capture, it has been possible to go quite a long way down the road to the development of a software system for the support of the behaviour described. How is this so? Just as models of the system were mapped into models of goals, and models of goals were mapped into models of methods, we can map models of methods into executable code. This is considered in the next chapter.

THINGS TO DO

- Create models of the system and models of goals for some familiar activities. For example, consider the process of house purchase. What would the models look like? Design some models of method using Role Activity Diagrams to show how house purchase might be carried out.
- Revise your models to accommodate some likely changes. For example, in the house purchase model it might be useful to think about a *virtual estate agency* (e.g. download descriptions and pictures of houses, make appointments to view houses via email).
- Consider alternative ways in which the Assessments Database and the Guidance Application might interact (Figure 7.36). Design alternative tool-integration implementations using Role Activity Diagrams. What are the implications for the integration of the Assessments Database and the Risks Sheet?
- Devise other ways of modelling processes (i.e. not using Role Activity Diagrams or Conceptual Models). What are the pros and cons of each technique?

8

Process Design

The previous chapter was concerned with describing the behaviour of an organization. This chapter goes one crucial step further. It considers how the models can be used to program the software support system for organizations and, through this, to shape the new behaviour of the organizations themselves. In extending the OPM method, this chapter draws upon the architectural idea of the coordination layer that was introduced in Chapter 5. Throughout, a number of examples from the PEF team are used to describe different aspects of process design.

8.1 Introduction

In this chapter, OPM is developed by adding the *active* model to the *what*, *why* and *how* models. The PEF corporate team again provides the case study illustration for the discussion. The chapter describes several design scenarios arising from this case study. These are grouped into three levels. *Reflection* is taken to be ad hoc, extemporizing change. *Refinement* is more formal, of greater consequence and planned. *Reinvention* is radical change, starting with a *tabula rasa* and constituting a whole new package of behaviour.

In the remaining sections of this introduction three different aspects of process design are discussed:

- An ecology of software design. This revisits some of the arguments about the nature of systems that were presented in Chapter 2. They are presented so as to describe the organizational environment of software design; the ecology which the software designer seeks to affect. It concludes with a quote from Simon on the nature of the design process itself.
- A solution as a state in an evolution. In this section some of the issues presented in the preceding section are given further emphasis, viz; that the organization is in a state of flux and that this serves to heighten the uncertainty of the design process. As a result each design solution can be seen as a state in an ongoing process of evolution. In turn this leads us to view the malleability of software as an important asset. This is a point that is picked up later when we consider the reflexive capability of the executable Process Modelling Language (Chapter 10).
- The politics of designing. In this section the political aspects of the design process are re-emphasized. This reminds us that the process of designing will need to be tailored to the extant political realities of the domain. It also highlights the fact that in some circumstances the design of software systems will be just one part of a broader multidisciplinary venture.

8.1.1 An Ecology of Software Design

Consider again the scenario of the complex organizational scenario that was described in Chapter 2. The modern organization was pictured as a building filled with people and desks. We note that these people interact with each other. They each have goals which they seek to fulfil by carrying out activities, by making requests of others, by delegating and by doing certain activities in order to satisfy some request. As they interact with each other inside the organization so too they interact with many people outside the organization. They also interact with software. Software systems can be a critical media for the interactions between people. Software mediated interaction can be indirect through shared facilities and databases. On the other hand, increasingly, software mediated interaction can be direct. For example, people can be linked by a workflow system which passes *documents* between on-screen *in-trays*. Then, of course, these days any organization is likely to be housed in more than one building. An organization might have different offices in different countries and continents, staff may work from home or on the road between the offices of clients. People might be dependent upon telecommunications devices and portable computing in order to interact with other people in the same organization, with other offices, or with clients or collaborators.

Now, a simple point about the ecology of software systems: in modern organizations where software plays a critical role, the design of the software system and the design of the organizational structure itself are mutually dependent. They cannot be designed in isolation of each other. Each affects the other.

We can put it like this: a software system in its real world domain of application can be thought of as a system within a system. Figure 8.1 depicts this with transports across each system boundary. .

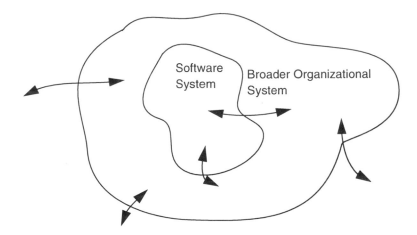

Fig. 8.1 An Ecology of Software Design: Systems Within Systems

We can use this simple model to reiterate some useful points:
- The systems interact.
- The relationship between the systems can be described as that of served and serving systems.
- Often the relationship between the systems is such that a change to one may affect the other in some significant way.
- The identification and labelling of each system as separate systems is based upon some formal or more probably informal, intuitive assessment of the distinctive emergent properties of

each. This leads obviously to the assertion that the two systems are not alike.

• The organizational system is necessarily in a permanent state of flux. For it, *there is no steady state*. Without human intervention the software system is essentially static. This presents us with a conundrum. The software system is a *serving* system and therefore ways must be found of preserving the quality of this service in the face of changes to the served system. Otherwise, function is usurped by dysfunction.

We have already seen how in OPM, the relationship between the organization and the software system is explored through the modelling of interactions, goals and the activities that are carried out towards the fulfilment of these goals. This gives a platform upon which the designer's role can be depicted as one of facilitation, or more particularly, *mediation* between the goals of people and the capabilities of software. As Simon writes:

'The artificial world is centered precisely on this interface between the inner and outer environments; it is concerned with attaining goals by adapting the former to the latter. The proper study of those who are concerned with the artificial is the way in which that adaptation of means to the environment is brought about – and central to that is the process of design itself.'

Simon, 1981

8.1.2 A Solution as a State in an Evolution

Consider again two factors:

• It is in the interests of organizations to change. They seek to adapt to changing circumstances and to change their environment to their advantage. They innovate, rationalize, extemporize and replicate.

• Organizations are immensely complex as well as dynamic. They are human activity systems and as such their purpose is ambiguous. A software designer cannot be certain of how a system will contribute to an organization. This is more especially the case because a software system of consequence will change its environment.

This leads us to conclude that software systems should evolve in a way which is consistent with the evolution of the organization or, taking the argument further, should even provide a *means* for the evolution of the organization. This means that design is not a one-off process. Moreover, it is characterized by uncertainty. We cannot be certain what the consequences of some new software design or revision will be. In this light, the malleability of software, which is in some senses problematic as it undermines the management of its form, becomes not only an advantage but provides the basis for our design approach. This shall become clearer later, in the presentation of the usefulness of the high-level constructs and reflexive features of PML in Chapter 10.

8.1.3 The Politics of Designing

Part and parcel of people working together is the sharing of ideas and the drawing up of agreed (implicit or explicit) agendas. Recently, much research has come to focus on the immeasurable difficulty of ensuring that some system (e.g. an information system) satisfies the needs of many different users. This is a political problem which is shared by complex design projects in all fields (e.g. architecture, roads, genetics). In Chapter 2, we have seen how information-systems research has sought to highlight and address the subjectivity of organizational analysis and design. This has motivated responses from several quarters, for example much interest has been afforded to methods which give a user focus to a systems design process (e.g. Mumford, 1981).

In Chapter 7 the task we set ourselves was to describe the behaviour of an organization through a language of agents, goals, roles, interactions etc. We have been working and making progress by working closely with end users (see Section 7.5). It seems highly appropriate and, indeed, to some degree essential that we do so. However, it is also worth reflecting on some of the many difficulties which surround user involvement in the design process. Users may not agree on what actions they should seek to carry out. There may be dispute over objectives. In moving from a description of what happens now to what it is desired should happen, disagreement is likely amongst those concerned. There are also questions over who should be involved in decision-making. Indeed, user involvement may not always fit within a given corporate ethos or be inappropriate because of the nature of the redesign proposed. Such difficulties may be of profound consequence for any process modelling project. The real world is a difficult place in which to undertake process design!

This leaves us with a broad problem and may imply a need for some sort of design process through which alternative schemas can be presented and evaluated. Such a process would act as a mechanism for seeking to achieve political reconciliation (or triumph). Moreover, as has already been stated, the problem is multidisciplinary in its nature. Neither this chapter nor this book attempts to deal with all aspects of the problem. It continually interfaces to those aspects just beyond its remit. The remit here is to consider the use of process models in relation to the software support of organizations.

8.2 Using OPM for Design

Utilising the concept of the active model from Chapter 3, and developing such a model using the Process Modelling Language (PML), provides the final refinement step in the OPM method. We now have:

• Model of the system – a *what* model – this is a structural view of interactions between agents. We use conceptual models for this.

• Model of goals – a *why* model – this specializes identified interactions by describing the goals that each can achieve. We use conceptual models for this.

• Model of method – a *how* model – this shows how the goals of the interactive behaviour can be achieved. We use Role Activity Diagrams for this.

• Active model – this is the software system that responds to and prompts behaviour in the organization. We use the Process Modelling Language for this.

In order to emphasize the difference between the modelling steps and their implementation technologies, we will continue to refer to system, goal and method models rather than Conceptual Models and Role Activity Diagrams. For the active model we shall do likewise. Its implementation technology, Process Modelling Language (PML), was originally developed within the IPSE 2.5 project (see Chapter 2). It has subsequently been developed for the ProcessWise Integrator (PWI) product and adapted for the Process*Web* system (see Chapter 10).

PML is described in Chapter 10. Here, we need only to note a few pertinent features. The language has four principal classes. These are interactions, roles, actions (activities) and entities. Interactions are uni-directional communications channels, roles encapsulate data and behaviour, actions are procedures and entities are records. Thus, although the precision of the mapping is something that will concern us later, we can see strong conceptual similarities between PML and RADs. This is one of the reasons for the choice of these two technologies.

8.2.1 Creating an Active Model

To create an active model of coordination (i.e. the coordination layer), a number of decisions have to be taken. Through these decisions, the following tasks will be accomplished. They are numbered not to signify importance or sequence but to assist referencing later in the chapter.

1. It is necessary to decide which of the goals expressed in the passive model are to be supported.
2. It is necessary to investigate the relationship between the roles thus supported (the inter-role logic).
3. It is necessary to decide which activities to support within the roles. We are not constrained by the model created in Conceptual Models and RADs. For example, we might consider some activities for the first time when creating the active model.
4. It is necessary to investigate the relationship between the activities within the roles (the intra-role logic). This may require that we create new models which express how activities relate to each other.
5. It is necessary to define additional roles which are necessary for execution purposes.
6. It is necessary to define instantiation rules for all roles.
7. It is necessary to define how non-functional attributes should be supported and how they shall affect support of the functional attributes.

8.3 The Design Domain at Parker, Ellington and Fitzgerald

8.3.1 Complex Systems, the Fruits of Success and the Need for Coordination

Returning to consider the Parker, Ellington and Fitzgerald corporate team, we have seen how underwriters and administrators coordinate, how brokers play a critical role and how databases and other IT are fundamental to the operation. It is a buzzing, ambitious organization. We have seen how the risk proposals are passed into the team by brokers in the form of fat submission files. These are moved around the team as a kind of analogue and approximate representation of the state of their processing. Each file moves from administrator to underwriter, underwriter to administrator, underwriter to underwriter and administrator to administrator. At the same time, different databases are used for different purposes. Details of the submission are entered into the In Progress database. This involves a search query to check that it has not already been entered. This is usually done by administrators but may also be done by underwriters. It may take place before or after an underwriter has looked at the proposal. The In Progress database acts as a coordinating mechanism between parties interested in a risk proposal. Underwriters assess risk with reference to defined criteria, contextual information and case histories. They use databases, spreadsheets and other tools. Data fields that are logged into the In Progress database may at sometime be replicated into the Business database. The Business database is used to record details of risks that are actually underwritten by the team. This is usually, but not always, done by administrators. Other databases are used to build up local profiles of submissions, relating them to brokers, business trends and favoured industry sectors. These are maintained and updated by administrators. They may require the further replication of data fields that have been added already to the In Progress database, the Business database and the notes attached to the fat submission files. So although IT is fundamental to the operation of the team there are many ways in which it disappoints. The team are creative but sometimes the IT seems to be obstructive.

Describing the situation to a colleague, the process modeller draws a rich picture (Checkland, 1981).

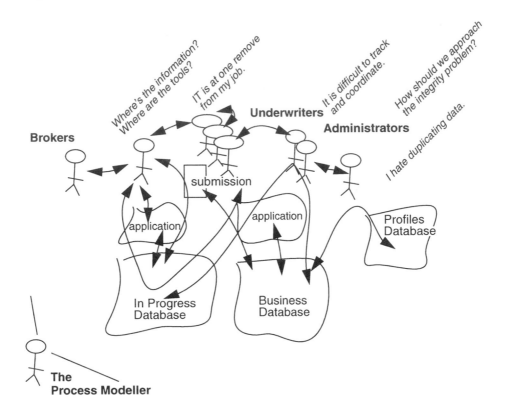

Fig. 8.2 A Rich Picture of the PEF Corporate Team

This complexity is, at least in part, a consequence of success. As organizations succeed, so they grow. In growing they take on new staff and develop new applications. Consider one case of this. The Profiles database is a recent innovation originally intended to aid the underwriters' review of submissions. It was implemented quickly on a PC when the team began to receive an increasing number of proposals from a major brokerage which had previously little connection with the team. The database helps the underwriter to evaluate risks accurately and to issue the lowest possible premiums. The intention is to give the PEF corporate team an advantage against the broker's more usual contacts. The database contains information about the interests and performance of a wide-range of companies in a certain industry sectors. This information is set in context by information about PEF's existing risk exposure in these industry sectors. This requires the sharing of data held in the Business database. Thus, the Profiles database, although in itself very useful, adds to the problems of duplication and integrity.

The demands of coordination are one of the characteristic differences between a multinational and a business that is just one man and his filing cabinet. Appreciating that a coordination issue is thus a consequence of success (i.e. of expanding, adapting, being dynamic), the intention is not to seek a tidy-minded approach which suppresses new innovation (such as the Profiles database). The intention is to provide a means by which coordination can be understood and supported, by which new interactions can be rapidly assimilated into the coordinative patterns and by which glitches and frustrations can be resolved.

As the process modeller describes it, it is a question of making sure that the serving system serves and does not replace informational problems with coordination problems.

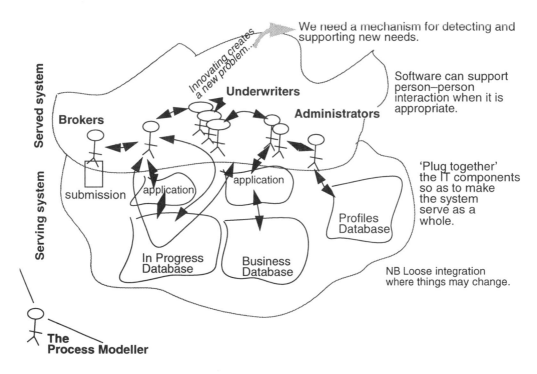

Fig. 8.3 Supporting the Coordination Needs of the Organization: a Rich Picture

8.3.2 The Good Butler

In this way the process modeller perceives the serving system as being made up of different components which have a combined impact upon the served system. An analogy can be used for describing how the serving system should contribute. It should be, suggests the process modeller, like a good butler to the served system. It brings you what you want, when you want it. It may even anticipate your needs and do a little extra work. It is also easy to communicate with and to give new instructions to it.

In this way the process modeller is concerned with the ways in which software elements relate to the lives of people in the organization and how software is applied to *knit* other applications together into a meaningful support system for these people. The increased scale of software systems and the greater reliance of people upon them mean that these concerns seem to become ever more important. Thus, the design frame of reference is made up of process co-ordination (many agents) as well as functions undertaken by single agents. This is something which we have already discussed in Chapter 2. Below, a diagram originally presented in Positioning is repeated in a slightly simplified form. This picture and the rich pictures presented above, should help to make clear that the process modeller's design strategy is not solely concerned with a *piece* of software (e.g. a database, a group support system), but rather with the *pieces*.

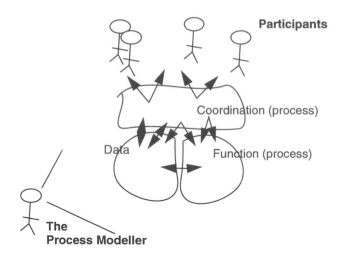

Fig. 8.4 Coordination, Function and Data

8.3.3 Identified Problem Situations

These issues can be explored by reference to problem situations in the PEF corporate team.
- A submission comes in from a broker. It can be received either by an administrator or by an underwriter. One thing is certain: the file will be passed around between them. For example, an underwriter will assess it but an administrator may log it. Whenever anything is done, a note is appended to the submission (e.g. when it is logged details are added such as its log number, log name and brokerage address). The net effect is that quite a lot of effort is expended just keeping track of submission files.
- A submission comes in from a broker. Details from it are input to the In Progress database. Later, after a quote is negotiated with the broker, these details are replicated into the Business database. Users regard this as frustrating and a waste of their time.
- An administrator maintains the Profiles database with information taken from company reports, the business press and newspapers. In addition, the administrator queries the Business database for certain information (e.g. the risk exposure in an industry sector). This information is reformatted and then duplicated to the Profiles database.

Each of these gives cause for thought.

The first case describes the difficulty of handling and tracking the submission files themselves. Underwriters complain that they cannot always easily get hold of a submission file. They can never be sure whose desk it is on. Often they want only to look at it for summary information anyway. Administrators complain that when submission files get lost they are often on the desk of the Underwriter who is looking for them. They also have difficulty because the submissions are moved around a lot and begin to fall apart. A number of procedures have been instituted to try and help with all of these problems. For example, administrators now fill in a movements form. In this they record those file movements that they know about. The last name in the list of movements is the person whom, as far as they are aware, had the file last. Each movements form is kept in a file which is itself shared amongst the administrators. The form is a little tedious to fill in but all the administrators seem to agree that it has helped. There is also a general awareness that document image processing might eventually be a solution. This seems a long way off as the submissions are very large, they contain photographs and occasionally, they are of very poor quality. Even if they do manage to scan the whole thing in, underwriters are wary because they feel that reading page after page on-line will be unpleasant and inconvenient. 'I like to read the files on the bus from Piccadilly,' says one.

Figure 8.5 depicts the problem.

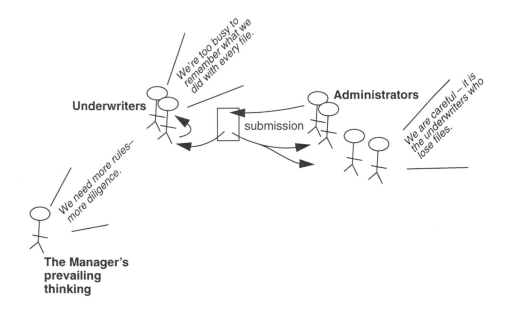

Fig. 8.5 The File Tracking Problem: a Rich Picture

In the second case, the difficulty seems to stem from the fact that the In Progress and Business databases are not integrated. They were developed at different times as different business needs arose (the In Progress database is newer than the Business database). There is also the complication of the brokers making submissions in a different media. This necessitates further replication. The problem of repeated data-entry (and thence integrity) is widely recognized. The extant thinking as the process modeller starts his study is that the In Progress and Business databases will have to be integrated. Furthermore, it is thought that a response to the problem of duplication of data to and from the submission file will have to wait until an age when risk proposals are submitted electronically. Figure 8.6 depicts the problem.

The third case is a little like the second. Before the middle of every month, an administrator is required to input details about many companies in certain industry sectors into the Profiles database. These details are taken from company reports, newspaper clippings and PEF internal information mechanisms. Another administrator gathers these information sources together every day and keeps them in a box file. Underwriters also gather information through the natural course of doing their job. They are asked to submit any information which they feel would be useful in the Profiles database to the administrator who updates it. This administrator provides short summaries of all the information on the database and organizes the information sources themselves (e.g. the newspaper cuttings) into a monthly file. The administrator also runs a query on the Business database. This output is reformatted by the administrator and entered into the Profiles database. Thus, the process by which the Profiles database is updated is not as regular as the updating of the In Progress and Business databases. The progress of a risk

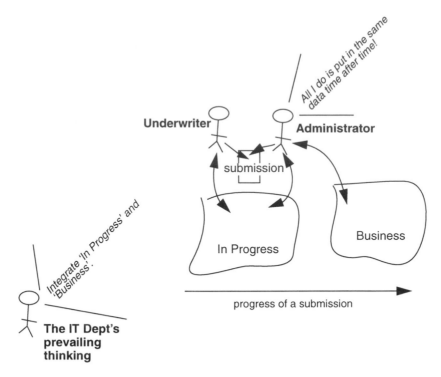

Fig. 8.6 The Replication Problem: a Rich Picture

proposal dictates that these latter two be updated in a regular way. For the Profiles database the task must be done before the middle of each month but the exact date is determined by the workload at the time. Also, as a problem, the Profiles database is perceived very differently. The underwriters think that the Profiles database is very important. For some submissions they rely on it to maximize their chances of issuing a competitive quote. They would like to see its coverage extended over more companies in more industry sectors. To the administrator, the Profiles database represents an arduous chore. A rota has been introduced to make sure that each administrator updates it as often as any other. From the perspective of the IT department, comes the view that the use of the Profiles database is not their concern. It was developed within the corporate team to respond to a particular business event (the making of links with a major brokerage). They did not create it, so they can hardly be responsible for looking after it.

Figure 8.7 depicts the problem.

8.4 Process Design Examples

In this section the focus is upon some process design examples from the PEF case study. There are five in total. The middle three relate to those problem situations described above in Section 8.3.3. The other two relate to minor change that occurs as a result of the modelling exercise and radical change where a substantial redefinition of the process is planned.

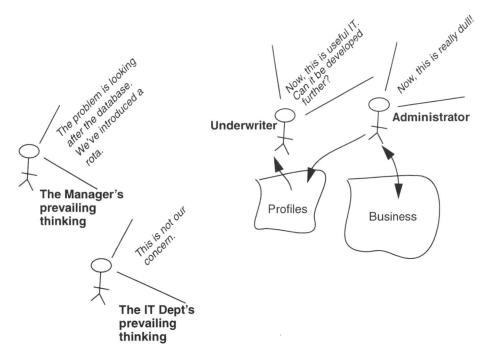

Fig. 8.7 The Local Innovation: a Rich Picture

A rough classification of levels of change is used to group the concerns:
- Reflection – minor change that just happens or is not formally planned.
- Refinement – change that has some element of formal planning but does not substantially eradicate existing patterns of behaviour.
- Reinvention – change that has some element of formal planning and either substantially eradicates existing patterns of behaviour or starts afresh where there was none before. This is a *tabula rasa* approach.

8.4.1 Reflection: The Modeller Intervenes

The first thing for the modeller to realize is that change has already started. What is more, just by building a model, the modeller is part of it. When users and groups are faced with questions about work activities, the production of prototype models and general discussions, they will initiate change through rationalization or revision. Model building (a reflective activity) is an intervention in the organization. It causes people to reflect upon their activities, to identify strengths or weaknesses, and to change the way they do things. The sands shift. This provokes us to ask, 'How can we model something that keeps changing?' We venture towards an answer to this question later in Chapter 9.

For now we conclude, as we model, that to some degree the process must be evolving. We need to be aware of this and it introduces uncertainty into our thinking. The critical level of change, wherein the change affects the design process, has to be found.

8.4.2 Refinement (1): Simple Coordination Through 'In-Trays'

If some change occurs simply because people reflect upon what they are doing, so there is another level of change within which change proposals need to be prepared and discussed. This level of change is known in this chapter as *refinement*. This section considers a very simple example from the PEF corporate team. It concerns the use of the movements file in the team and the development of an *in-trays* support facility to assist the underwriters and administrators in keeping track of the submission files.

Currently, because it is difficult to track the whereabouts of the submission files there is a partial tracking system in place. This is implemented via the movements form which is filled in for each submission that comes into the team. Each time an administrator gives a submission to someone else, he or she fills in the movements form for that submission. The movements forms are kept together in a couple of large ring-binders (submissions A–L and M–Z). This system seems to be generally regarded as an improvement upon the previous arrangement wherein there was simply no clue as to where a lost submission file might be. There are problems of course. Filling in the movements form is a rather dull task for the administrators to perform. Sometimes the ring binders containing the movements forms are not available when an administrator needs them, and sometimes the movements forms are incorrectly filled in. The underwriters are not required to fill in a movements form and so the system is useless for finding files that have been passed several times between underwriters.

Then, at a meeting of administrators and underwriters, someone says, 'What if we had a computer system which gave us a workspace; it gave us the services we need to carry out our work? What if it included on-screen in-trays for all administrators and underwriters? What if we allocated the proposals to people on-screen and then that person was responsible for the submission file? Wouldn't that be another step in the right direction?' This idea is explored in a series of models.

Initially, the focus is upon the specific case of submissions that arrive by post or are given to an administrator. The system and goal models that represent this activity remain the same.

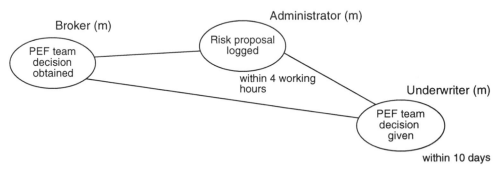

Fig. 8.8 Giving, Logging and Evaluating Proposals

What does change is that a new method is devised for achieving these goals. The existing model is as follows:

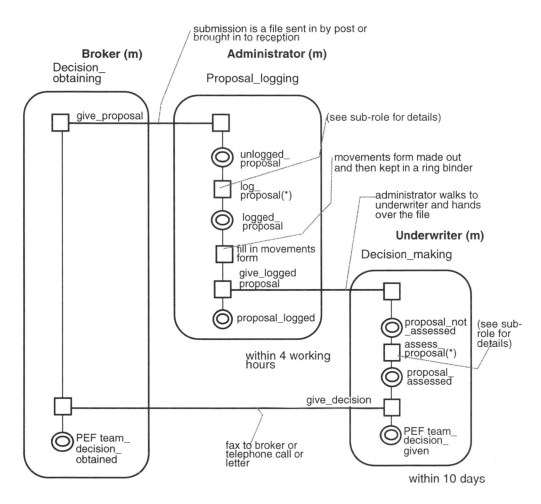

Fig. 8.9 Giving, Logging and Evaluating Proposals (Method 1)

Implementing on-screen in-trays as part of a more general support system would seek to make it possible for everyone to track files more accurately. Any team member would know who is working on a submission, and hence who should actually have the file. This simple idea is described by the following method model (Figure 8.10).

The process modeller progresses by putting the two diagrams (method 1 and method 2) together in a report and circulating them amongst the team of users. The idea is simple, but there are a number of important implications for the way in which work is organized. These are discussed amongst the team. There are also a number of alternative technology scenarios. Initially, as the users seek to identify as many issues as possible, the debate focuses upon how the allocation of submissions to administrators and underwriters might be handled by a support system. A user might ask to allocate a submission by clicking on a button and then fill in the name of the person to whom it should go. This would cause the system to place an icon with the name of the submission in the in-tray of that person. Taking a file out of the in-tray could then be the cue to the system to assemble the necessary IT services for the activity in hand. In this very simple example, no capability other than a demonstration of the coordination layer itself will be developed.

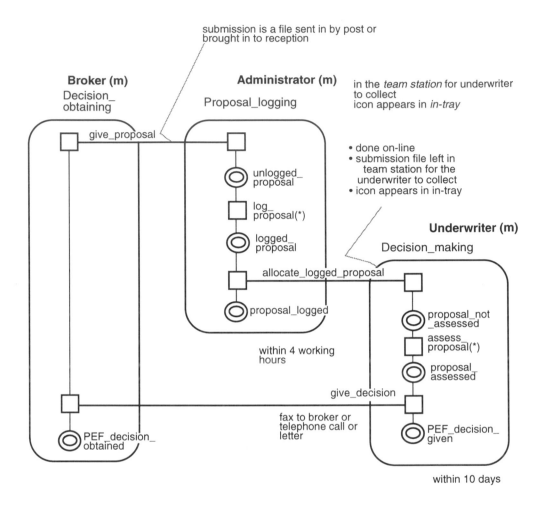

Fig. 8.10 Giving, Logging and Evaluating Proposals (Method 2)

The model shown in Figure 8.10 represents the behaviour from the supporting software system and thus the task is to map it into an active model. Two caveats need to be applied to this. First, the system will not support any interactions with the broker. This accomplishes decision number one in the list given in Section 8.2.1. The decision is justifiable as Figure 8.10 shows that the media used for these interactions are variously post, by hand, fax, telephone and letter. There is, at this point in time, no intention to add software support for coordination to this. Secondly, for purposes of simplicity, the sub-roles will be treated as primitive activities and thus the design process will do nothing other than create a button on the screen for them (e.g. 'assess proposal'). Applying these caveats leaves the task of mapping the following from a passive model to an active form in PML:

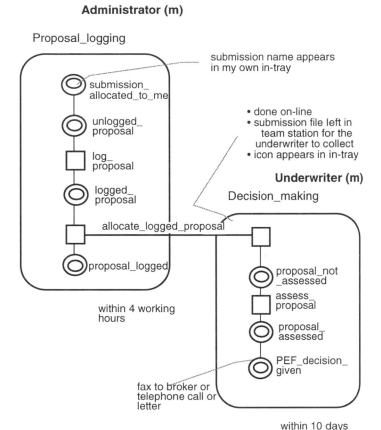

Fig. 8.11 The In-Trays Model Illustrated

Below, the roles 'Proposal logging' and 'Decision making' are described in PML. This gives executable capability to the model and hence, the design process has moved into active modelling. Note that in mapping to PML a 1:1 relationship has been enforced for the role boundaries and activities. Less obvious, but also important, is the fact that the RAD state model has been interpreted strictly so as to give finish/start sequencing (decisions three and four in Section 8.2.1). The first example shows the role 'Proposal logging'.

```
Proposal_Logging isa Role with

resources !**the resources of the role
        intrayentry : InTrayEntry
        referproposal : giveport InTrayEntry
        proposal_logged : Bool {false}

actions !**the actons that the role can execute

        log_proposal :
        {UserAction (agendaLabel = 'Log this proposal');
        ViewObjectNow (object = 'Sorry sub-role not implemented yet!')}
        when log_proposal = nil
```

```
allocate_logged_proposal :
{UserAction (agendaLabel = 'Refer submission to underwriter');
Give (interaction = referproposal, gram = intrayentry);
proposal_logged := true}
when log_proposal ~= nil


termconds proposal_logged
end with !* Proposal_Logging
```

Fig. 8.12 PML for 'Proposal Logging' Role

The second example shows the role 'Decision making'.

```
Decision_Making isa Role with

resources !**the resources of the role
        intrayentry : InTrayEntry
        takereferral : takeport InTrayEntry
        pef_decision_given : Bool {false}

actions  !**the actions that the role can execute

        loggedproposalallocated :
        Take (interaction = takereferral, gram = intrayentry)
        when loggedproposalallocated = nil

        assess_proposal :
        {UserAction (agendaLabel = 'Assess this proposal');
        ViewObjectNow (object = 'Sorry sub-role not implemented yet!');
        QueryAlertNow (question = 'Have you finished assessing the propos-
                                                                al?',
        answer = pef_decision_given)}
when loggedproposalallocated ~= nil

termconds pef_decision_given = true

end with !* Decision_Making
```

Fig. 8.13 PML for 'Decision Making' Role

It is decided that for this example a role should be instantiated for each work package handled (this relates to decision six presented above in Section 8.2.1). Thus if 'Dedalus & Dedalus Shirt Retail' and 'Finnegan & Henchy Hotels' are submissions presented to PEF, there will be a role instantiated for each of them. The behaviour of these roles can then be illustrated as follows. Take an administrator, Catherine, and an underwriter named Andrew. The description starts with a risk proposal ('Dedalus & Dedalus Shirt Retailers') allocated to Catherine (see Figure 8.14). Catherine has an on-screen in-tray which is a window on her workstation. The risk proposal is shown in this. An example of what the in-tray might look like is shown below in Figure 8.15. Note that the issues concerning the look and feel of the UI are beyond our remit here. What we are most concerned with is the way that the technology is developed.

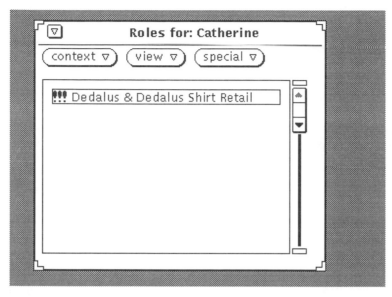

Fig. 8.14 An Example UI for the Proposal Logging Role

If we follow the description of the role in Figure 8.11, we will note that Catherine can log the proposal and then allocate it to an underwriter. If Catherine allocates the risk proposal to Andrew it will appear in his in-tray. The arrival of the proposal in Andrew's in-tray is shown below in Figure 8.15. This time there are a number of other risk proposals also in the in-tray (i.e. Finnegan & Henchy Hotels and Dangerfield Wine Importers). Note that the RAD in Figure 8.11 shows that Andrew can assess a proposal when it is allocated to him. In the example UI shown below, Andrew has selected the risk proposal causing a new window to pop up with the action 'Assess this proposal'. It can be imagined that by selecting this action the system would present Andrew with the databases, expert systems, spreadsheets, fax facilities and whatever that he needs to complete the action.

In this way a highly transparent mapping between the passive, diagrammatic models and the active models has been achieved. It might not always be so neat and tidy. Many compromises might be made and it is easy to create more convoluted relations between the passive and active models than those that are illustrated here. Reflecting upon the use of OPM in this example, it is useful to highlight two aspects. First, that the goal originally established in the *why* model has become a unit of modularity in the executable code (as a role). In other words, after a process of dialectics we have been able to modularize the executable system around meaningful descriptions of goals. This is very valuable because a high level of transparency has been maintained and it is thus easier to comprehend the relationship of organizational behaviour and the software support of that behaviour. Secondly, the activities which describe how this goal is achieved have themselves been mapped into the active model. It is not always easy or useful to do this. The intricacies of behaviour might sometimes be better expressed in the semantics of executable languages rather than in graphical form. Therefore, in OPM it is sometimes necessary to use simple, graphical models for user communication and for defining modules, whilst requiring more complex descriptions of executable behaviour.

In order to emphasize the first aspect whilst relegating the significance of the second, this example has utilized a *principle of structural integrity* to guide the design process, viz: whenever a goal is expressed in a passive model and supported by an active model, the active model must contain a module specifically designated to the support of that goal.

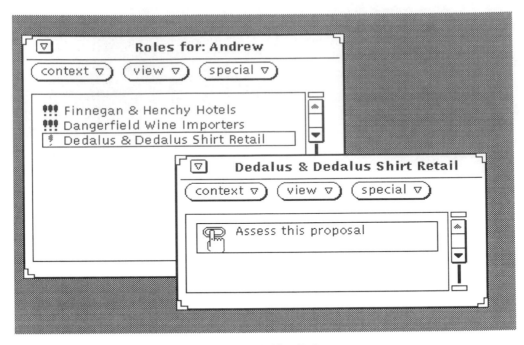

Fig. 8.15 An Example UI for the Decision Making Role

One detail of the method model shown in Figure 8.11 has not been mapped into the active model. This is the non-functional requirement to give the decision to the broker within ten days (i.e. decision seven of those given in Section 8.2.1). This can be supported in a range of ways by the active process model. For example, it could interact with a calendar program so as to put reminders into it. If a decision has not been sent to the broker, the underwriter would then receive a reminder after a pre-set (possibly user-defined) number of days. Imagine though the debate within the PEF team about this superficially trivial piece of functionality. When they discuss it, one manager suggests that the active process model should, on the tenth day, allocate proposals to him. This way he can see who has failed to respond to proposals and can chase them up in person. Other managers believe this measure to be heavy-handed and out of step with the professional, cooperative ethos of the organization. However, all the managers begin to discuss revising the non-functional goal to 'within eight days'. This does not immediately perturb the underwriters themselves who point out that all but difficult proposals can be decided upon within about six days anyway. The underwriters themselves have mixed views about a calendar facility. Some believe it would be very useful to have a reminder flashed onto the screen. Most agree that seven days would be an optimum time. A few do not like the idea of a message being flashed on their screens. One underwriter comments that he has always used his diary to track the proposals and does not want to fix something that is not broken. Eventually, after a lot of debate, a very simple implementation is adopted (see Figure 8.16). It is created in the form of a usable mock-up so that people can experience using it every day. It allows the user to define the number of days upon which a reminder is flashed (it can be set to zero – do not send reminder) and allows each underwriter to enter his own bespoke reminder message.

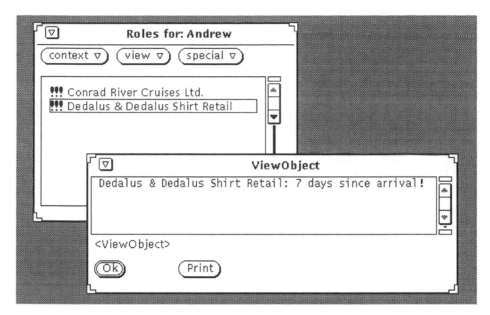

Fig. 8.16 An Example Implementation of the Reminder Facility

A similar strategy is adopted, with less disagreement, to provide the administrators with a reminder facility appropriate to their needs.

8.4.3 Refinement (2): A Tale of Two Databases

The problems of coordinating the In Progress and Business databases are well known within the PEF team. In simple terms the problem is understood to be that the databases share a common set of data entries but require these at different stages in the processing of a risk proposal. The problem is exacerbated because the same information is also written on to a summary sheet that is placed in the file. If you think about it, what is happening is that through a combination of IT inflexibility and organizational procedure, the team members are made to conform to a rigid pattern of behaviour. Modelled in detail it would show activities such as 'log details to In Progress' followed by 'log details to file', followed sometime later by 'log details to Business database'. It is *strict process enforcement*, although it was probably never explicitly designed as such.

Stepping back a little, Figure 8.17 expresses a typical scenario. The diagram emphasizes the goals that the agents seek to achieve (these are shown as states). The ellipses are used to hide the detail of the activities that occur and the interactions are not specified in detail.

Thus the diagram shows three interacting roles which are carried out by the agents 'Broker', 'Administrator', and 'Underwriter'. The burden of data replication falls mostly upon administrators. In logging a risk proposal and in logging the business (the two goals of 'proposal_ administrating'), the administrator would repeat data entries between the file, the In Progress database and the Business database. This will become clearer later.

Alternative high-level scenarios could be mapped out as easily. For example, underwriters may initially choose to log a submission in the In Progress database themselves rather than delegate the task to an administrator. For the purposes of our description, however, we can restrict

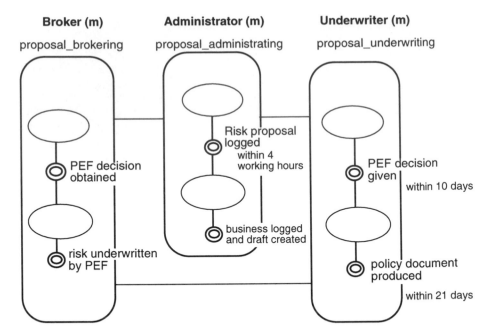

Fig. 8.17 A Typical Process Scenario

ourselves to the more typical scenario wherein the administrator logs the proposal. Thus, we start again with the process depicted in Figure 8.9 which is refined in Figure 8.10. In Figure 8.9 we see a method model which describes how the goals 'PEF decision obtained', 'Risk proposal logged', and 'PEF decision given' are obtained.

Note that the role 'Proposal logging' in Figure 8.9 makes reference to the sub-role 'log proposal'. This sub-role describes the way in which proposal details are entered to a search mechanism ('Enquiry Line'), to the 'In Progress' database and to the file. It is shown below in annotated form in Figure 8.18.

log_proposal

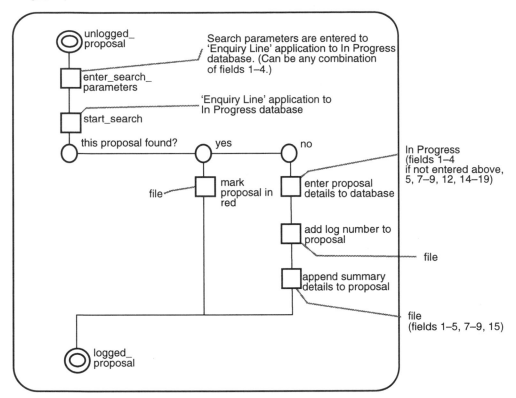

Fig. 8.18 Sub-Role 'Log Proposal'

Moving onwards, the example can be developed by considering the later part of the process after a decision has been given to a broker (i.e. after the goal of PEF decision given has been attained). For the purposes of this illustration, two assumptions are made. First, that the decision was to issue a competitive quote. Secondly, that the quote has subsequently been accepted by the broker on behalf of his or her client. What will happen in these circumstances is that the broker will contact the PEF team to ask that they underwrite the risk. The goals towards which subsequent activity contributes are identified in Figure 8.17 as 'Risk underwritten by PEF', 'business logged and draft created', 'policy document produced'. A method model is shown below in Figure 8.19. This describes a possible way of achieving the goals.

The Business database is updated when a quote is accepted by the broker and the PEF team need to record details of a risk. Thus, in the model shown in Figure 8.19 there is a reference to the sub-role 'book business'.

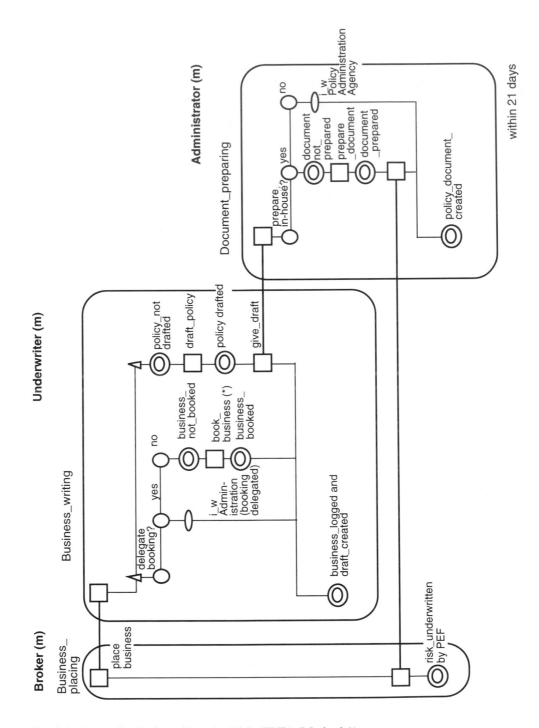

Fig. 8.19 Formally Underwriting the Risk (FUR) (Method 1)

The following figure shows the sub-role in which the Business database is a supporting mechanism.

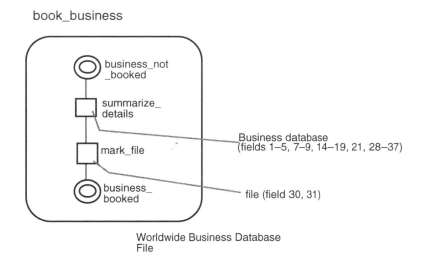

Fig. 8.20 Sub-Role 'Book Business'

Through these various diagrams we have considered in some detail the way in which the high-level scenario presented in Figure 8.17 is currently carried out. It has been possible to exemplify the problem of repeated entries to the In Progress database, the Business database and the submission file itself (Figure 8.18, Figure 8.20).

Earlier the creation of an active model that could coordinate members of the PEF team through in-trays on their terminal interfaces was discussed. This was motivated by the suggestion that the activities carried out by the team could be better coordinated if there was a clear way of assigning a proposal to a person. Hence, Figure 8.14 and Figure 8.15 show the administrator Catherine assigning a proposal to the underwriter Andrew. That simple example showed that the active process model could serve as a coordination layer between people. This can be represented as follows.

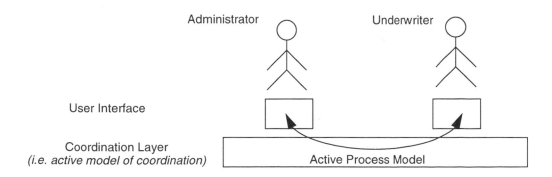

Fig. 8.21 A Representation of the Coordination of People

Using the active process model in this way is akin to handing an icon with the name of a proposal on it to a central coordinator (or *good butler*) who passes it on your behalf to some other person. Just as this coordination between people can be supported, so too can coordination between tools. The idea is the same: we give the data to a centralized source from where it shall be given to the In Progress and Business databases. We also need to be able to embed the business rules so that the coordinating system knows when to update each database and what to do if there is a problem. Keeping these business rules separately from the operational data and in a traceable form ensures that they can be more easily changed.

When these ideas are discussed amongst the PEF team members the process modeller suggests a number of graded design alternatives. The schema that is most popular provides a screen into which data is input. It uses the process model as a partial results area and updates the various other tools that need the data. In the normal processing of a proposal the users will no longer directly interface to the In Progress database, the Business database or even the Enquiry Line application (see Figure 8.18). 'I won't miss paging through those In Progress screens', comments one administrator.

The idea is that the active process model will present what is known as a *top sheet* for each proposal being presented. The team members can input all information on to this. When a proposal is assigned to a team member's in-tray, they can bring up the top sheet simply by pressing on an icon. In this way the summary information that is normally put into the file will always be available on screen. The process modeller suggests that given this new way of recording information, the team might no longer need to add the summary information to the file in paper format. There are mixed feelings about this suggestion. Some like it, some do not. It is decided that the best way forward is to ensure easy access to laser printers so that any team member who wants to can print a top sheet at any stage and add it to the file.

As these issues are discussed, a number of new method models are created. These depict how the work shall be carried out with the coordinating software in place. An example is shown below in Figure 8.22. This can be contrasted to Figure 8.18 to see the likely impact of using the active process model upon one sub-part of the process. In a general sense it illustrates how in designing the support system the organizational process is affected and vice versa. These method models do, after all, represent people's activities in the context of their work with other people and the various technologies that they use.

log_proposal

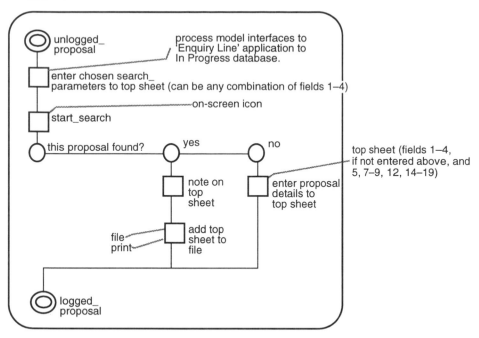

Fig. 8.22 'Log proposal' Using the Coordination Layer

By proposing to use the active process model to implement the top sheet, more of the coordinative activity in the organization is to be handed over to the technical system. The idea is akin to that expressed in Figure 8.21, only this time the emphasis is upon the integrative capability of the process model rather than the collaboration of people. The coordinating role of the active process model can thus be represented as follows:

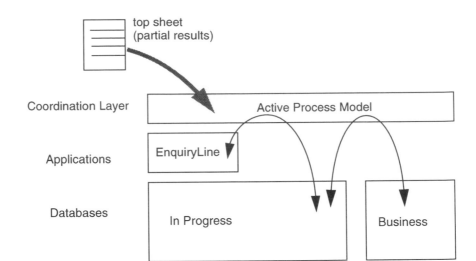

Fig. 8.23 A Representation of the Coordination of Tools

We have thus looked separately at two halves of a picture. The first concern was with the co-ordination of collaborating people and the second was with the integration of tools. The con-joined picture is shown in Figure 8.24.

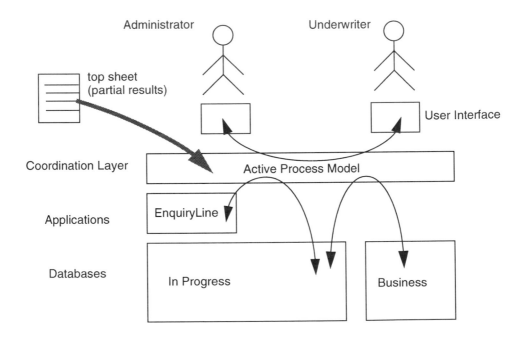

Fig. 8.24 A Representation of the Collaborative and Integrative Aspects of Coordination

Quite soon, a team of volunteers (underwriters and administrators) begin work on the design of the top sheet. They propose to take a simple approach which eschews functionality that they believe might be confusing to the user. This approach was particularly motivated by the underwriters for whom 'clarity or nothing' became a motto. Nonetheless, there is some talk of using a GUI builder to give a modern look and feel. In the meantime the team members experiment with a mock-up in Figure 8.25. This is incorporated into the coordinative harness of the active process model so that the users can see what it is like to pass proposals between in-trays, click on the appropriate icon and enter or read data on the top sheet.

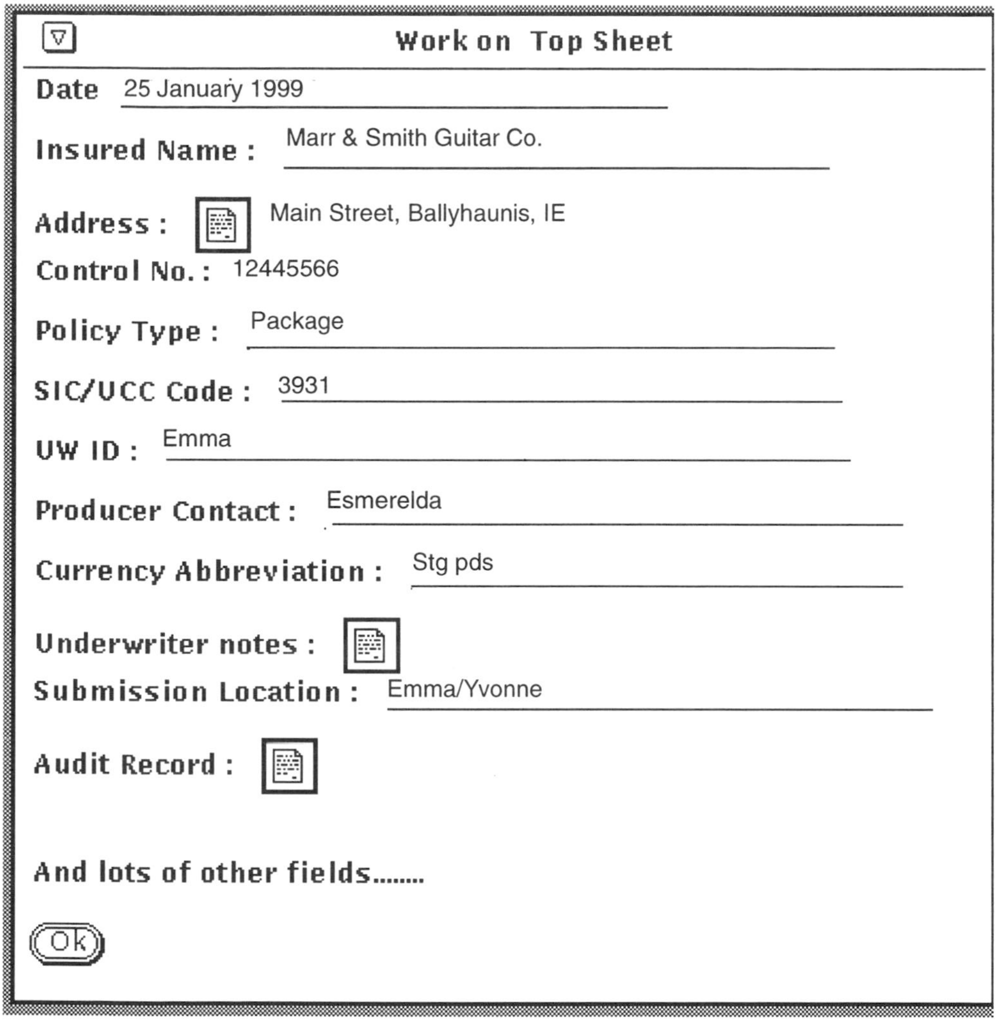

Fig. 8.25 The Top Sheet Mock-Up

8.4.4 Refinement (3): the Third Database

Later, with an active process model operational, the PEF team begin to consider the issues surrounding the Profiles database. This database is used to give underwriters extra information about certain companies and their industry sectors (see Figure 8.7). They find it very useful and would like to see it extended. The administrators have found updating it, and maintaining the file of information sources (e.g. company reports, newspaper clippings and PEF internal information) to be an onerous task. As well as repeating information that they have already placed in the Business database (or now the top sheet), they have to reformat data by collating figures about risk exposure. In the early discussions the process modeller questions whether a relational database is the best tool for the job. Would a groupware system, a kind of shared and structured email system, be better? Such a system would allow underwriters to update or retrieve information from common spaces organized by themselves whilst retaining some relational capabilities. In the longer term the database could be integrated with document image processing facilities so as to handle the miscellaneous information sources. After considering the process modeller's comments, the PEF team rule out this departure in the short-term. However, they acknowledge that the long term expansion of the Profiles facility will be supported by such new technology.

In any case, some of the problems that exist now would also exist given a groupware facility. Most obviously, the need to replicate data that is input to the Business database, to process this data and to enter it into whatever data store there is. Clearly, this is another example of the need to coordinate tools. Once a month the Profiles database needs a collated subset of the information that has been put into the Business database. This time, rather than passing information directly from the active process model to the Profiles database, a new application is built to automate this collation function (see Figure 8.26). Having achieved these innovations, an additional benefit is that the active process model shall be available to assist the migration from the existing database implementation to a new groupware implementation.

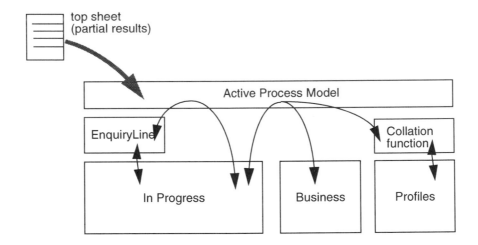

Fig. 8.26 A Representation of the Coordination of Tools Including the Profiles Database

8.4.5 Refinement Epilogue: the Fax Facility

Discussing the interactions between brokers and underwriters, the process modeller noted how closely they often had to work. There was a widespread consensus about the need for easy communications between these agents. For example, underwriters wish to quickly and clearly inform the broker of her or his decision on a proposal. On other occasions, the underwriter may need clarification of some details contained in the broker's proposal. By common consent, one of the most valuable tools is the fax facility. Recognizing this, a decision was taken to supply each underwriter with an on-line fax facility rather than to continue to rely on a few shared machines located around the office. This on-line facility is available for use as and when the underwriter wants it. It is simple to operate: the underwriter can select the fax icon on her screen, fill in the name, company and number to which it is being sent, type out the message, check the details and click 'OK' to send. At the same time, as the on-line fax facility was introduced, the active process model was developed so that it too could call up the fax facility. This gives an alternative way of using the fax facility. Its operation can be illustrated as follows. The underwriter may have already selected a particular proposal in her in-tray. She may, for example, be making reference to the top sheet of the proposal concerning *Marr & Smith Guitar Co.* A fax icon relating to that specific case is provided by the active model. The underwriter can click on this. She types in her message and after a brief check over the details, and clicks 'OK'. The active process model fills in the name, company and number to which it is being sent, these details having already been entered into the top sheet as part of the 'log proposal' sub-role.

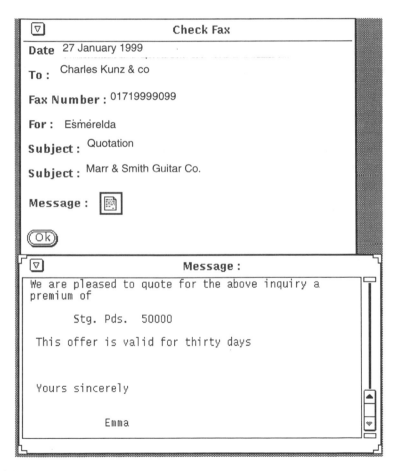

Fig. 8.27 The Fax Facility Illustrated

The use of the active process model to relate a generic fax facility to a particular item of work is illustrative of how working contexts can be assembled for users. The approach is extensible, allowing users to call upon different sets of tools according to the class of role that they are undertaking and that are specialized to the particular instance of that role. For example, to assess a proposal an underwriter might also need a spreadsheet, expert systems (e.g. to help diagnosis of risk) and databases (e.g. details of PEF's current exposure). The active process model can present these to the user when the user needs them and can specialize them to the particular circumstance (e.g. by automatically putting basic information into the spreadsheet). The right user receives the right tools at the right time and in the right form.

8.4.6 Reinvention: the PEF Blue Sky Directory

We call the most radical level of change *reinvention*. This is planned change that either substantially eradicates existing patterns of behaviour or starts from a *green field* situation. For reinvention projects there may be little or no purpose in taking cognizance of an *as is* situation. The idea is to start with a *tabula rasa* and is akin to the Business Process Reengineering blank sheet of paper approach (see Chapter 2).

PEF corporate team decide to radically reinvent themselves. Their purpose is to offer a new service which is quite unlike any other available on the market-place. This is motivated by the recognition that a lot of potential business submitted to the PEF corporate team is, in effect, turned away at the door. This is because PEF have strict rules about the kinds of proposal that they will insure. For example, they like to specialize in hotel chains, retail outlets and certain industry types such as publishing, telecommunications, software engineering and advertising. However, there are some industry types that they will not insure because the potential risks are thought unfavourable (e.g. cold food storage and cigarette manufacture). Other industry types are in a grey area, they are neither favoured nor excluded. These strict policies are important to PEF and they do not want to do away with them. However they begin to believe that all proposals that come to them are a resource, even the ones they will not themselves consider (e.g. Felicity Thaw's Cold Meat Storers Ltd).

After consultation with brokers it is decided to offer a new service under the name *PEF Blue Sky Directory*. The idea is that, if at all possible, a quotation will be given for any insurance proposal, no matter what the industry type. This will be accomplished in the following way. Brokers will be encouraged to submit all proposals to the PEF team. The brokers will be told that they will almost certainly receive a quotation and may even receive several. Each proposal will then be quickly appraised to ascertain whether it might be of interest to PEF. If there is the possibility that PEF will underwrite the risk it will be evaluated further by an underwriter. If there is no possibility that PEF will underwrite the risk then they will offer it to other insurers. This shall be achieved by reference to a new database. This database is known as the Blue Sky Directory. Insurance companies are encouraged to register themselves in this database together with details of the industry types that they will consider. It costs them nothing to register or update their entry on the Blue Sky Directory although they have to agree to pay the PEF team a very small percentage of any premium they receive as a result of being registered. All the external insurance company has to do is pass a decision on a proposal to the broker within an agreed time-frame. Thus, the PEF team functions as a second tier broker on those proposals that they do not underwrite themselves. The perceived business advantage is not the collection of funds for this referral service but the likelihood of attracting more proposals from brokers and hence more risks that they can underwrite themselves.

Originally, as the proposal is first discussed a number of rich pictures are drawn to express the concepts in the designers' heads. One is shown below in Figure 8.28.

From this point on, the design is expressed using the techniques set out in Chapter 7. The intention is to map quickly to the creation of an active process model which is initially used as a demonstrator to assist further design work.

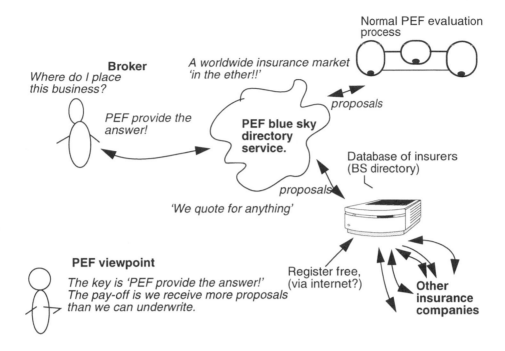

Fig. 8.28 A Rich Picture Expressing the Reinvented Insurance Team

The context model looks as follows:

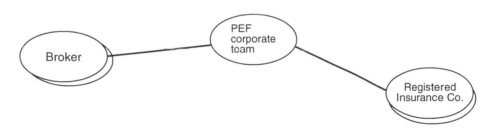

Fig. 8.29 Blue Sky Directory: Simple System Model

A pivotal role in the new process is played by a number of specially trained administrators. These become colloquially known as *gatekeepers*. Their task is to receive proposals that are sent into the PEF team and assign them either to a PEF underwriter or, via the Blue Sky database, to external insurance companies. In order that the gatekeepers are able to work with maximum effect, and to help them evolve their role, they are involved in the design of the process and the support system from a very early stage.

As well as 'gatekeeper,' the process designers come up with other items of jargon to describe important aspects of the process. A proposal is *assigned* when it has been given either to a PEF underwriter or external companies. A *RICo* (Registered Insurance Company) denotes a company that is registered on the database. A *release* is a proposal that is made available to the external insurance companies (i.e. to the RICo's). The term *BS top sheet* describes the summary form (top sheet equivalent) which is filled in for each release.

The rest of this illustration will focus only upon the role of the gatekeeper. Figure 8.30 is a system model describing *interacts with* relationships between the gatekeeper and brokers, underwriters and registered insurance companies.

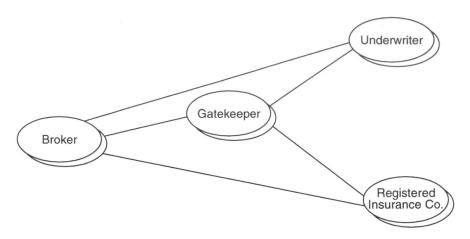

Fig. 8.30 The Gatekeeper: Simple System Model

An important goal model is shown below in Figure 8.31. Proposals are passed by the broker to the gatekeeper. The gatekeeper seeks to assign the proposal either to a PEF underwriter or alternatively, to a RICo. There are also possible variants of this behaviour. For example, a broker may pass a proposal directly to a PEF underwriter. The underwriter may then proceed with the assessment of it in the normal way. However if it is found to be unsuited to insurance by PEF, the underwriter will refer it outwards to the gatekeeper.

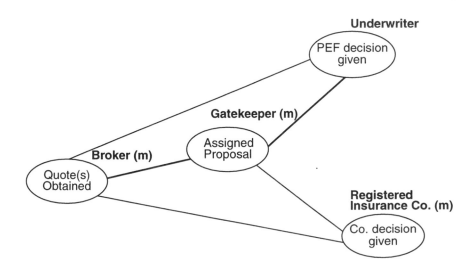

Fig. 8.31 The Assigning of a Proposal

There are obviously aspects to the work of the gatekeeper in addition to those described in the diagram (e.g. the proposals that are rejected by a PEF underwriter are re-assigned by a gatekeeper for assignment to a RICo). The gatekeeper also has an important managing role, trying to ensure that the BS directory is always up to date and that RICo's are responding to proposals advertised to them. These details are not considered here in order that we can keep the illustration compact.

A method model which depicts how the goals of 'assigning a proposal' (Figure 8.31) may be fulfilled is shown below in Figure 8.32.

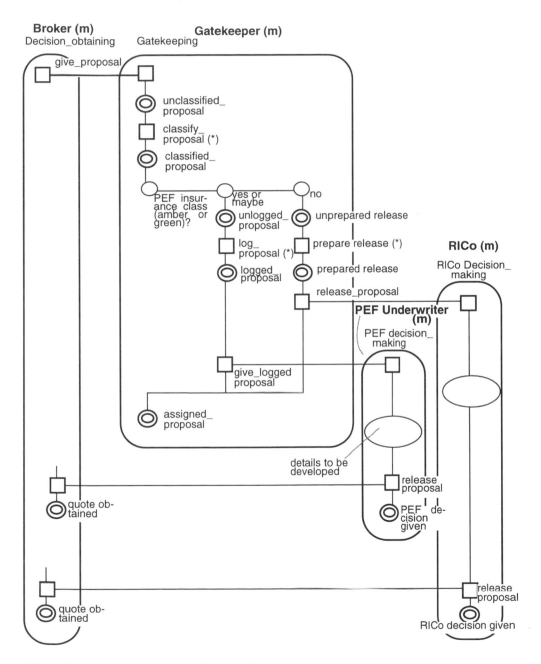

Fig. 8.32 Assigning a Proposal (Method 1)

Figure 8.32 describes how upon receiving a proposal the gatekeeper will seek to classify it. This classification seeks to establish whether it is of a type that the PEF team will insure. If there is any doubt the gatekeeper will pass it to a PEF underwriter. If it is to be passed to a PEF underwriter the gatekeeper will log it in a corporate database first. Alternatively, if the proposal is to be passed to a RICo the gatekeeper will prepare it for release. This preparation involves a number of activities including the interrogation of the Blue Sky database to ascertain which RICo's might be interested. The detail of the way in which the activities of the gatekeeper are carried out is considered in more depth later.

In order to help gatekeepers classify proposals, the PEF team have red (will not underwrite), amber (will consider) and green (favoured) industry-types. Individual proposals are given a classification according to an industry-wide system of numbering. This is known as the Insurance Classification System (ICS). Each industry has been assigned a number which has an approximate correlation with their English alphabetical ordering. For example, abattoirs have the number 0100, zinc mines are 9134. Sometimes the broker will provide a classification number on the submission. More usually gatekeepers will look through the proposal and assign a classification themselves. This can be difficult. It involves care and judgement. Often a single proposal will span a number of industry categories. If there is any doubt or difficulty about the classification the gatekeeper will pass the proposal to a PEF underwriter. There are also special cases where a proposal is passed to an underwriter whatever its classification. This can be because an underwriter gives a specific instruction or because it comes from a broker who is particularly important to the PEF team.

Figure 8.33 shows the sub-role Classify Proposal. The activity 'Query status' sends a query to a new Classifications database. The database returns the current status of an industry classification (e.g. 0100, abattoir, red). The management of the PEF team plan to use the Classifications database to give them an additional control mechanism over the exposure that the team accrues in different industry sectors. They can change the rating of an industry type at any point in time and this may involve changing the status between any of the red, amber and green groupings. For example, after insuring a major chain of hotels (e.g. 'Finnegan & Henchy'), they may consider that they have sufficient exposure in the hotels sector and change the status from green to amber or red.

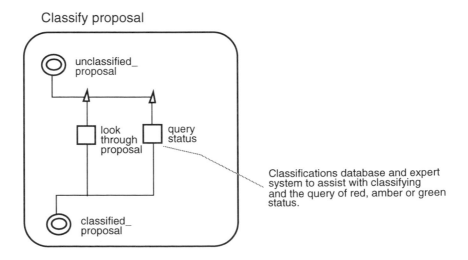

Fig. 8.33 Sub-Role 'Classify Proposal'

The new process is to be given a trial in the London office of the PEF company whilst the other offices of the company do not participate in the reinvention programme (i.e. Barcelona, Tokyo, Nairobi etc.) Thus it is decided that one of the more important metrics applied to assess the new process should be the number of proposals that London receives from brokers overseas. Among the motivations for the reinvention programme is a hypothesis that by using electronic media and offering a new service the PEF company will begin to attract more business to London from countries where they do not even have an office (e.g. Germany, Belgium).

Figure 8.34 shows the sub-role 'Prepare Release.'

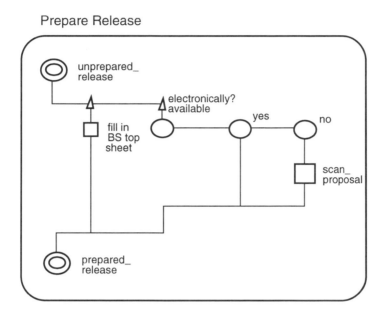

Fig. 8.34 Sub-Role 'Prepare Release'

Note that after preparation for release the gatekeeper will activate the release (see Figure 8.32). The BS directory is automatically interrogated on the basis of the information entered into the BS top sheet. Automatic faxes or emails are then be sent to every RICo with an interest in that industry class. A fax will include the details from the BS top sheet (e.g. broker's name, proposal details, due date) plus the directory path where the proposal can be found in electronic form. If an email address is available it is used. The email message takes the same format as the fax but includes an iconic link to the electronic version of the proposal. The gatekeeper's telephone number is available if there are any problems.

As work progresses on the coding of the Blue Sky database, and even before the design of the Classifications database has been prepared, the process modeller presents the team with an active process model. This is presented in a workshop so as to serve as a basis for further discussion and invention. Underwriters and administrators are then encouraged to take half an hour each week off from their normal duties in order to simulate the processing of a proposal with it. They are also encouraged to use it in coffee breaks or at lunch-times. Those administrators who are to be trained to work as gatekeepers use it more often and for longer periods. The process modeller is by now more or less resident in the office and able to discuss its use and enhancement at almost anytime. The modeller developed a role structure through the system, goal and method models and retained the integrity of this structure in moving to the active model. Through and within the role structure the modeller sought to maximize the flexibility available to the users. For example, the active model clearly permits the user to make a mistake (e.g. it can be passed to a PEF underwriter before it has been logged). These issues have been discussed. So far, under simulated conditions, no one has asked for more constraint or prescription from the support system. They prefer to rely upon the skill and experience of the users and thereby, potentially, permit more ad hoc, extemporizing ways of working. The process modeller is also involved in the design of the new databases. A database designer has been hired in from a small software house in Manchester to work on the Classifications database. The designer uses the active process model in order to understand the contribution the Classifications database shall make to the process. The designer reinforces this knowledge with a discussion of the method, goal and system models. When the Blue Sky and Classifications databases are complete, there will be some further work integrating them into the active process model. The whole system will then undergo further testing before being used for real.

Catherine is one of the administrators who has gained a promotion to become a gatekeeper. Figure 8.35 shows the user interface of the active process model as she explores its behaviour prior to implementation of the new process.

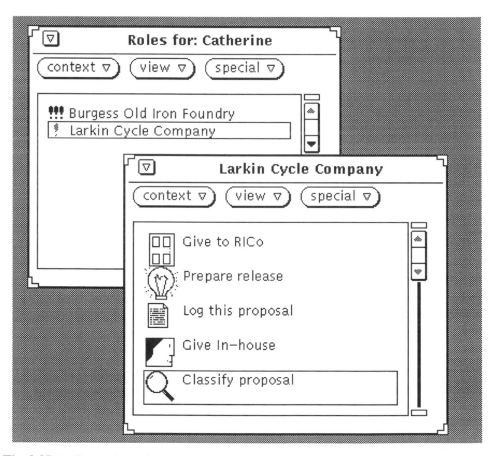

Fig. 8.35 An Example UI for the Gatekeeping Role

Figure 8.36 shows the active model code for the role 'Gatekeeping.' It is written in PML.

```
Gatekeeping isa Role with

resources !**the resources of the role
        intrayentry : InTrayEntry
        referinhouse : giveport InTrayEntry
        release : giveport InTrayEntry
        proposal_assigned : Bool {false}

actions !**the actions that the role can execute

        classify_proposal :
        {UserAction (agendaLabel = 'Classify proposal', icon = 'Magnify');
        ViewObjectNow (object = 'Sorry Classifications DB not implemented yet!')}
        when proposal_assigned = false

        log_proposal :
        {UserAction (agendaLabel = 'Log this proposal', icon = 'Text');
        ViewObjectNow (object = 'Sorry sub-role not implemented yet!')}
        when log_proposal = nil

        prepare_release :
        {UserAction (agendaLabel = 'Prepare release', icon = 'Idea');
        ViewObjectNow (object = 'Sorry sub-role not implemented yet!')}
        when proposal_assigned = false

        give_logged_proposal :
        {UserAction (agendaLabel = 'Give In-house', icon = 'Face');
        Give (interaction = referinhouse, gram = intrayentry);
        proposal_assigned := true}
        when proposal_assigned = false

        release_proposal :
        {UserAction (agendaLabel = 'Give to RICo', icon = 'Door');
        Give (interaction = release, gram = intrayentry);
        proposal_assigned := true}
        when proposal_assigned = false

termconds proposal_assigned

end with !* Gatekeeping
```

Fig. 8.36 PML for 'Gatekeeping' Role

8.5 The Broader Dialectic

The design activity concludes the broader series of dialectics that has been depicted and explained in Chapter 6 and Chapter 7. Assuming that the task of process capture precedes the design activity (i.e. that a *tabula rasa* approach is not taken), the series of dialectics can be depicted as follows:

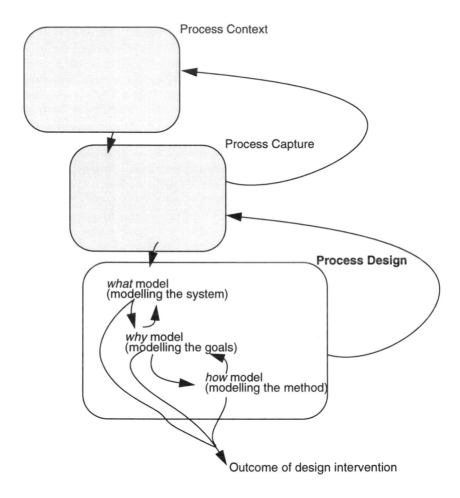

Fig. 8.37 Third in a Series of Dialectics: Process Design

8.6 Conclusion

8.6.1 General Issues

A number of general issues are worth briefly revisiting. A presentation of some more specific issues shall follow.

Essentially, what we have been concerned with in this chapter is the designing of people's behaviour, the designing of the behaviour of software systems and the relationship between the two. A few words of caution are in order lest we fall into the trap of thinking that we could ever *design people's behaviour*. At least we need to be aware of why we should not want to. We have explored the relationship between the social and technical systems and concluded, simply, that the former is served by the latter. If in a fundamental sense the software systems used at work are more hindrance than help, if they rigidly enforce behaviour and prevent users from exercizing initiative, then it is not a better *technical* understanding that is needed, but there are questions to be asked about the *social* system. What was the designer's rationale in creating the system? What was the impact upon work that he or she envisaged? Who commissioned the software, anyway? Were they looking for a way of ensuring that users work to a fine-grained specification? If so, did they seek to understand the real difficulties of the job first? Does the system, perhaps, say a lot about the lack of understanding of organizational behaviour of those who commissioned and designed it?

A prime difficulty in designing software systems for organizations is to achieve the correct balance between providing flexible and adaptive systems and, on the other hand, maintaining and promoting group working. For reasons too obvious and many to mention, the design of support systems is not simply a case of assembling all the tools one can think of and providing the users with an executable permission. As a member of a group each of us can, through collective action, achieve more than we could do alone. On the other hand, dependencies exist between the group members. People rely on you, you rely on other people. Work takes place in a context; individuals have a role in the group. You may wish and indeed need to be as free as possible to handle tasks in the way that you see fit, but still those who work with you need to know how your output will affect them. The goals of each person's interactions need to be understood by those who participate in them. The well being of the group and the well being of its members are mutually influencing.

Indeed there are circumstances where fine-grained procedure and rigidity are important (perhaps a nuclear power plant) and there are circumstances where they are not (e.g. a commercial insurance company). 'Systems designers' (in the broadest sense of that term i.e. managers, analysts, staff etc.) will respond to the environment they are in and will seek to tailor the organization accordingly. Thus, to take our particular example, a system will fail if we seek to make the levels of control that are suited to the nuclear power plant apply in the insurance company. Why? Because the operational environments are so radically different. The operations of the nuclear plant are deliberately inflexible and isolated from outside interference. The whole system is *designed* to make it so. Mission success (i.e. safety) depends upon minimizing the number of variables that operational procedures have to manipulate. The operations of the PEF insurance company are quite different. They have to be open to the outside world, to be flexible and innovative and to be able to identify threat or opportunity. Mission success depends upon being able to manipulate and respond to the ebb and flow of the commercial insurance market. Therefore the operational procedures have to cope with a much greater variety of circumstances and have to be much more flexible. Each company has its own fingerprint.

It follows that a process modelling design exercise of the sort presented in this chapter should be made more or less granular to suit the fingerprint of the organization concerned. How we judge the suitable level will depend upon our appraisal of the organizational context. In the PEF corporate team the emphasis has been much more upon the establishing of role contexts, and upon understanding what people contribute to each other, than upon the sequencing of individual activities. If we were to apply the same techniques to the nuclear power plant we would seek to prescribe in advance all the states of the system and hence the sequencing of activities would be subject to formal analysis.

The OPM method presented in this book works very well from a user-centred perspective. Through a vocabulary of interactions, goals, and roles etc. it seems we have a language which can be shared with users, used to explore their domain, and utilized to configure an active process model of coordination. It seems almost foolish not to take advantage of this. Yet there is probably nothing intrinsic to process modelling that means that the modeller must take a user-centred approach. If it is thought to be a good idea, one can start designing a process for an organization without ever meeting a single user. Perhaps a high degree of automation or a blank sheet approach is just what is needed in some circumstances.

One of the goals of this work is to create adaptable systems which continue to support the group as needs change. We have described change as endemic to organizations so it is a question of need rather than choice. Just as the usability issue affects the granularity of our process modelling effort so too does the issue of evolution. If the behaviour of an active process model is prescriptive in a fine grained way, then in an environment of change it is going to become out of step with the needs of the organization more often than a model which allows greater flexibility. It will be less resilient. Therefore a high-level modelling approach not only helps to make the software more robust to changing circumstances, but when things do change we can more easily trace their likely impact. Perhaps, for example, certain goals change or are obliterated; we need to be able to work out how the active model is affected; which roles?; which activities?

8.6.2 This Chapter

Leaving Process Capture with some simple diagrammatic models, in this chapter we have been able to propose and illustrate how they might be mapped into an active form using the Process Modelling Language. A number of issues have been presented. The architectural approach has been to utilize the active process model as a coordination layer which helps to manage interactions between users, between users and tools and between tools. Examples from the PEF corporate team have been developed to illustrate the design approach. These have spanned different levels of radicalism in design, from reflection through refinement and to reinvention.

THE FOLLOWING CHAPTERS

The issue of process evolution has already been raised a number of times. In the next chapter we consider how the process modelling approach can be developed to address evolution directly. Following this in Chapter 10, we look in more depth at support technology.

THINGS TO DO

From here we can propose a list of specific, architectural issues which have been touched upon but not explored in depth.

• We have made reference to a number of existing databases in the PEF case study (e.g. In Progress, Business) but do they contain functionality that might be better managed by the active process model? How do we determine the boundary between the coordinative system and the operational systems? How do we determine or interpret which is which? By analogy, how do we tell the conductor from the orchestra, the cellist from the violinist?

• How do such notions relate the various concerns of process and object?

• What *roles* are held by the various software tools? How are the tools integrated into the active process model?

• We have used the active process model as a coordination layer, but what alternative architectural roles are there for process support technology?

Something else of interest is the principle of structural integrity which was utilized in mapping from the passive, diagrammatic models to the active process model. The principle of structural integrity states: whenever a goal is expressed in a passive model and supported by an active model, the active model must contain a module specifically designated to the support of that goal.

• What advantages have we gained through the adoption of this principle? It allows the simple graphical models to be correlated very easily to the actual code, but how significant is this? How might it assist the PEF team as they go through a further series of changes? How might it be difficult to maintain this simple mapping in other examples? Why does the principle not require a more detailed mapping be maintained (e.g. to the level of activities).

Finally, it is worth noting that although we have not yet considered the issue of process evolution (that follows in Chapter 9), we have been designing with change in mind already. How do the following contribute to an adaptive, evolvable system?

• The concept of the coordination layer.

• The active model: a high level Process Modelling Language – the simple mappings between the diagrams and the executable code.

• Allowing users to work flexibly.

9

Process Managing

Organization processes are not insulated from their environments. They are subject to influences from many sources and, as a result, every process is subject to change to a greater or lesser degree. As a natural progression from Chapter 8, this chapter will address the subject of change in practical terms. Assuming we have designed a process model, what has to be done to make it evolvable? This is now explained using the Process for Process Evolution meta-process model, which has already been introduced. It will be developed using the method described in the previous chapter and will be illustrated with reference to the insurance example.

9.1 Introduction

In Chapter 2, we were reminded that, 'the modern study of organizations is dominated by issues of complexity and change'. These issues constitute the reason why we need the kind of meta-process that was introduced in general terms in Chapter 3. Our model, the Process for Process Evolution (P2E), was introduced in Chapter 5 and we can now discuss the practical application of P2E to support the managing activity associated with any operational process.

We choose to use the term *process managing* in a restricted sense. We do not mean managing in the sense of planning, leading, troubleshooting, or any of the other human-centred roles of the typical manager. We mean managing in the narrower sense: monitoring the state of the operational process; monitoring influences relevant to this process (influences emanating from within the process and external to the process); assessing if the process definition ought to be changed and, if so, the instigating and carrying out of a change. In this chapter, a scenario will demonstrate how an active model can guide, first of all, the adaptation of an IT-supported business process, and later how it can guide the creation and implementation of, and subsequent evolution of, the operational process.

The model does not make any presumption about the power relationship between those who manage and those who are managed. An individual might be responsible solely as a manager, remote from the day-to-day operation of the process, or they might in fact be one of the participants in the operational process who has this additional responsibility. In the latter case, the individual would be responsible for two roles. The first relates to the operational process. The second relates to its managing process.

As we mentioned earlier, in this example we are not concerned with the managing of individuals, resources or the finances of the process. Our sole concern is with the process activity, and these other concerns only become relevant if they impact upon the process necessitating behavioural changes.

There are very many influences on a business process and in many cases it is not possible to define the process such that it can cope with all possible influences acting over its entire life.

This is not important for the many operational processes that are quite isolated from the business environment and thus are likely to remain unchanged for many years. The common business expenses-paying process is typical of such a process. Others have a great variety of products, are susceptible to influences from outside of the business, need substantial intuitive thought in interacting with the process, and are in a state of almost constant flux. The software development process is an example of this. With such processes, we appreciate very well that we do not know exactly what to do to achieve the desired results under all conceivable future situations, and that we do expect to introduce many corrective changes to maintain an optimally efficient and effective process.

If this change is always ad hoc or reflective, undertaken to solve problems as they arise without concern for the long-term consequences, then it will lead to premature extinction of the process because it will become very difficult to maintain. Our interest here is in evolutionary change: change based on the existing shape of the process (i.e. based on the existing definitions), rather than ad hoc change which is not necessarily predicated on existing definitions. The significance of this difference is that under the former kind of change, complexity should not increase. Under the latter, typified by process workarounds to avoid specific problems, complexity may well increase. And, as mentioned above, increasing complexity will eventually make the system correspondingly difficult to maintain and thus accelerate its demise.

P2E represents a very general approach and thus a highly suitable architecture to use as the basis for structuring change, but it is not the only one. For example Pasmore (1988) describes a model for environmental adaptation of a process. This model modifies the conventional feedback control loop operating on a process that converts inputs to outputs. The control loop incorporates detection and filtering devices; comparison and decision devices and a response mechanism; new behaviours and organizational learning. We will make reference to this model as we go through our example to emphasize the generality of our chosen approach.

We will populate it by real models of methods, and design the support for the meta-process in just the same way as we have done for the operational process. The same principles and methods apply. In the previous paragraph we mentioned efficient and effective processes. As well as having a process to ensure efficiency in the operational process (doing it right) we also have to ensure effectiveness of the process (doing the right thing), i.e. we need a process to ensure the goals, objectives and constraints that we are setting are indeed appropriate from the point of view of the organization (they fit with other goals) and the operations (they are not being asked to achieve the impossible).

Real-world process models are very complex, and so the discussion will be effected in the context of a very simple example. The example used in this chapter is that of a single business process being guided by an active model. The process is that of Formally Underwriting the Risk (FUR), whose model of method is described in Section 8.4 and illustrated in Figure 8.19. The meta-process model is P2E, introduced in Chapter 5.

A number of scenarios will be used to assist explanation. We will initially assume an active model being used to drive an operational process, and then describe what is needed of the managing process such that the model of the operational process might be changed in a systematic, evolutionary manner at run time in response to the changing needs of the business. This will give us a model of the managing process method, together with minor changes to that of the operational process which will allow the two to be integrated. The combined model of methods can be implemented as a single active model which, when established, can be used to support a scenario of change which will be used to help explain just how the managing process and operational process interact to achieve the desired outcomes.

9.2 The Problem and its Context

The discussion so far in the book has been about single processes: how to capture them as models, how to design new models, and how to support them using an active model. The focus of this chapter is on support for some of the manager's concerns. A typical business situation can be succinctly expressed as a rich picture, and Figure 9.1 is used to express the underwriting manager's viewpoint: 'OK – we have a process producing insurance policies, it's supported by IT, but how do I control it? How do I change it?'. This is a common kind of managerial prob-

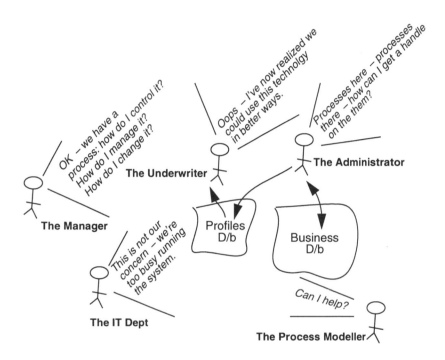

Fig. 9.1 Rich Picture of Management Concerns

lem, and we want to demonstrate that the OPM modelling approach can be usefully extended to this context. This will achieve the benefits of being able to follow a consistent process for each change and of being able to ensure the changed models are consistent with earlier models. As long as the underwriting manager's concerns and goals can be realized as a defined process (or processes) then they can be supported by means of an active model.

In the process domain, we can study the processes with which managers interact, so-called management processes, not only to see how they can be supported to help enhance the performance of managers, but also to provide a basis for improvement. Quality concerns should not be restricted to the operational processes, and can be extended to the processes of management. We are however interested in only one application area of the management process, and that is the operational process, so our attention is focused on the *process-management* process.

Now the management process is a kind of control process. It uses feedback and feedforward as in classical control theory to manipulate process resources to achieve desired outputs. We are less interested in manipulation of process resources as manipulating the processes themselves, and our approach is to do that by manipulating the model that shapes real-world process activity. Furthermore these changes are part of a continuum of change: they are process evolution.

In reality of course, there may be very many operational processes, all interworking and all having to evolve. The scenario described in this chapter relates solely to a single process but there is no reason why it cannot apply to multiple instances of that process model, and indeed to multiple process models. They all have to evolve for the reasons described in Chapter 3. The change process that we intend to support is not ad hoc, but systematic. It follows a pattern of activity which can be described as a process, and this process can itself be captured and supported by an active model.

In a very few simple cases, this evolution could be implemented by simply taking away the old model instance and putting in a new one. However, the process instance may in fact have a life of many years, and there may in be many instances in existence, all in different states. To preserve the information already associated with these instances, changes have to be applied with discretion but to all instances where the changed behaviour lies in the future. If the change is applied to the part that has already been executed then it will obviously have no effect. There is an analogy to the adding of amendment slips to a procedures manual. Add a new slip, then the next time that rule is needed, and it has been read by the corresponding participant, the new steps will be followed. But what happens if a chain of activity has already been started? There have to be special rules for this situation, and we need these rules to be built into the active model.

It is useful at this point to indicate a number of interesting similarities and differences between process-managing processes (or process-evolving processes) and operational processes:
- Operational processes have goals that involve the attaining of some state at which the instance concludes, whereas the goals of managing processes involve maintaining operational process performance within certain bounds on a continuous basis.
- There may be very many instances of an operational process being controlled by a single instance of a managing process. Even if there is only one instance of an operational process (such as in a project structure) there is still one instance of the managing process.
- The products of the operational process can be objects, or services interpreted in terms of objects, and they have value to some customer or end user. The products of the managing process are changes which are ultimately applied to the enacting model of the operational process, and their value is less discernible.
- The managing process is partly continuous and partly cyclical. There is continuous monitoring of the operational processes and the environment, but each application of change is a discrete instance.

We will use the insurance process discussed throughout this book as the example of the operational process. We will revisit this process and integrate it with a meta-process structure which will allow it to evolve in the longer-term interests of the organization. In the following section, the general approach to addressing the concerns of the manager will be described.

9.3 The Meta-Process as a Solution

The requirements for an implementable meta-process have been expressed in Section 3.8.3. They can be combined with the problem-solving process and expressed in a behavioural model known as the Process for Process Evolution, introduced in Chapter 5. A viable model must be able to relate the social context of organizations, where problems are perceived, identified, and need to be addressed, and the technical context of methods, techniques, and IT System which provide the means of solving these problems. This socio-technical system has been much referred to earlier in this book.

Four distinct encapsulations of behaviour can be identified, and these are now described before describing the relationships between them (referring to Figure 9.2). The descriptions are derived from the problem-solving process introduced in Chapter 3.

Deciding what to do

Managing is the component that is concerned with behaviour which perceives the state of the operational process, decides on certain desired goals, initiates change, assesses progress towards these goals or objectives, and reassesses the objectives themselves if appropriate.

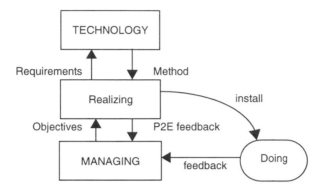

Fig. 9.2 The Process for Process Evolution P2E

This Managing component perceives the state differences which we want our operational process to address. This is translated into a set of pragmatic objectives which, if attained, eradicate that state difference. By goal, or objectives, we mean a statement of the high-level requirements which the system must fulfil, any constraints (such as the use of a particular method for doing so), and an indication of the metrics against which performance will be evaluated. There are two concerns which must be borne in mind when dealing with objectives. The first is that, on many occasions, the context of the solution will be well known, so it need not be reiterated, but if the context of the solution is not known, or different form the usual, this has to be included in objectives. In fact the objectives could become more akin to a terms of reference, i.e. including both goals and constraints. The other concern is that it might not be possible to establish a solution process for given goals, so a dialogue with Realizing is needed regarding the practicability and risk of failure of the solution, and this is indicated by the arrow labelled *P2E feedback*.

Devising some course of action

This activity is achieved in two distinct components, Realizing and Technology. Realizing is the step that contributes towards the towards fulfilment of the Objectives by the provision of a process model specialized both for these objectives and for the relevant organizational context, and the implementation of this model in the real-world. Realizing translates the objectives received from Managing into requirements that can be used in Technology to furnish a suitable method (a process model) for addressing the objectives. It is then responsible for the assembling together of all things that are necessary to carry out the operational process, which could include knowledge, methods, tools, resources (human and machine), etc., and also installing the method, causing the process activity to be executed or enacted in the real world. This enactment is represented by the Doing component. The Technology component encompasses behaviour related to the maintenance of libraries of methods, behaviour for searching this library, and for assembling process components together into methods. It would also have to include support for process model development methods, the means by which the process models themselves are produced.

Carrying out this action

The Doing component represents the real world performing of process activity both to achieve the goals and to provide feedback to Managing according to certain measures. Doing is where the usual kind of operational or production process takes place. It takes various inputs and transforms them into outputs intended to address the overall process objectives. The only condition imposed on this activity is that of the monitoring of process state and the passing of this information to the Managing activity. In this abstract model there is no need to define this feedback any further.

Relationships between components

There are various information flows or transformations between the components. Feedback is an indication of the state and performance of activity for use in the control mechanism. P2E feedback is needed to reflect back to Managing the internal condition of the P2E: for example, if there is no suitable method to address the stated objectives, then this state of affairs has to be reflected back to Managing for further action. This is of particular importance in the case, discussed later, of the individual components themselves being P2Es. This is because the components represent process behaviour and hence are manageable themselves using P2E processes. Process feedback is information about how well the operational process is progressing towards the achievement of the stated goals.

Requirements are definitions that are adequate to determine a technical method, either from a knowledge source, or as a design brief for a new method. The method is an abstract process model of the operational process. It may need specialization, to a greater or lesser degree, to enable it to address the objectives, and to relate it to the organization in which it will be implemented. Install is a different kind of information flow. It represents the transformation of a real world without the process, to a world with participants interacting with each other in an understood process. In pragmatic terms this refers to the implementation of the design in a suitable system, the installation of the system in an organizational environment, the assignment of resources to the task and the training of staff to use this system.

Now this model, so far described, is abstract. Its description is only sufficient to bring out the concepts embodied in the model and their relationships. For it to be useful in the real world this model must be adapted and refined. We will now see what further properties are needed of the model to fully satisfy the requirements for the example.

9.4 The Approach to the Solution

The recommended development phases of OPM have been described as System model, Goal model, Model of method, and an Active model. These different phases will be followed where appropriate in this example. The result will be an active model which will structure and support the managing process of the underwriting manager of the PEF team.

The specific phases in this development are:
• Identify goals and requirements.
• Decompose goals by role and interaction.
• Elaborate on role-oriented requirements.
• Map these to the structure of the P2E model.

- Map P2E to its model of method.
- Adapt the FUR model to interface with the P2E model of method.
- Link both models of method, ready for translation to an active model.

Thus the solution is a method model which is the integration of the model of the operational process method and of the P2E. Subsequently, various scenarios will be described which explain further the use of P2E.

At this point we will recapitulate briefly on why we need the P2E model. So far in this book, the models have been designed on the assumption that they are correct. We know from experience that this is unlikely to be the case, and we also know that the demands placed on the business are likely to change over the years. So we need a mechanism to manage this change. The prime reasons for using P2E is its wide applicability, its potential for specialization, and its potential for enaction. It is a generic model which, as well as addressing the objective of handling change, also addresses non-functional goals of, for example, minimizing inconsistency. We only need to take this as a template and adapt it for our purposes. The modeller's skill is then applied to this process of adaptation rather than of invention.

In following this scenario, we can assume that the context of the process is well understood and that a system model would not add anything to our knowledge, thus we can proceed straight to establishing goals and requirements.

9.4.1 Elaborating Goals and Requirements

The underwriting manager is responsible for the totality of goals but of course, in the normal way, has to delegate some of the responsibility for achieving them to the PEF underwriting team while retaining the accountability to higher management. So the activity unique to management is that which is associated with addressing the efficiency component of the goal, maintaining awareness of state and influences, and objective setting.

Another agent needed to manage the operational process effectively is the process modeller. The process modeller has the responsibility for, and the necessary skills and experience to undertake, the provision of generic process models in response to objectives determined by the manager. In addition, the process modeller will adapt these models specifically to the objectives, and to the nature of the organization as it exists for the PEF team, and to introduce the model into the live operational process.

The design approach involves identifying essential business objectives, and decomposing them until a level of granularity is arrived at where it is possible to define or develop a minimum set of activities and tools which can satisfy these objectives. In other words, until the objectives are rendered tractable by utilizing the resources (knowledge, skills and tools) available in the organization.

First of all, the organization objective, here represented by the goal of the Underwriting Manager, can be decomposed with respect to the agents. There are three agents involved in this aspect of PEF insurance: the Underwriting Manager, the Process Modeller, and the PEF Team. A generic goal decomposition is shown in Figure 9.3. The goal of the underwriting manager is, in generic terms, to satisfy business goals, and for our particular example we can say that she needs to efficiently document the underwritten risks. It is necessary for the manager to interact with both the process modeller and the underwriters in the PEF team to achieve this. The goal of Process Modeller is to provide a process model which will address the goals, and in this case the model will be that of formally underwriting the risk. Of course we can be rather more specific and add the word *maintain* as well to emphasize that this is an ongoing responsibility. The goal of the underwriters in the PEF team is to enact the process (which means in this case essentially the work of the drafting of policies) to attain the objectives of that process. In this situation, the goal of the underwriting manager subsumes the goals of the other agents, i.e. the goals of the Process Modeller and the PEF Team are sub-goals of those of the Underwriting Manager.

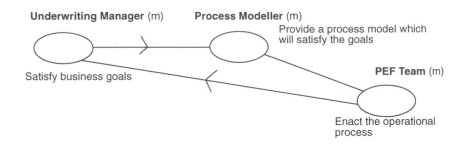

Fig. 9.3 Generic Goal Model

This then is the statement of requirements which we intend to satisfy by use of an active model. If there is no existing managing process to capture then the design of the process model can proceed on the basis of these functional and non-functional goals.

By adopting a P2E model we address the following non-functional goals mentioned in Chapter 3, which are essential if the changes developed for the process are to be evolutionary:

• Consistency: there must be a way of detecting the state of things of interest in the performing insurance process. Some kind of early warning or analysis mechanism is needed in order to assess these states and to assist in determination of issues that have to be addressed.

• Integrity: change should always be made with reference to the generic process model, maintaining existing forms and structures wherever possible, and it should not increase the complexity of the model.

• Complexity: provide a way of making problems tractable.

We will now see how these goals can be addressed by making use of the generic meta-process model, P2E.

9.4.2 Adapting P2E

P2E is an abstract process model (Figure 9.2), it provides the basic structure which allows us to continuously adapt an operational process and allows us to achieve a number of non-functional goals. For practical use it has to be specialized. We do part of this adaptation in the model of method, and a part in the active model. We will describe the behaviour which is to be associated with each of the P2E components, and also the interactions which are needed. After the behaviours are described, it will be possible to define communication links more exactly.

The agents, and thus the goal model, can be mapped to the P2E model as shown in Figure 9.4. With this architecture, our knowledge of business goals, and our detailed knowledge of the FUR model, we can sketch out the necessary behaviours which would support these goals. This results in a more detailed model of method for each of the individual P2E roles, shown in Figure 9.5, and is of course the model of method, or the RAD model for the meta-process.

Managing

This is the activity which is the responsibility of the underwriting manager, and which can be represented as a role in a model of method. When addressing the requirements of a manager's goals, what has to be done frequently depends on some existing or anticipated situation: it cannot be defined in advance. Managers do not achieve their goals by directly producing anything of value, they achieve them by controlling the activities of others. The term *control* means to regulate something, or in other words, to manipulate something in order to achieve desired ends. To do this for an enacting operational process, there has to be some way whereby the manager can be made aware of the state of the process – and just what measures are adopted to engender this awareness can be very important. The existence of a feedback loop to achieve this is a key characteristic of a control process.

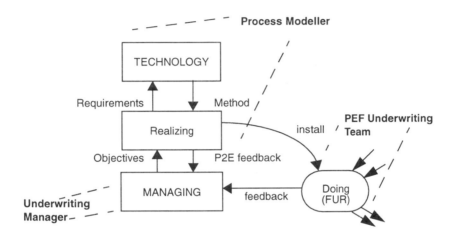

Fig. 9.4 The Agents Managing, Maintaining and Operating the FUR Process

In order to address the goal of satisfying the business objectives, the manager has to undertake at least four things:
- Know what the current state of the process is, obtain information about inconsistencies between the modelled process and the desirable process.
- Receive relevant information about the external environment.
- Study all this information, map it quantitatively to stated objectives, and, if necessary, seek to correct any apparent or emerging adverse circumstances by:
- Setting new or revised objectives for the operational process.

These considerations provide the information necessary to make informed decisions about the model of the process. It may be that some issues cannot be resolved in the model – if, for example, participants were unaware of the potential of the support available to them, then some training might be required.

Support for these four responsibilities from the process model can take the form of three activities: *See Suggestions* a text window allowing the participant to read messages; *See Statistics*, allowing scrutiny of service statistics automatically collected from the enacting FUR model; and *Prepare Objectives*, a way for the manager to draft a set of objectives for transmitting to the Realizing role for subsequent action.

The model of method for these behaviours is shown in Figure 9.5. Of course the real world being so much more complex than our model, it seems obvious that it might well be beneficial to extend and to automate some parts of this activity such as data filtering, statistical interpre-

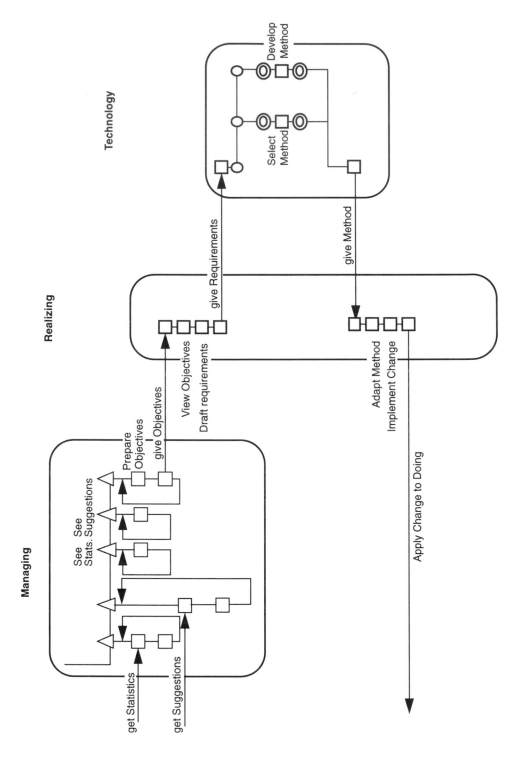

Fig. 9.5 The P2E Model of Method

tation, and decisioning. There may be a quite well-defined process relating statistics (and indeed external sources) and suggestions for objectives through some decision support process. This is analogous to Pasmore's *Filtering, Comparison and Decision* devices.

Realizing

The goal of the process modeller is to find a generic process and to adapt it for use by the PEF team. It is the activity foreseen by Pasmore as *Developing a new Response*, and then *Introducing New Behaviours* in the operational process. There are two distinct facets to this activity. The first is the translation of objectives into requirements suitable for searching for or developing a new process model. The second, once the method is obtained in the form of an abstract process model, is its adaptation to the detail of the particular objectives and for the organization in which it is to be implemented. This requires knowledge of the organization (the mapping of people to roles), machine resources, and also the mapping of roles to behaviour, as well as the current definitions for each of the roles, and the interactions between them.

In its simplest, the first can be a text window to enable the incoming message about objectives to be read, and recast in terms better suited to formalizing in a model, so some knowledge of the kind of models available in technology is needed and how they are characterized. The second activity involves taking the abstract model, and restructuring it so that it can be installed. It depends, for example, on the architecture of the components in the repository accessible to Technology. It is also very contingent on the architecture of the active models. The aim of the Implement Change activity is to incorporate the new behaviours into the existing enacting process activity as quickly as possible and with a minimum of disruption.

Technology

This behaviour encompasses the activity of selecting and of developing the generic method in a specialist domain. Selecting can be associated with some library of relevant generic methods suitable for (in this case) the insurance business, along with activity associated with lodging, searching, retrieving methods. Support for a model development process would also be within this component. We are not concerned with the physical architecture of the repository containing the library, we are concerned only that it is capable of storing the data on generic process models and process model fragments. In the exemplified insurance domain, typical fragments might be: Setup policy document; Policy document life cycle; Approving, Credit checking and so on.

Using the set of requirements obtained from Realize, the process modeller interacting with Technology has available the Select Method action to search the library for appropriate process fragments. If one is available, it is passed back to Realize. If none is available, the Develop Method action will provide tools to produce a new method, in the form of a process model, probably using a mixture of existing fragments and new constructs. Associated with each generic fragment would be a guide to its adaptation. Not shown, but very important, would be the behaviour associated with maintaining the library: making corrections to generic methods in the light of experience, new ways of adapting generic to customized.

Both these roles of the process modeller provide facility for what Pasmore refers to as *New Behaviour* and *Learning*. In any quality approach to process models (e.g. Madhavji et al., 1990), the fruits of experience with particular examples of generic methods ought not to be lost, but incorporated into the repository of methods. Thus in a real application of Technology provision would have to be made to assess and log the results of experiences with process models.

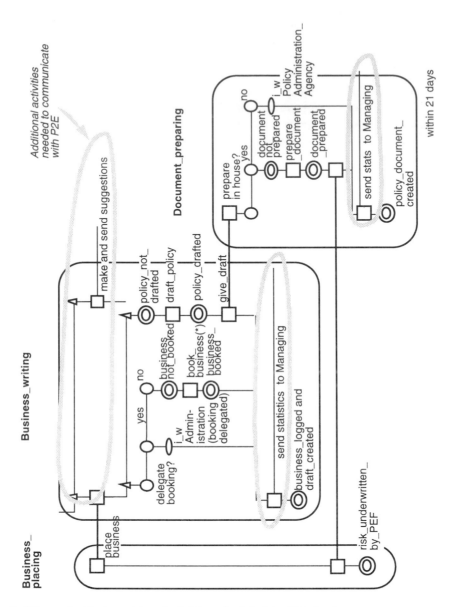

Fig. 9.6 Formally Underwriting the Risk – the Model of Method

9.4.3 Adapting the FUR model

Doing encompasses the operational process (or processes) and in this case represents the responsibilities of the PEF team of underwriters. The model of the FUR method is shown in Figure 9.6 and it is almost exactly as described earlier in Chapter 8. The differences relate to the need to have certain outputs from the process made visible by a manager, and also a mailing facility to communicate complaints and suggestions from staff involved in the operational process (i.e. what Pasmore refers to as a *Detection* device). In Business_writing, the user always has access to a Make and Send Suggestions action, and in both Business_writing and Document _preparing there is automatic dispatch of events such as when a policy document is started, and when it is finished. These interactions have corresponding behaviours in the Managing role.

The Doing component is the target for all changes, including the one that sets up the process in the first place. The actual way that this is done is not using an interaction in the conventional sense of a message-passing channel, but specific to the technology adopted. The effect of this is to integrate the management control process with the operational process. The application of change to the operational process is through the IT system's coordination layer.

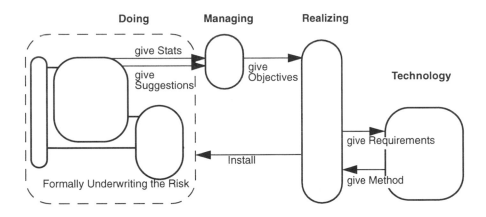

Fig. 9.7 The Model of Method for P2E Adapted to Control the FUR Process

9.4.4 The Combined Model of Method

The model of method for P2E comprises the roles of Managing, Realize, Technology, and it is linked to the model of the FUR method by interactions to pass suggestions, give statistics, and change Doing. The combination is expressed in Figure 9.7.

This combined model is now ready for transforming into an active model, in exactly the way as was described in Chapter 8. Once installed, the model will not only guide participants in the operational process, but concurrently with this, a part of the model will be guiding the manager and process modeller as they go about adapting the model to needs arising from considerations of state and need.

9.4.5 Recapitulation

The aim of this example is to provide IT support that will help real-life underwriting managers deal with one very important aspect of their responsibilities: that of ensuring that the operational process is always optimal. We have decided that the manager can achieve the goal of satisfying business objectives using the operational process. It can be done by enacting certain activities which can be structured as a process model. Now these activities could be defined in an ad hoc model of method, but matters become easier if we have at hand a generic model which can be adapted to the needs of the manager, and which has the potential to structure the future evolution of the operational process.

This generic process is P2E. Not only does it save us from inventing a structure from scratch, but using it gives us further distinct advantages. These are as follows:

• It encourages us to keep the models for our operational processes in a library in a generic form.
• It facilitates the building up of complex processes from simpler components.
• It facilitates the inheritance of methods from higher levels in the organization, passing them on to lower levels.
• It facilitates reuse of process fragments.
• It is implementable, so the technological support offered to professionals engaged in operational processes can also be offered to those engaged in managing processes.

P2E represents a way of integrating the managing process with the operational process, so making the former more responsive to the latter, and the latter more responsive to the former.

We have set up a process model to support coordination by means of which the operational process can be maintained in some optimal state, and have integrated this model with that of this operational process. The goals for the underwriting manager and the structure of P2E were brought together in a model of method. The FUR method model was slightly adapted to provide activities which would furnish needed information to the managing role, and both methods integrated in a single active model.

What do participants such as the Underwriter get out of it? It might be the knowledge that the Underwriting Manager has up-to-the-minute information on what is happening, leading to improved decision-making; the facility to have process inconsistencies dealt with by the Underwriting Manager. It might be that if Underwriters find that they have inadequate time to carry out necessary risk assessments, means can be found for improving the retrieving and presenting the risk data.

What do Underwriting Managers get out of it? They have a better awareness of process state because of the run-time links. If there is a sudden rush of business (or a lull) they can respond as appropriate. There is a common understanding about what is going on; more fruitful discussion on the basis of value-free process models, there is faster response to any emerging need for change; the change process is a normal process, so it is less disruptive and it will become a more normal part of business routine. This will allow more attention to be paid to non-routine change. All changes will be based on the generic model of the process, so maintenance will be easier and software will be maintainable for longer.

With the enacting model implemented, and the broker, underwriter and administrator going about their tasks guided by coordination from the active model, how exactly is change brought about? The following section describes such a scenario.

9.4.6 Evolution

There are two features which distinguish evolution in a system or process from simply change itself. One is the relevance of the earlier form, or structure, or function of the system to the new one. Evolution is always based on the earlier form. The change is achieved by altering that form in some way. When we refer to evolution, we understand a series of related changes, a part of the ongoing flux which allows the system to continue to suit its environment even though the latter is changing, but, most importantly, *not* becoming more complex in so doing. We might expect complex requirements to lead to a complex system. But if change is handled badly, the end result can be a system which really addresses a simple set of requirements, but which has become a very complex system indeed. Such systems are difficult to understand, difficult to maintain, prone to errors, and prone to the situation where solving one problem propagates more problems. This can come about if the changes to the system are not implemented with a view to minimizing complexity, and results in a shortened useful life of the system.

The second feature is that of feedback. By *feedback*, we mean that some parts of the outputs of a system are utilized to control that output. Part of the output is manipulated and fed back as one of the inputs, or used to vary the inputs to the process. This is the way that the system can detect difference between what it is doing and what is desired of it. If we support feedback then we can support this goal-seeking process.

How do these features help the manager to control the operational process? They help because the defined thread of the evolution activity always makes reference to the library of generic methods. This encourages the practice of making changes in the most appropriate domain of process – for example in that of model definition if all future occurrences of the process have to be changed, or in the enactment domain if the currently active occurrences of the process have to be changed. It also encourages the inheritance of methods, i.e. it is then possible for an organization to have available certain standard methods at hand when new methods are being constructed. Obviously pressures of time and money may require that, from time to time, some changes must be implemented on an ad hoc basis. The trade-off between unstructured change and quick implementation, and evolutionary change and longer implementation can be assessed taking into account both the short-term and long-term interests of the business.

By referring to Figure 9.7, we can follow through a typical iteration of evolutionary change. It begins with the feedback of information made available from the enacting model of the operational FUR process. Statistics are generated and made available to the manager as individuals work on-line and are connected through an IT system. These are real-time views of activity. From time to time, members of PEF team might send complaints and suggestions about their process: things that ought to be done, different ways of doing things, things that are wrong with the model, etc. They do this by the Make and Send Suggestions activity. On the basis of these, and possibly, in addition, reflecting on some environmental influences (such as change in state legislation), the underwriting manager can initiate periodic change to the operational process.

This is done by first of all formulating new objectives for the FUR process incorporating the requirements arising from considerations of performance statistics and apparent inconsistencies. Referring to the generic model in Figure 9.7, these are dispatched to be dealt with in the Realizing role. Here, the process modeller can translate these objectives into more technical requirements. The Technology role has responsibility for finding a method to meet these requirements. This role provides the process modeller with a way of finding an existing model, or creating a new one. The activity of Select Method might involve searching a database of models and model fragments to find one which matches the requirements most closely. If none exists, the action of Develop Method can be used to create a new one. Of course Technology also has the responsibility for maintaining a repository of models, or indeed maintaining access to some external repository.

In Realizing, the selected generic method is adapted for the specific details of the manager's objectives and the organization into which it is going to be implemented. The strategy for implementation will be decided. It will probably not be possible to implement these changes simply by removing the old model and substituting the new one, so the sequencing and timing of changes to be applied will be important and need careful consideration. The last phase is the actual changing of the active model of the FUR process to reflect the desired evolution, and in such a way that the enacting process model is at all times in a consistent state. This may mean the modelling and enaction of a transient change process, to ensure that changes are applied to specific instances in specific sequences with established fall-back states if unexpected failures arise. The Install arrow indicates change of behaviour in the Doing component from an existing version of the FUR model to a newer one.

Of course while all this is going on, the work of the PEF team continues, statistics continue to be collected, and suggestions continue to be made. In fact this illustrates how P2E can be used to evolve an existing process. The same mechanism can be used to install a new process and this is described in the following section.

9.4.7 Using P2E to create a process

We have said that evolution is change based on an earlier form. Thus the creation of a process model is not, strictly speaking, evolution. However, in our context the process by which an existing model is evolved is similar and P2E can be utilized to create a model ab initio. In this case we start off with a Doing that is empty. Creating a process first of all implies that the manager becomes aware of the opportunity or problem that can be addressed by using an active model. This awareness can come from many sources including ideas from people involved in existing processes, ideas from outside, or a visionary organization strategy. This notion is made somewhat more rigorous by establishing it as an objective to be addressed by the active model. The idea is that if we can define a process model intended to satisfy these objectives, then enacting it will in fact realize the objectives, and so solve the initial problem.

In discussing how to create a model, we shall use the same example as before. The prime difference between the use of P2E to evolve a model, and P2E to create one, lies in the way that the objectives are established. In the last case, the new objectives were based on some analysis of feedback from the performing process – automatic collection of statistics, and ad hoc messages regarding issues of concern from staff. As mentioned earlier, there are other sources of issues of concern, and these are external, ranging from say changes in legislation, through the results of market research, to emerging awareness of competitors' initiatives. These kinds of issues have to be addressed by the manager in an informal way, but the outcome of such an analysis is the same; a statement of objectives. For a new process, this is the only source of information available upon which objectives can be based, as there is no operational process in existence to provide feedback at that time.

This objective can be refined in Realize as before, a method sought to address it, then the method adapted for the detail of the objectives and organization. In this case, installing it is not simply a matter of changing an existing active model in an operational environment. Human, machine and software resources, with appropriate capabilities, have to be mobilized and made available and to be capable of being associated with the roles of the model of method. The physical environment has to be created before the process model can be installed and enacted. There have to be people and desks, network servers and PCs, people to maintain and support them, the IT system incorporating the active model must be installed, the PCs catalogued. People may have to be trained – in simple IT skills as well as any specifically associated with the process. With this in place, the process model enaction can be started up and bound to real users. Individuals can then log in, open their system roles, and commence working in the process environment, accepting the business, booking, preparing policies and so on, generating feedback for the managing part of the process

So we have shown P2E in its role as a managing process, creating and evolving an enacting process under management control. We will now discuss the use of P2E as an empowerer – as a facilitator, rather than as a definer, of process solutions.

9.5 A Role as a P2E

So far in this book a role has been described in terms of specific activities that can be undertaken by an agent – be it an individual, a team, or a department. However, it is often the case that it is not possible to define a role explicitly at the outset – a project type of activity is like this. At the beginning of a project, there is an awareness of the general shape of its process, but much of the detail does not get filled in until some way into the execution, or unfolding, of the project. In fact for large projects, this filling in is a continuous activity lasting almost as long as the project itself. There are two main reasons for this. First, there is the need to commence productive activity as early as possible. Secondly, the project organization has to learn about and understand all the implications of its objectives before it is in a position to prescribe activity needed to address these selfsame objectives. This might suggest that we cannot define a model for a project. In fact we can, in this case we can substitute a P2E. The only requirement is that the goals of the P2E can be defined, and the high level inputs and outputs identified as the project unfolds, so new methods can be found and implemented before they are needed for enactment.

As with a project, so, at the other extreme, with an individual. For many more demanding activities it is unacceptable to be explicit about the activity that is to be undertaken. In many cases a statement of objectives together with some policies is wholly sufficient for suitably skilled agents to produce satisfactory deliverables. The risk to not attaining goals is managed, not by defining the specific activities that must be undertaken, but in matching the skills and experience of the individual to the task. In this case, the specific activities needed to achieve a goal are defined by the individuals themselves, and just as design engineers have an armoury of techniques at their disposal, so the individual users can have access to a range of pre-defined processes, which they can select as they see fit. The difference from the use of P2E as a constraining control process is that in this case the subject process is seen as remote from the control process, using different agents, whereas in an empowerment situation, the subject process is tightly bound to its managing process, and there is only one agent.

A possible use can be seen in the role Document Preparing (referred to in Figure 9.6). This has a fixed set of activities allowing documents to be prepared in-house or externally. There is no provision for, for example, doing part of the work in-house and part by sub-contract. In fact we can ask if is it really necessary to specifically define the activities of the role? If we used a P2E then we could make available a number of methods for preparing documents, and also the facility of constructing ad hoc processes for dealing with unusual situations. The library of methods would be available via the associated Technology inherited from the parent, the domain of Doing could in fact be fully reflexive. The net effect is that we do not have to specify exactly how each particular document will be prepared. That decision can be left until the appropriate moment in the process and, if none are found to be suitable, a new one could be developed, or assembled, implemented and used. We then have a powerful empowering mechanism. The precise methods to be adopted being left to some individual with local responsibility, with support available when needed to develop or assemble new methods.

The methods available thus represent the degree of autonomy which is given with Document Preparing. Constraints are represented by a limited range of methods, whilst autonomy is represented by many and by the ability to generate new methods. The kind of restriction on method would be the kind of restriction imposed by the need to adhere to organization policies, and also the need to ensure that process activity elsewhere was not adversely impacted.

9.6 Conclusion

In present day organizations, most IT-supported processes exist in isolation. They have been designed and installed to deal with specific workflow-type problems and the issues of process interaction and long-term evolution have not been addressed. The fact is that these IT systems will have to evolve if the business is going to evolve and, if it is going to evolve it will have to be managed. Evolution can be supported by means of an active process model. Such a model could contain the complex network of operational processes and managing processes, and furthermore model the coordinations between them.

This chapter has explained and demonstrated how the evolution of an enacting process model can be brought about by integrating it with another process model, the meta-process model. The use of such models as P2E, or some similar structure, is absolutely essential to address the problem of legacy systems, the penalties of locking-in business process into IT systems are now becoming known. Experience with the growing problems of such legacy systems serves to indicate that even processes initially thought of as simple, sequential, stable (unlikely to change), and conflict-free, may themselves become legacy systems over the years as new methods, new technologies change the way that objectives can be achieved.

The relation of the meta-process model to the model of the operational process has been made clear, and an example has been described of just how P2E can be adapted to specific needs of the manager and of the operational process.

As well as supporting the evolution of a process through its active model, P2E also supports the creation of that active model, and P2E can itself be represented as an active model. It can thus be enacted and guide users or participants in the creation and the evolution of their operational process models.

The potential advantages of using a P2E in integrating managerial processes with the operational process are many and include: a better integration of the concerns of management and the concerns of operations; real-time status information; evolutionary change rather than ad hoc change; better consistency between model and real world, a much longer system life. It is a way of supporting the co-evolution of business and its information system.

THINGS TO DO

- What concerns of management *cannot* be addressed through a process model?
- Technology deals with determining process models suitable for addressing the objectives set by Managing, either by reusing an existing definition, adapting one, or creating a new one. What kind of information systems would be useful in Technology?
- Think of project managing in terms of P2E. What different sources of feedback can you imagine which might lead to changes in the project process?
- P2E is a particular view of problem solving in an organizational context. Is it relevant in say for the clinical process, where the challenge is a) to diagnose the illness in a patient, and b) to treat the illness so diagnosed?
- If we establish an evolution process based on say P2E, do you think it important for that process to be able to evolve itself?

10
Process Support Technology

Our process approach to business information systems is not based on a specific technology. It enables organizations to understand their processes, and to exploit this understanding through systems which are aligned with organizational needs. It does not go beyond this to presume a specific technological panacea. However, technology can be part of the solution as well as part of the problem. As well as taking a process approach to the design of business information systems, it is also possible to have systems which are themselves process-based. In this chapter we specifically look at technology which is based on the notion of supporting processes. Our ideal technology would enable a clear mapping between the goal and method models drawn at the design stage and the active model. It would offer excellent facilities for integrating other software tools to the active model, and include the ability to respond to change by offering support for evolving active models.

10.1 Introduction

Chapter 8 described the final stage in the OPM method: developing information systems which are matched to the business processes they support. Active models were identified as providing a coordination layer within a broader systems architecture. There was an emphasis on developing adaptable systems, a theme which Chapter 9 extended in advocating systems which evolved in a managed fashion. As we seek to develop a good match between an organization's processes and its information systems, these two chapters represent the organizational *pull*. In this chapter we switch perspective and consider the technology *push*. What features make a technology suited to developing active models, a coordination layer, and evolvable systems?

Our aim is to include a process-aware component within our IT architecture. By embedding a process model in an IT system, we can use the model to coordinate the agents, both the people and the other IT systems, involved in the process. The model becomes an active model, changing as the state of the process changes, and providing appropriate signals to coordinate the behaviour of the agents.

In developing such an active model component the technology available is one important factor. We use the term process support technology to emphasise our focus on providing support for processes as a whole rather than just supporting the individual activities within those processes. Active models can be used either reactively to provide gauges which monitor the process at an appropriate level, or proactively to provide advice and control to ensure that activities are not overlooked or process integrity compromised. In an analogy with database technology, we can think of process support technology as providing facilities to describe and manipulate a collection of 'process values'.

In this chapter we will illustrate process support technology through Process*Web*. This is an exemplar: our process approach is not exclusive to this technology. The chapter therefore discusses general features of process support technology before using Process*Web* as an illustrative example. (One of the benefits of using Process*Web* is that we can show some small models in the Web pages which support this book.)

A simple, low-tech approach to process support is the process manual or wall chart. This is essentially support based on a passive model. The participants have to recognize how their current situation maps on to the manual, wall chart, etc. We could use OPM and make a selection of Conceptual Models (CMs) and RADs available to process participants. These would promote a better understanding of how an individual's work contributed to the process as a whole. The advantages of such a low-tech approach are its small initial cost and flexibility. The disadvantages are that people have to do substantial clerical work to ensure that everything goes smoothly (as exemplified by the problem situations described in Chapter 8), and the CMs and RADs can easily become out of date so reducing their usefulness.

In this chapter our emphasis will be on process support systems which are based around an active model; a model which is kept in step with the current situation. The technology to support an active model will be a computer system. This will include a language in which the model is written, and connection facilities which support the two-way mapping between the process and the real world. This means that information input by the process participants can be supplied to the model, and that feedback from the model can be communicated to the relevant participants. Without such connections the active model cannot be kept in step with the real world.

There are many ways in which computer technology can be used to support process participants. For example, the specialized databases and transaction processing systems which are used by travel agents in booking holidays and airline flights. Our interest is in generic technology which can be used to support many different processes. This means that we place emphasis on a clear, understandable mapping between the process in the real-world domain and the active model in the computer system. An understandable mapping is particularly important given our interest in being able to evolve the process support as and when the process evolves. In this chapter we will concentrate on Process*Web* as an exemplar of process support technology. This technology fits with our methodology and thus provides a convenient way of illustrating the possibilities of process support technology and the main issues. We expect that many organizations will wish to target other technologies to provide process support.

It is important to recognize that developing and using active models is more intimately connected with the process than developing and using passive models. For example, producing diagrams which capture the current insurance application process can be done quite separately from handling any particular application. Indeed, such modelling can be done by people distinct from those who handle the applications. Active models are used to provide support to the people performing the process as they are actually doing it. An active model forms a core part of the organization's serving system.

This chapter will be too general and too specific. It is too general because unlike earlier chapters, it does not discuss how to develop active models in the same depth as we discussed system models, goal models and method models. It is impossible to discuss active model development in detail without adopting a particular technology and considering how its specific strengths can be exploited. As there are several, and emerging, technologies in this area (Finkelstein et al., 1994; Lawrence, 1997) this would be inappropriate. This chapter is too specific because we do discuss Process*Web*, and its major component TeamWARE's ProcessWise Integrator, in more detail than any other technology. This is to show that our ideas have been grounded in implementation. By using Process*Web* as an illustrative proof of concept we expect to make our general comments about process support technology more comprehensible.

Process*Web* is available on the web site which accompanies this book. Interested readers can log on to Process*Web* and try out some example models. At least one of the example models will be based on the PEF corporate team discussed in Chapters 7 and 8.

10.2 Views of Process Support Technology

In the Process Design chapter, we describe how the active process model provides a coordination layer which supports interactions between users, between users and tools, and between tools and tools. The active model knits things together so that the users (process participants) are provided with an appropriate serving system, rather than just a large array of tools and files accessible from their PCs or workstations. The technology to support an active model can be divided into two parts: the facilities provided by the technology which determine the architecture of the coordination layer, and the language used to express the active model which uses those facilities. From this we can identify three distinct views on the technology:

• **The User View.** The user view deals with how a system will appear to the process participants who use it as part of their day-to-day work.
• **The Developer View.** The developer view deals with how the system appears to the process designers who will develop and evolve the active model. It may be that the users are also the developers of a system, but they will still distinguish using and developing the system.
• **The System Manager View.** The system manager view deals with how the system appears to those responsible for ensuring that it is up and running on a day-to-day basis, and for dealing with any machine or communication failures.

These different views can be summarized through Figure 10.1. Each user essentially takes a personal view of how much the system helps them to understand what is going on and to progress their work. Developers are interested in the facilities provided to make it easy to produce and update the process descriptions. A system manager is concerned with the overall scheme, in particular how easy it is for users to access the active models and the reliability and performance of the links to databases and other external tools.

10.3 Motives for an Active Model

In developing an active model our focus of attention moves from the served organizational system to the serving software system and its connections with the served system. It is therefore appropriate to review the purpose of the model. Our aim with the active model is a serving software system which better supports the organization both as it is now and in the future. The general approach is to use computer technology to take care of routine, relatively simple concerns and thereby allow people to work effectively. Computer support is often found in the augmentation of individual effort, such as in word-processors or spreadsheets. However, with the ever increasing networking, computer technology can also assist in the coordinating effort, which can consume so much of an organization's resources and be responsible for poor performance. The active model can also provide a focus to promote organizational learning. The model can provide step-by-step support to those with little experience and establish a common vocabulary to discuss problems or suggestions. The model provides a way in which best-practice can be propagated throughout an organization.

There are a number of reasons why an active model might be appropriate:

• Clerical assistance. The main benefit of an active model may be as a tireless and careful, but not intelligent, clerical assistant. This includes cases where the same data has to be entered

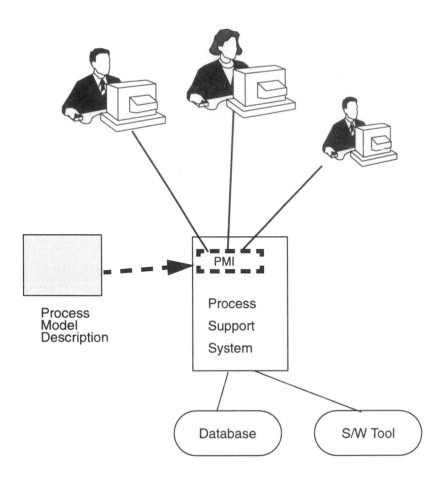

Fig. 10.1 Process Support System as a Coordination Layer

into multiple systems, perhaps in slightly different forms, where a number of documents and tools can be collected so that the participant has everything to hand, and cases where careful account needs to be kept of time spent of different activities.

• Virtual group. An active model can be used to help process participants work together effectively when they are not co-located or not all working at the same time. The active model can provide the participants with a shared understanding of the current state of the process.

• Predictability. An organization may want to use an active model to improve the predictability of a process. If an organization adopts a standard process, an active model can be used both to make that standard easier to follow than alternatives, and to gather monitoring data to improve predictions of future performance. This has been of particular interest in the software development process community, especially with the increased use of fixed price contracts.

• Conformance. There may be legal requirements or business reasons, such as ISO Quality Accreditation, which mean that an active model which performs activities automatically or ensures that they are not omitted is appropriate. This does not mean that the active model must control the process at a fine level of detail; it may give users complete flexibility within agreed bounds. Conformance may also be important where an organization has advertised response times: 'We will reply to a request for quotation within 7 working days!'

From this range it is clear that in some cases the benefits are primarily for the organization and in others the beneficiaries are primarily the process participants. This can be polarized into two styles. One, top-down, is to support the organization view of how things ought to be done, by guiding or controlling the activities of individuals so that they do their work in a way which is perceived to be correct by management. In particular, this view is concerned with coordinating activities across the organization to ensure the right things appear at the right place at the right time. The second style might be thought of as bottom-up, the assistance to individuals to help them to do their work in a certain way and work together more effectively. This might, for example mean that standardized word-processor templates are made available for use on company documents, or it might be that certain documents needed for a task are fetched automatically, rather than the worker having to call them up individually. Ideally there will be a judicious combination of both top-down and bottom-up approaches. There is an essential dilemma in process support technology. To get the full benefits from computer support you need to supply precise descriptions of what you want the computers to do; however this can implicitly restrict your own freedom of action.

The potential benefits of an active model are most obvious if there are clear dependencies between activities which the model can monitor and act upon. However, such clear dependencies are not an essential prerequisite for applying active model technology. Sometimes there is no doubt which activity must be carried out, but the dependencies on other activities are subtle and context sensitive. There is no reason why such activities cannot be supported, leaving the dependencies to be decided upon by the user at the time. An active model provides people with a shared context to talk about: the current state of a process, the process itself and how it might be improved, and how IT systems and tools contribute.

10.4 Requirements for Active Modelling Technology

Our basic scenario consists of a community of process participants being supported by an active model-based system. The active model system must be reactive. While it can send prompts to participants saying that some data is required or a deadline is approaching it can exert no control over the rate at which the participants proceed. In contrast the participants will hope (expect) the system to respond almost instantaneously to any requests which they make. The system therefore must always be able to respond to any participant, and not suspend awaiting a specific input which might never arrive. We should also note that the users of such a system could include not just the participants, who are performing the process, but also auditors, whose job it is to check that the process is done properly, and designers, who are evolving the process. From this scenario we can identify several general requirements for active modelling technology.

10.4.1 Multiple Users

The system must enable the process participants to interact with one another. Usually several of them will be connected to the system at the same time, each independently progressing their contribution to the process. There may be some participants who are in a waiting state, unable to do anything until others finish their activities and the appropriate information reaches them.

This waiting must be intrinsic in the process not imposed by the technology.

The system must have a user-interface component which allows the current state of the process to be presented, and which allows data to be communicated between the users and the model. This user interface will be personalized in the sense that participants will normally be interested in their view of the process rather than its complete details. Often the role, which an individual participant adopts within the process, is used to achieve this personalization.

10.4.2 Multiple Threads

Given multiple users and our desire for a clean mapping to the real-world process, the active model must be a concurrent system. There must be multiple threads of execution, at least one for each user. The threads mean that each user can participate in the process as it is convenient for them. This is particularly important when the process is expected to last for many days, weeks or even months, specifically when the users will make multiple connections to the system during the lifetime of the process.

10.4.3 Communication between Threads

To support collaboration between the multiple users there must be facilities for communicating between the threads. We believe that these facilities are very important, based on the importance which we attach to interactions when understanding and designing processes. These facilities will be used both to communicate data between threads, and to synchronize the threads when required. The ideal support technology would be able to cope with the full range of interaction types (synchronous, asynchronous, one-to-one, many-to-many etc.) which we might use during process design, not force an active model to be designed using only one or two interaction types.

Multiple threads may be achieved by using time-slicing, in the same way that multi-user operating systems handle multiple programs. The communications between the threads might be achieved by shared memory or message passing. The exact implementation details are not a major concern, though they may have implications on the ability of the active model technology to scale up. What is important is that the technology supports a network of connected threads, including the facilities for dynamically creating new threads and new connections between them.

10.4.4 Connections to Tools

In many situations the process participants will already be using a range of computer-based tools, such as word-processors, spreadsheets and databases. The active modelling technology should provide facilities which allow such tools to be orchestrated and presented to the user as required. This may include providing input to tools to relieve the error-prone burden of entering the same information many times, and providing parameters to configure tools as appropriate to the user's participation in the process. In the same way that we want multiple users to be handled in a flexible manner so that changes to individual participants can be accommodated easily, we also want the tool connections to be flexible to provide the ability to improve and change tools.

10.4.5 Availability

An active model-based system to support a process needs to be available for the duration of the process. Processes may last over many working days so participants need to be able to disconnect from the system, and then later reconnect and pick up from where they left off. The system should also be resilient to the computers on which it is running being stopped (or crashing) and restarted; after all some processes may last for months or even years.

The availability of active models to support a process will also depend on the ease with which models can be started when required.

10.4.6 Distribution

Among the potential benefits of this technology are virtual teams: the ability for a group of users to collaborate without having to be co-located. Through the system users can interact in the same way whether they have neighbouring offices, are independent home workers, or even on different continents (ignoring communication delays). This depends on the system's ability to support distributed connections, including the additional availability and reliability issues which this entails. Ideally the system should be able to cope with mobile users who cannot remain in permanent contact but regularly connect to re-synchronize with others.

10.4.7 Evolution

Active model technology needs to enable and improve an organization's ability to evolve its processes rather than restrict or hinder such evolution. There must be facilities which enable the active model to evolve as the process it is supporting evolves. The pressure for change will come not only from ideas on how to improve the process being supported, but also from desired changes in the relationship between the process (served system) and the technology (serving system). Anecdotal evidence suggests that the introduction of any active model process support will lead to: either suggestions of further support which could be provided by the model; or suggestions of where the technology provides over-enthusiastic and narrow support and more flexibility should be introduced; or suggestions of both types. In short the very introduction of support technology provokes accelerated co-evolution of the process and its support.

There are a couple of features which we expect to see in any system which needs to evolve. The first is incremental development. In the case of an active model it must be possible to define an additional part of the model and then bind this in with the existing system. This incremental change should not just be restricted to growing the model; removing parts of the model which are no longer appropriate is also important. The second is reflexivity: the ability for the active model to be manipulated as data. This is key to being able to provide meta-process features as described in Chapter 9 (Process Managing).

10.4.8 Relating Requirements and Views

As users, developers and system managers take different views on active modelling technology they will place different emphases on the requirements.

From the user view the key requirements will be multiple users and connections to tools. The multiple threads and communication between threads to support coordination of users will be expected, as will availability and distribution. For users the ideal is to be able to get on with the work, hardly noticing how the system makes things easier. They are also much more likely to be influenced by how effectively a particular model supports them, than the generic capabilities of the technology.

From the developer view the key requirements are multiple threads, communication between threads, evolution, connecting to tools and multiple users. The developers' prime concerns are the facilities which enable a clean mapping between the real-world process and the active model to be established and maintained.

From the system manager view the key requirements are availability and distribution. System managers require a system which is easy to install and maintain. A prime problem for system managers will be participants unable to connect to the active model. This means that how new users are introduced to the system, and new tools, will also be a concern for system managers. There are other administrative issues such as the ease of system installation, security and resource conflicts with other systems which we do not address in this chapter.

Most organizations which adopt process support technology will want to provide support for a number of their processes. This means that the support technology will provide support for a number of distinct models. A developer will normally be focused on only one model, while a system manager will often want an overall view of all the models which are being supported by the technology. A user will often have several responsibilities in the context of different models. This gives a requirement for the user interface to provide support for handling multiple models, rather than requiring users to have a separate interface for every model.

10.5 Manage Documents or Manage Workspaces

There are two broad categories of process support technologies: those which focus on managing documents which are sent between process participants, and those which focus on managing the workspace, or environment, of the participants. As with any programmable technology, these differences are more apparent to those programming the system than those using it. With sufficient programming a system designed around moving documents can appear to be managing the workspace of participants, and vice versa. Whether one approach is better than another also depends on the particular active model which is required.

10.5.1 Managing Documents

Systems which focus on managing documents are usually based on the notion of an electronic form. The notion of a business form which is passed through a chain of people, each completing their section, is quite familiar. The advantages of transforming this to an electronic form include: increased traceability, no more phoning round or rifling through in-trays to discover the whereabouts of a particular form, and automatic routing. Not only can forms be transferred from person to person quicker but sending them to people on holiday or who have just left the organization can be avoided. In addition, better integration with computer-based tools can be accomplished. (Many of these systems also have document imaging components allowing electronic versions of external documents to be attached to the electronic form.)

Central to document focused systems is the notion that the organization will have to handle many instances of each form, whether it is an overseas travel application or a mortgage request, and these instances are independent. Each process is represented by a form type and there is a central definition of how all forms of this type are to be handled. This usually consists of some kind of flow chart describing the path of the form through the organization. For each type, there will be a specific set of users who have the authority to create a new form instance. Document focused systems also tend to assume that the process is stable. (This is not surprising given the form analogy. If the process was not stable it would not be worthwhile developing a specialized form for it.) If a change is required this is achieved by creating a new form type, and retiring the old one. When new form instances are created they will follow the new definition, but existing documents will continue to behave according to their existing definition.

The concept of modelling in terms of an electronic form flowing through an organization from inception to completion has proved effective. Several organizations have reported dramatic reductions in processing time (Fischer, 1995; Lawrence, 1997). Much of this depends on the fact that forms are independent: reducing the time spent transporting forms between people can be converted directly into reduced processing time. The advantages of independent forms needs to be balanced with the inability to model interactions between them. A system which processes individual expense claims very efficiently, may provide little support for identifying any unscrupulous employees who submit two, or more, claims for the same expenses.

10.5.2 Managing Workspaces

Systems which focus on managing workspaces are usually based on a network of activities which are divided between the participants. Each user has a workspace, managed by the system, which displays what that user can do next in the context of the process. Often there will be a selection of alternatives available to the user. When a user completes an activity the system will ensure that the relevant results are transferred to the workspaces of those users waiting for them. The advantage to the user is that the workspace specializes his or her computer to the current tasks in hand, rather than offering a vast array of tools and files. In contrast with the notion of an electronic document being passed from one user to another until it is completed, the basic notion is of a community of participants collaborating to achieve a goal.

The concept of multiple instances of a process is nowhere near as fixed in workspace-focused systems. Often if there are processes which could be regarded as separate instances these will exist as sub-processes within a process which is responsible for starting the instances and maintaining connections between them. For example, an insurance handling process might include some preliminary checking or negotiation before starting a *request for quote* sub-process, and might monitor the quotes being considered for their value and business spread. In many workspace-focused systems there is the notion of having a template or generic model which is then parameterized to the current environment. Sometimes this parameterization is confined to an initial phase when the process is started; sometimes it is ongoing with later parts only being parameterized as required.

In contrast with document-based systems there is no general style of process description in workspace-focused systems. Some processes have an assembly line style where there is a fixed network of activities, linked to the participants, through which items flow. For example, a standard document review and correction process used for all project documentation. Other processes are more case-oriented with a network of connected sub-processes being created and passed between participants according to their skills and availability. (In the restricted case of one sub-process per case, this is similar to the document based style.) Other processes are organic in the sense that they can grow to an appropriate size for the task in hand. Such processes usually have a basic core, and the ability to clone this core in a standard fashion. The Process for Process Evolution is a good example of this style. While assembly-line, case-oriented and organic represent alternative styles possible with these systems, a real active model may involve a judicious combination of all three.

Most workspace systems do not assume that processes are stable and change only slowly relative to the number of instances. We have already mentioned parameterization which is used to cope with expected changes. Beyond this are the evolution facilities offered by reflexive systems where one of the activities can be to view the existing model as data, and make changes to the model. In this way a process can evolve itself, without prior knowledge of the type of changes which it might have to make.

Many current workspace-focused systems originated in the demands from the software engineering domain to support software developers in high-level, long-term creative activity. The initial focus was on the integration of tools, which was a serious problem for programmers. The notion that a quality product needs a quality process, and the idea that an ideal process would produce ideal software, led to a process view of the developers' activity whereby developers were constrained in their choice of tools (or possibly given no choice at all) so as to ensure the software was designed and implemented in a controlled manner. This stemmed from the view that the, 'effective execution of rigorously defined processes assures that an organization will behave in ways that can be predicted' (Osterweil, 1987). This position is now widely contested (Lehman, 1987) and current systems aim for flexibility, capable of providing the appropriate degree of constraint deemed to be needed in any situation.

10.5.3 Views of Document or Workspace Management

The document or workspace distinction is usually obvious from a user view. In a document focused system each user will have some sort of mail box containing a number of different documents requiring attention. If two documents have the same type then they are separate instances of a process. In a workspace-focused system each user will connect to a workspace which usually contains icons for the different activities which can be done. The user will expect items to arrive in the workspace when things need to be done, and disappear as activities are completed.

For the developer the document-focused system provides a strong paradigm of the electronic form. In many cases the ability of the developer to use a graphical tool to design new processes has made the systems widely acceptable. In a workspace-focused system the developer has more flexibility, particularly when dealing with concurrency. The cost of this greater flexibility is more programming. The systems also make different assumptions on the frequency of process change.

From the system manager view, the document or workspace distinction is largely irrelevant. There will be other aspects of individual technologies, such as their operating systems or networking requirements, which have a greater impact on how system managers classify them. In general there is a tendency for current workspace systems to be centralized with one component managing communications to and from the active model, while in document-based systems the process information is distributed over the network.

10.6 An Example Process *Web* Model

In this chapter we will use a Process*Web* model based on part of the PEF process described in Chapters 7 and 8. (There will be at least one version of this model available on the web site.) There are three roles involved: decision obtaining which is associated with a Broker, proposal logging which is associated with an Administrator, and decision making which is associated with an Underwriter. As there is a one-to-one correspondence in this case, it is often more convenient to talk about the Broker role than the decision obtaining role, although strictly Broker is the name of the agent rather than the role. In this example Role Activity Diagrams have been used as the basis for the interface to the model. A user progresses the model by selecting one of the activities from the RAD. (Figure 10.2 shows the Broker at the start of the process when *give*

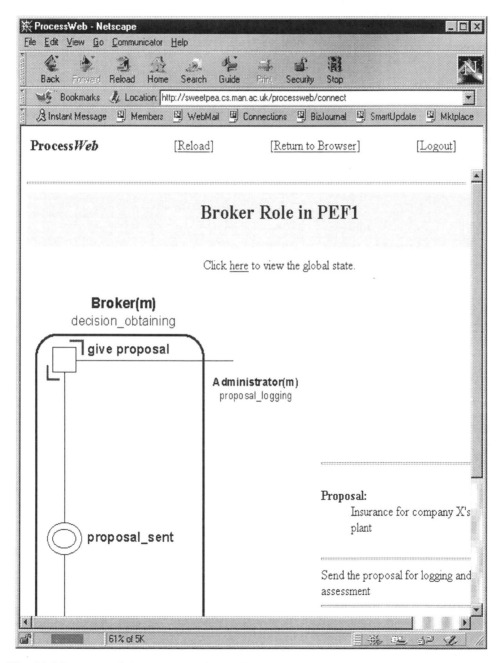

Fig. 10.2 Process*Web* Example (Broker Role)

proposal can be selected.) The state of the model determines which activities are available and these are highlighted. For example, when the model starts there is nothing which the Administrator can do until the Broker has submitted a proposal.

In this example the model is constructed so that it deals with one proposal from submission to decision. To deal with another proposal you need to create another instance of the model. This choice of creating three roles for each proposal, and the RAD interface, was adopted because the model is designed as a Process*Web* exemplar. If the PEF company were implementing a system for their regular use a different design might be more appropriate.

10.7 Generic Process Support System Architecture

The core of a process support system is some sort of process engine. This engine will run a collection of active models providing users, the process participants, with their personal view of the state of the process. As users input data, this causes the state of the active model to change and the engine to output the appropriate messages to users and tools.

The process support technology must provide a number of features which are independent of the particular models. First, there must be a language for describing the active model, and there must be some facility to load this description into the system. This will usually include the facility to make multiple instances from the same model. Secondly, there must be facilities to manage the repeated connection of users. Users need to connect to the process engine to get and update information about the processes in which they are involved. As these can last for a long time there must be facilities which enable users to disconnect from the system and later reconnect perhaps from a different computer. Thirdly, there must be facilities to allow connections with other computer tools and databases to be established. Finally there must be facilities which enable the engine to save its state in case of any machine failure, and to restart from a saved state when required.

10.7.1 Process*Web* Architecture

Process*Web* is a process support system which is designed to work across the World Wide Web. It makes use of a web server and the ProcessWise Integrator (PWI) system (Bruynooghe et al., 1994; Greenwood et al., 1992). (ProcessWise Integrator is a commercial development from earlier work in the Alvey IPSE 2.5 project (Snowdon, 1989; Warboys, 1990). In 1998 it was transferred from ICL to TeamWARE and is to be renamed TeamWARE Process Manager. ProcessWise is a registered trademark.) This means that users access the system through web browsers, with the connection and disconnection of users being handled by the standard facilities of the web server. The pages which a user gets from Process*Web* are different from standard web pages in that they are personal and they are dynamically generated. The web server acts as an intermediary, forwarding user input to the process engine (PWI) which generates the content to be displayed on the browser.

The Process*Web* system reacts to the actions of the user when they enter data into their web browser. The data may simply be a query on the current state of an enacting process, or it may change the state of the process. If the state of the process is changed, it may affect other users; such changes are propagated through the Process*Web* engine and the relevant users' displays are updated to reflect the change.

The core of Process*Web* is the ProcessWise Integrator Process Control Manager (PCM). The PCM executes models written in a process language, PML (ICL, 1996). In addition the PCM also provides facilities, accessible through the PML language, which manage the connection and disconnection of users and software tools. The PCM has no control over when connections will be established or broken. In some circumstances Process*Web* will cache the information which would otherwise be sent to a user or tool. The information can then be sent as soon as a connection is re-established. In other circumstances it is necessary for Process*Web* to report to the making and breaking of connections so that appropriate responses can be initiated.

Within the PCM there are a number of PWI *roles* connected by *interactions*. (Both Role and Interaction are primitives in PML.) The PML language distinguishes between on-line roles, which are fully described in the language and represent threads of control, and off-line roles, which represent users or software tools. Interactions are unidirectional communication channels which allow roles to exchange data. On-line roles have two basic states: waiting (for data to arrive via one or more interactions with on-line or off-line roles) and ready (data has arrived and must be processed). The PCM provides a scheduler which examines each role to determine its state. Roles in the ready state are executed for a time, after which the scheduler proceeds to the next role. When a role is executed, it will process the data which has arrived, changing the role's state and perhaps causing it to send data through another interaction. This new data may cause another role to switch from waiting to ready; changes to the state of the active models are propagated in this way. Process*Web* provides facilities which allow a user's web browser to be treated as an off-line role.

There is no specific part of PWI which is responsible for copying the current model state to stable storage (a database or file on disk) to guard against machine failure. The PCM makes use of a persistent store which means that data (in this case our active model) is handled in the same manner whether it lasts for 10 milliseconds or 10 years. The scheduler periodically ensures that a complete and consistent copy of the system is written to disk, so that even if the computer running the PCM crashes, no communication between threads in the PCM will be lost in transit. (Users might see their user interface return to a previous state if the last data they sent had not arrived before the crash.) This means that when developing an active model in PML, there is no need to manage explicitly the conversion to and from a file or database format.

One of the key parts of a process support system is how the process is divided between the process participants. In Process*Web* this is done by allocating off-line roles to process participants. Process*Web* allows a model to create and destroy dynamically any number of off-line roles, and also manages their allocation to actual process participants. Most off-line roles are unbound when they are created, that is the off-line role is not allocated to any Process*Web* user. An unbound role must be explicitly acquired by a user (currently there are no security/authentication procedures – any user may acquire any role). The role can be relinquished later, which will return it to the unbound state. A role may only be allocated to one user at a time. If two users request the same unbound role, the role will only be allocated to one of them. While at any time a role can only be allocated to one user, a model can make a role viewable. This allows other users to see the state of a role but not interact with it.

Figure 10.3 shows a Process*Web* user's browser page. This is the page which allows the user to look around the system and to decide on which role to interact with next. At the top there are some standard links. Next there is some information about the model in focus. In this example the model PEF1 contains three roles, one of which (proposal logging) is allocated to this user, Brian. Below that is a list of the active models in the system which a user can use to change the model in focus.

The first version of Process*Web* had a browser page which just gave a list of roles. This proved hard to manage as the list grew in length. The version shown in Figure 10.3 only shows the roles for the model in focus, and there are options for filtering this list.

At the bottom of the browser page (not shown in Figure 10.3) is a link to the Process*Web*

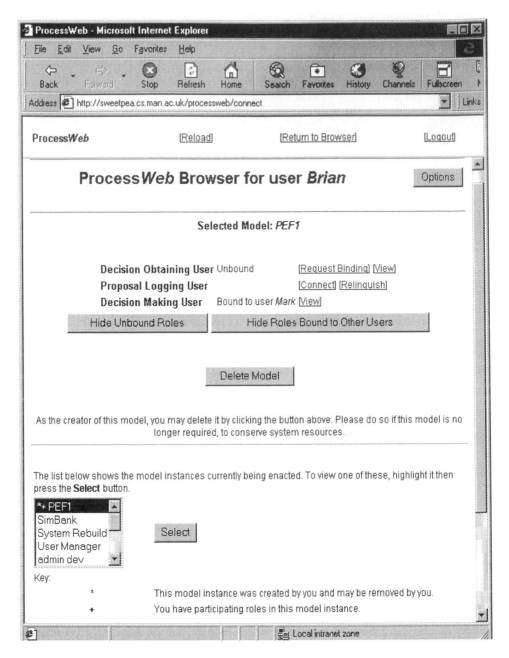

Fig. 10.3 Process*Web* User Brian's Browsing View

library. The library contains a number of descriptive models (i.e. models written in PML to describe a process) which may be instantiated by any user. Creating an instance of one of these models transforms the descriptive model into an active model and adds it to the list of active models. Users may then select the new model instance and bind to the roles it has created.

10.8 From RAD to Process*Web* Model

In this chapter we will not go into details of the PWI's PML language which we use when writing active models for Process*Web*. Some examples and the code will be available on the Web pages supporting this book for those who are really interested.

PML is a typed, concurrent language which supports multiple users, connections to external tools, and is developed in an incremental fashion. There are four principal classes in the language: entities (records), activities (procedures), roles (encapsulations of data and behaviour) and interactions (communication channels). For the designer the active model to support a process is a PML application. As with any application in a class-based language, the developer must not only define the classes, but also the particular instances of those classes which are to be present in the application.

The fact that PML uses roles as its main construct for structuring a model makes it easier to establish a close relationship between a Role Activity Diagram and the corresponding PML code.

While a RAD, such as the one in Figure 10.4, is a useful way of describing a process, it does

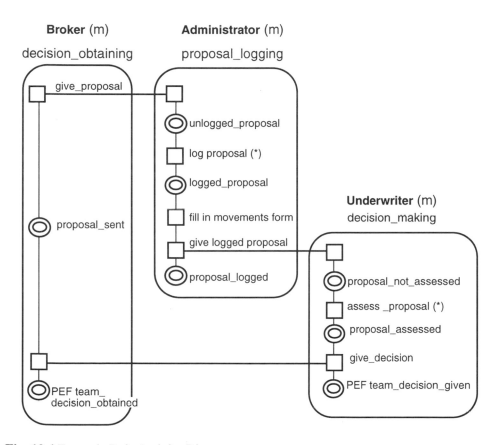

Fig. 10.4 Example Role Activity Diagram

not by itself contain enough information to enable us to develop a useful active model.

There is no detail of the data entities given in a RAD. From our example we can conclude that a proposal is passed. We will have to decide how this will be represented within our active model. One alternative is to have a data structure within the model which represents the proposal. Another alternative is to have the active model contain a reference which can be used to identify the proposal when required. The choice of data structure to represent a proposal is affected by the choice of how the active model deals with multiple proposals. In our example, where a new set of three roles is created for each proposal, the proposal could be identified by the name given to the active model instance.

The RAD also gives no detail of the user interface which is required. Process*Web* has a very flexible user interface, and we must decide what the model should present to the user, and how it should be done; of course, this has implications for the design of the process model. For example, consider the Administrator role. This is a linear sequence of activities, triggered by the arrival of a proposal. We must decide what level of detail to provide to the user: this might range from a simple prompting whenever data is required (i.e. the process is controlled by the model), to a display of all possible options, and having the process model refuse inappropriate actions. If we opt for the former, how do we ensure that the user knows what state the process is actually in? It may confuse the user if too much activity is performed automatically. Should we provide on-line help? If we opt for the latter, how do we ensure that activities are performed in an appropriate order? This may require changes to the process model. A Process*Web* model may adopt any strategy within this continuum at the choice of the developer. Also, more detail is needed because of the specifics of PML interactions. In RADs interactions are not directional; they are synchronous and can involve more than two roles. This is quite different from the uni-directional, asynchronous, many-to-one interactions in PML. If the precise RAD interaction semantics are required then this can be programmed using several PML interactions.

An active model must deal with some activities at a finer level of granularity than the RAD model, so development time goes into tasks which are not modelled at all at the RAD level. These may include parsing and interpreting data from the user, updating the state of the role and ensuring that the user's display is consistent with the state of the model. What happens if the user mis-types something? Should we allow users to enter information repeatedly, and only proceed when they confirm their input in some way?

The Process*Web* developer may also adopt a framework (e.g. the P2E) to allow the active model to support its own evolution.

An implementation of the Administrator role is shown in Figure 10.5. The user interface in this case is designed to show the mapping between the RAD model and the active model. The state of the model is depicted by a marker which highlights the activities which are appropriate in that state. In the case depicted, the proposal has arrived, so 'log_proposal' is the only appropriate activity. This is a sub-role (as indicated by the *), so when a user selects it a new RAD for the sub-role will be presented, with the current state highlighted in the same way.

10.8.1 PML Facilities

The previous section discussed the issues involved in moving from a RAD model, which describes a process, to an active Process*Web* model which can be used to support it. We can now give a more general overview of the features of PML. PML is an object based language; models are composed of classes. A developer can define new model specific sub-classes of the three main classes: Role, Entity and Action. The model is expressed in terms of instances of these classes, and instances of Interactions, which are not sub-classed.

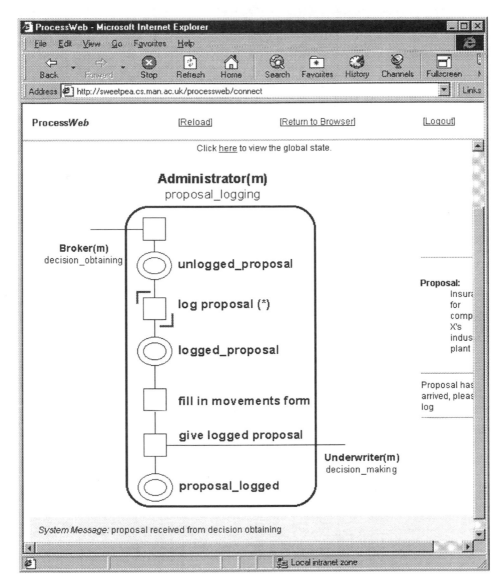

Fig. 10.5 Process*Web* Example (Administrator)

Roles

These objects represent on-line roles. Each role instance in the model is a separate thread of execution with its own local data and its own independent behaviour. A role may interact with other on-line or off-line roles via interactions. Off-line roles are represented using a special subclass of Role: Agent. An Agent is only available for communication when the external application or user is connected to it via a server running outside PWI.

Entities

These objects are used to structure data. They are similar to records or structures in imperative programming languages. The primitive types (Bool, Int, Real, String) are defined as sub-classes of Entity. The PWI PML language also provides two forms of data aggregation: collections (indexed by integer) and tables (indexed by String). Both forms are typed.

Actions

Actions are procedures. They are a way of abstracting behaviour. Like roles, actions have their own local data and behaviour. However they do not have a separate thread; they are executed by the thread of the role which called them. Parameters are used to pass values when calling an action, and to return results when an action call completes. These parameters are referenced by name rather than position. PML provides a number of standard actions and Process*Web* extends this set. Developers can then define further actions which are specific to the active model. In the PEF example we may use a user-defined action to model a sub-role.

Interactions

Interactions are used to support communication between role instances. Conceptually there is an interaction class, but this does not concern the developer. The developer does not define new interaction classes, just creates interaction instances. Interactions are asynchronous, buffered and many-to-one. When an interaction is created two values are returned: one *giveport* for sending data and one *takeport* for receiving it. As the interaction is asynchronous, a role giving a data entity to an interaction does not wait for the message to arrive at another role before continuing. Interactions buffer their data so the role can send a second message before the first has been received from the interaction. The many-to-one facility is achieved by the ability to clone the giveport of an interaction.

One key feature of interactions is that giveports and takeports can themselves be included in the messages passed through interactions. To achieve synchronous communication between two roles, the sending role creates a reply interaction and includes its giveport in the message it sends (by defining a structured entity class to hold it). After sending, the role waits for a confirmation message by listening to the takeport of the reply interaction. When the message arrives at the receiving role, it must send a confirmation message through the giveport contained within the message.

Instance Creation

One of the features of PML is that dynamic instance creation is part of normal behaviour. There are specific PML actions for creating new role instances (*StartRole*) and new interactions (*NewInteraction*). Entity values are created by value constructors and Actions are only instantiated on invocation and last for as long as their execution. Thus Interaction instances are represented by the giveport and takeport, role instances by a pointer, entity instances by their value. Action instances are not represented at all as they are not values in the language. This instance creation means that a PML active model is more dynamic than any diagrammatic process representation. New roles and interactions can be created as required. Interactions can be passed across interactions so that the network of inter-role connections is dynamic, not static. A rather poor analogy is the difference between a mobile phone network and the static wires of a traditional phone network. Process*Web* also allows off-line role instances, which enable users and tools to connect to the PCM, to be created and destroyed dynamically.

The converse of instance creation is instance termination. Role instances must be explicitly destroyed. Interaction instances may be destroyed implicitly when a Role instance terminates or may be explicitly disconnected. Entity instances are destroyed by simply discarding them.

User and Tool Communication

In PML the communication with users and tools outside the process engine is performed through interactions in just the same way as communication between roles within the process engine. In the case of Process*Web* the communication with users is through their web browsers. When a user inputs data, this arrives in the model through an interaction as if it had been sent from another role. (Figure 10.6 is at the point where the insurance underwriter has typed in

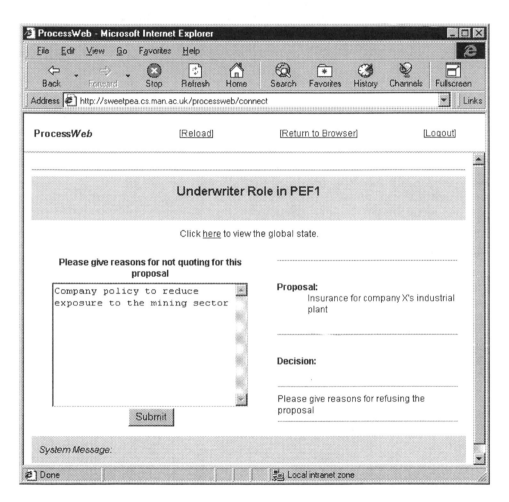

Fig. 10.6 Process*Web* Example (Underwriter)

some information and is about to send it to the model.) The web browser is an off-line role. To interact with the web browser the process engine needs to establish a connection with it. There is an intermediary program which manages this connection. It takes data, supplied by the user through the standard web common gateway interface (CGI) facilities, and transfers it to process engine in PML format. Similarly it takes the HTML, which is sent by the process engine, and ensures that this will be appropriately interpreted as new web pages or frames. The approach to communicating with a software tool such as a database is essentially the same. The database is an off-line role, with an intermediary program which handles the conversion of data between formats and the invoking of the appropriate database functions. The net effect is that a role in a model can communicate with the database as if it were another role. ProcessWise Integrator provides facilities for creating these intermediary programs. There are also facilities in PML for handling errors reported by these intermediary programs.

Incremental Development

PML includes a number of features which support incremental development. There is access to the compiler within the language. This enables one process to manipulate another process description as text, and then call the compiler to add the new class definitions to its existing ones. The compiler is given a set of class definitions which form the environment for its compilation, so the process description can be a small modification or addition to be added to the existing process. All the ProcessWeb models are added into the system in this way. Each model is a set of classes. Initially there are just the basic ProcessWeb classes which provide general facilities such as exchanging data with web browsers, and binding users to roles. A number of PML class definitions are then compiled, extending this initial set. These PML class definitions are often loaded from a file, but they could be produced by another ProcessWeb model or typed in directly by a user. The compilation will check the syntax of the definitions and also check consistency between all the classes now in the set. Once all the PML definitions have been successfully compiled the model is now ready to be enacted. It will either be started or placed in the library so that instances can be started on demand.

The compiler accepts PML class definitions as text and converts then into their enactable form. There are also facilities for doing the reverse: taking a PML role instance and obtaining its class definition as text (that is, a PML String), and also the text definitions of other classes to which it refers. These abilities to convert between textual process descriptions and their enactable form is a key part of being able to define flexible meta-processes where one process manipulates another.

PML also has facilities which enable a meta-process to manipulate the data and behaviour of role instances. These enable the meta-process to make changes which were not foreseen when the role class was written and compiled. Together these incremental development features are key to the ability to create process models as reflexive systems, that is systems which can refer to themselves, and thus control their own evolution.

10.9 ProcessWise Integrator User View

When the earliest version of PWI, then called IPSE 2.5, was implemented it was easy to describe what it looked like; there was one user interface and a set of pre-defined *UserActions* in the PML language. This gave a simple, uniform appearance to models, but was restrictive. As models were developed there was an increased demand not to be restricted by this proprietary user interface but to allow more specialized user interfaces.

The original user interface server is illustrated in Figure 10.7. When users connected to the system they were given a role agenda window with one entry for every role currently allocated to them. Selecting a role from the role agenda brought up the action agenda for that role. The entries in the action agenda were the user's current choices in the context of that role. When the user selected an action agenda entry a further window might be brought up displaying or requesting information. This user interface was constructed automatically from the state of the model and parameters given to the pre-defined UserActions.

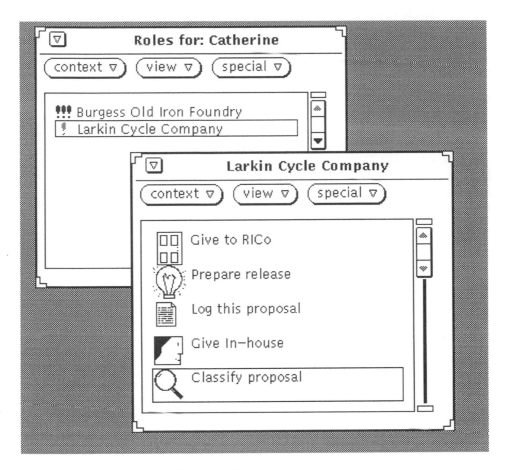

Fig. 10.7 ProcessWise Original User Interface

With the advent of Windows on PCs and tools such as Visual Basic, users became far more demanding. The PWI approach to this was to allow users to develop their own interfaces using Visual C++, and later Java. Rather than a general interface style which was used by all models, interfaces could now be model-specific. This gives users what they want but can be harder for developers since the mapping between the user interface and the model is no longer standard but may vary from one model to another. Developers may have to include considerable code in the model if fine-grain control of the user interface is required.

Process*Web* can be seen as a development of PWI based on using standard Web pages as the user interface. Initially the user interfaces developed have only used simple facilities of the standard HTML language used for writing Web pages. However, as Web developments continue there will be further opportunities to develop new interface styles.

10.10 Other Process Support Technologies

ProcessWise Integrator (PWI) is not the only process support technology. Process Weaver and Staffware are two other systems of similar maturity. Process Weaver is also a workspace type of system but does not place as much emphasis on evolution as PWI. Staffware is a document type, workflow system.

10.10.1 Process Weaver

The Process Weaver (Fernström, 93) toolset is aimed at giving process support to software development teams. It includes tools for both model development and model enactment. The system has its origins in the European Software Factory (ESF) project. One of the principal aims of the project was to enable effective communication between the users and tools involved in software development. The project developed a reference framework which classified tools involved in the production of software according to the way they communicated. A key motivation was to provide hooks to the tools which an organization was already using, such as project management tools and software configuration management tools. Like several other tools designed with software development processes in mind, Process Weaver has adapted to support business processes in general rather than software processes in particular.

System Architecture

The key element of the Process Weaver architecture is the software bus which is used to connect components. When a component connects to the software bus it provides a filter which identifies the types of messages of interest to it. This provides very flexible connections since the component sending a message does not need to identify specifically the component which will handle it. Components can be replaced or updated as and when required without major upheaval. The software bus is provided by a Broadcast Message Server (BMS). The BMS can itself be treated as a component, and there is one local BMS for each user carrying such components as the user's agenda UI. The models supported by a Process Weaver system are structured in terms of projects. The BMS can be shared by all projects but care must be taken to avoid unintentional interference caused by separate projects having the same message types.

Developer View

The developer does not work directly in the underlying Process Weaver process modelling language but through a series of views. These views are supported by graphical tools. At the highest level a process is described in terms of a hierarchy of activity types. This is done using the method editor. This is an *is-part-of* hierarchy. For example a software maintenance process might be broken down into three sub-processes: management, implementation, and review. These are functional components: defined only by input, output, and associated roles. There is no sequencing information.

The next level is concerned with *cooperative procedures* which are the implementations of the activities described at the method level. The control flow between activities is described using a transition net, a formalism of extended Petri Nets. For the non-leaf activities in the method description, the control flow between the activities at the next level of decomposition is described. For the leaf activities, control flow is described between *process steps*. A process step is a primitive part of a process – a user activity which is not broken down into its constituent parts. In Process Weaver this is termed a *work context* and consists of: a description of the work to be done, information about the data and tools which may be used, and control buttons to provide status information.

User View

Process Weaver users have an agenda tool on their desktop. This allows them to access the *work contexts* that are currently assigned to them. The agenda is an addition to the users' environment, and does not interfere with their normal interaction with other tools. The normal pattern of events will be for a user to select a work context and activate it. After completing the required work the user indicates this, by pressing a completion button, so that Process Weaver can schedule any further work contexts which had a dependency on the one just completed. The agenda can also be used to delegate a work context to another user, or if allowed, to be deleted.

10.10.2 Staffware

Staffware, an example of a workflow (Lawrence, 1997) management tool of a similar vintage to ProcessWise Integrator, is a convenient exemplar to use to contrast the workflow and process approaches. (Staffware is the registered trademark of Staffware Plc.) The general background for these tools is office automation. It was recognized that many processes were defined in terms of forms which were completed by a variety of different people. Often using paper forms causes problems. They can be lost or mislaid, and the speed with which they can be transferred between people is limited. By having a computer-based form, the location of each form could be tracked, and they could be transferred around an organization almost instantaneously. The term *procedure* is often used to reflect the fact that the organization usually had strict guidelines on the processing of forms.

System Architecture

The system is viewed as a network of nodes, all having equal status. A node is equivalent to a *shell* of an organizational role, the behaviour of the role is defined in the procedures. For each procedure, one node is designated as the *host* node, from where the procedure is started and stopped, and the others associated with this procedure are then *slaves*. The host node holds details of the procedure, and stores all data relating to cases being processed under that procedure. The slave in a procedure can start cases of the procedure and receive work items (i.e. steps). Communication of documents between nodes is handled by email facilities.

When an event takes place at a slave node, this is communicated to the host. The host interprets the procedure definition, and sends the consequent event to the appropriate node. Within a Staffware installation, developing scripts to interface between Staffware and other corporate applications and databases is usually seen as a system configuration task rather than an integral part of process model development.

There are four different classes of user, in order of increasing authority: user, manager, procedure definer, and system administrator. Roughly, both user and manager correspond to this chapter's user view, procedure definer to the developer view, and system administrator to the system manager view.

Developer View

A Staffware procedure is composed of steps (sometimes referred to as Document for Response and Action). Each step is composed of an addressee, a document, an action, and optionally a deadline. The action parts describes what has to happen to the document when the current addressee (user) is finished with it, usually process another step, or stop. Thus one step can spawn other steps and the sum of all the steps is a procedure. The addressee is usually a role, identifying the group in the organization with the skills and authority for the step, rather than a specific individual. Often the assigning of users to roles is performed at an organization level rather than for individual procedures.

The basic scheme is that the addressee will complete part of the document and indicate that they have completed the step. This basic form-filling capability can be extended by developing scripts to run other applications, or invoke transactions with corporate databases. The mapping from role to user for the addressee part of a step is handled by the system which knows the roles assigned to users, which users are currently available and their current workloads.

User View

All users are provided with a basic menu which provides a mailbox for receiving work items (steps), email, notepad, and personal database. In addition, users can start cases of procedures, depending on the particular procedure definition and authorizations. A manager user can, in addition, obtain status and historical information about procedures and about individual cases of procedures.

For normal procedure-governed activity, the user selects a document from the mailbox, provides the needed data, and removes it from the mailbox. This act causes the action part of the step to be processed, and usually causes a subsequent document to appear in someone else's mailbox.

10.11 Managing, Learning and Developing

This chapter has discussed process support technology almost exclusively from the perspective of *doing* a process. That is, what makes a technology suitable for developing process-based information systems, which incorporate the notions of active models and a coordination layer. What technology is appropriate to support processes as a whole, and provide an effective match between people (served systems) and their information systems (serving systems)? The emphasis has been on the interaction theme highlighted in Chapter 2. In this section we turn to the evolution theme. Any organization which develops process-based information systems will evolve as these systems are used. It needs to consider how they will be managed, how people will learn them, and how they will be developed in the future.

As outlined in Chapter 9 the management of a process is itself a process. An active model of this meta-process can also be implemented and supported through process technology. This involves identifying the goal which the managed operational process addresses, and the feedback which will be sent from the operational process to the managing meta-process. In the context of our Process*Web* example the existing model would be the method for obtaining the PEF company decision on an insurance proposal, and an adapted P2E the meta-process. The existing model would have to be adapted to give feedback: perhaps the industry sector and the income from the proposal. The meta-process model would be able to provide information on which sectors were growing and which declining. Based on this information there might be an initiative which targets specific sectors. Alternatively, a new variant of the process might be developed so that the highest-value proposals could be given extra attention. (Note that this implies a further issue for the managing process: how to decide which proposals fall into this higher-value category.)

A Process*Web* model like the one outlined earlier in this chapter could be used by PEF as a training aid. This would allow people to act out the handling of a proposal. In such a situation the active model is synchronized with a simulated world. It would have the feel of a flight simulator or role-playing game rather than a traditional business simulation where the emphasis is on averages, event distributions, and resource utilization. The use of an active model to act out hypothetical scenarios in detail can be of value either in training new process participants, or in giving people a realistic impression of how proposed process changes would work in practice.

We can look on OPM as a process and consider how process technology could be used to support it. There might be tools to assist in the drawing of Conceptual Models and Role Activity Diagrams. If we were targeting Process*Web* as our support technology, the features for incrementally developing Process*Web* models are also relevant. We could also consider how to describe OPM as an active model to support the process as a coherent whole. Figure 10.8 shows

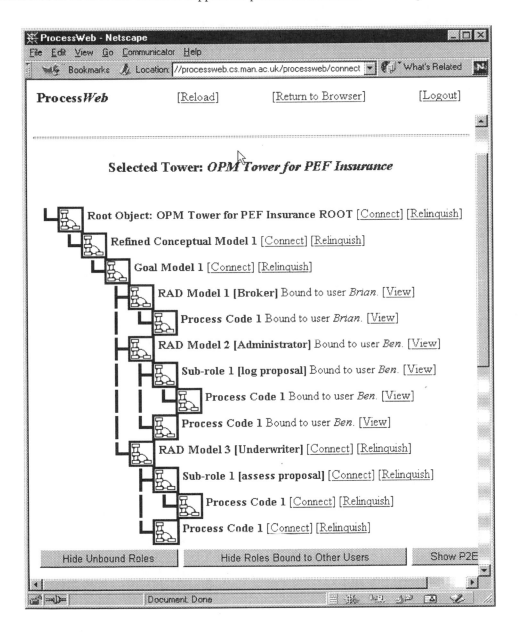

Fig. 10.8 Process*Web* Model for OPM

one possible model applied to the PEF company example outlined earlier in this chapter. This model does not capture the process of applying the OPM method in purely generic terms, it exploits the structure of the PEF process. That is rather than have one role *Develop RAD method model*, there is one for each agent, Broker, Administrator and Underwriter, identified in the goal model. Similarly, where a sub-role has been identified, a separate role has been created to deal with its development. This model is organic in the sense that while the rules for creating roles are defined, the exact number of roles depends on the particular model which is created. If the initial system model had six rather than three agents things would look quite different. This model also illustrates that it is possible for an active model to provide support at quite a coarse level. Each of the roles in this OPM process model corresponds to either a diagram or fragment of PML code. These could be modelled as having just three states: not started, in progress and finished. The Process*Web* active model would provide an overview of the structure of the model (which could itself be incomplete), a view of who is working on which parts, and a summary of how the modelling is progressing. There is no need to model in detail how one constructs a RAD diagram or writes a PML class definition.

This model of the OPM method is based on a generic design hierarchy model, which we have termed *tower* models (Greenwood et al., 1996; Yeomans, 1997). In the same way that models based on P2E have a common structure, tower models are based upon design decomposition. In designing large systems there are usually models at multiple levels of abstraction. A top-level model is decomposed into a set of related models at the next level, which can themselves be decomposed further. This hierarchic approach to tackling complexity is well known (Simon, 1981). In the OPM case shown in Figure 10.8, the top-level system model, a Conceptual Model, is decomposed into one goal model, which is decomposed into three RADs, and so on. Note that although the structure of the model is developed top-down, this does not mean that the detailed modelling must be done top-down. It might be more appropriate for higher-levels to be sketched roughly at first and then refined once lower levels have been developed in detail.

The generic tower model could be combined with the P2E model to support the evolution of the OPM method as it is applied in a particular context.

10.12 Conclusion

In this chapter we have used Process*Web* to illustrate the kind of active model-based process support technology which is now possible. One of the advantages of active models is that they provide a rigorous test of any designed process. While it is possible to read a number of process diagrams and not be 100 per cent sure what would happen in real life, an active model makes things precise.

In developing an active model we are forced to address the issues of instance creation and model evolution. These issues are not really specific to the technology; they would apply to any attempt to apply a set of RAD, or similar, models in an organization.

In describing Process*Web* we have tried to illustrate the requirements of an active model technology rather than the specific nuances of this particular system.

The descriptions serve to give only a flavour of the many different systems that are available. It is very difficult to compare technologies without an in-depth assessment for the particular kind of support desired in an organization. Many requirements of organizations only emerge after a significant amount of process analysis work has been done. In addition, some aspect of a system's architecture or formalism, which is relatively insignificant in theory, can have a significant effect on the acceptance of a system by an organization. It is for this reason that we have resisted the temptation to make detailed comparisons between the different tools that are currently available.

THINGS TO DO

- Go through a PEF insurance model on Process*Web*. This will involve getting a guest login for Process*Web* if you have not already done so (at http://www.cs.man.ac.uk/ipg/bisbook/), and creating a new instance of the model from the library. In particular, note how the interface updates to reflect changes in a role's state which can be either as a result of user input or a message from another role.
- Using either a PEF insurance or another Process*Web* model, experiment with logging on and off the systems while enacting the model. In addition, use the Process*Web* facilities to switch the bindings and relinquish roles from users. You should verify that the model's interface only changes as the enacting model's state changes. It is unaffected by users logging in and out, and by being bound to or relinquished by users.
- The PEF insurance model outlined in this chapter has a basic design consisting of creating three roles for every proposal. This is a simple design and works well for demonstrating Process*Web*. An alternative is to have each of the three roles maintain a queue of proposals in progress. Identify factors, such as the number of proposals under consideration at the same time, which could affect the choice of the best design for the PEF company. Try and envisage further possible mappings of agents, roles and proposals.
- This chapter's PEF insurance model uses RADs as the basic structure of its user interface. This is effective in illustrating the map between the static RAD models and the active Process*Web* models. Sketch out a proposal for a user interface appropriate for people working in the PEF company who are involved in handling proposals on a day-to-day basis.
- The PEF company are concerned about their proposal handling process. They are interested in both a better knowledge of the current status, and historical data of how previous proposals were handled. Identify a range of information in which they might be interested and try to evaluate which could be provided as feedback from a modified version of this chapter's Process*Web* example.

11

The OPM Case Study

This chapter follows from the chapters which set out the Organizational Process Modelling (OPM) method earlier in the book. It gives an example of a model which was created for the Parker, Ellington and Fitzgerald case study. It is designed to serve as a reference for the OPM method as it shows the various parts of the model and how they relate to one another.

11.1 Introduction

This chapter presents a model of the corporate team of Parker, Ellington and Fitzgerald (PEF) Insurance Company. Some of the diagrams contained within this chapter have been seen in earlier chapters. Others are new and help to make the presentation more complete.

The model is a *snapshot*. That is to say, it is not finished. But then, why should it be? The organization goes on. We can imagine that as the underwriters and administrators use the support system, new needs and new ideas arise. Meanwhile, strategists mull over new strategy. Tacticians think up new tactics. Some things work well, some things do not. The organization *lives*.

Most of the diagrams are quite simple, but taken as a whole they cover a lot of issues. The chapter starts with a review and then describes three views of the system under investigation. The following section describes the sub-role models which underpin different models of method from all of these views.

11.2 A Review

11.2.1 The PEF Corporate Team

The Parker, Ellington and Fitzgerald (PEF) Insurance Company is fictional. It was founded, we suppose, sometime after the Napoleonic Wars and before the Great Depression. Today it operates across the globe from a number of offices. The corporate team are the subject of the model. They are based in London. Their concern is with the underwriting of commercial insurance business. They work closely with insurance brokers to evaluate, quote for and underwrite risks associated with major commercial activity. They might, for example, underwrite the property risks of a high street store-chain or a large pharmaceutical manufacturer. Thus, compared with other insurance sectors (e.g. motor policies) the business of the PEF Corporate team is low volume. Each risk proposal is unlike any other and therefore the professional evaluation of risks by underwriters is an important feature of the process. The OPM example describes the work of underwriters and administrators, and their interaction with brokers.

11.2.2 The What, the Why, the How and the Doing

Remember the four modelling stages which were described in Chapter 7, viz:
- Model of interacting agents (model of the system or *what* interacts). A high-level, structural view of the system is given by describing the interacting agents. This is a context model which helps in setting the scope for the investigation. It describes the agents that interact with each other. The system described in the context model is explored in more depth by developing other models. These represent segments of the overall scope. They too describe the agents that interact. These models of the system are given the mnemonic *what* models.
- Model of goals (*why*). The purpose for the interaction is added to the description of the agents. Throughout, the focus is upon the coordination that takes place in the system being investigated. Thus, having identified the interactive behaviours they can then be specialized by declaring the operational goals that they seek to achieve. This model of goals is thus a *why* representation of the behaviour under investigation.
- Model of method (*how*). The way in which the agents achieve these goals is described. Upon the description of what interacts and why, a model of the method by which the goals are achieved can be created. This model describes *how* the goals are achieved. It requires the unbundling of the interactive relationship thus far depicted so that a more complex mosaic of interactive behaviours between people and people, people and tools and tools and tools can be created. The data input to these tools is described so that it is possible to identify which data is shared by activities within or between roles.
- The active model (executable). The creation of the *active* model considers which of these interactive behaviours are to be supported in a coordination layer, and the logical dependencies between the behaviours thus supported.

The *what* and *why* models are represented as Conceptual Models (CMs). The *how* model is drawn as a Role Activity Diagram (RAD). Models are executed using the Process Modelling Language (PML).

11.3 The Context

11.3.1 The Model of the System

This model tells us *what* interacts. To set the context, the diagram in Figure 11.1 was created. It expresses the PEF corporate team as an agent interacting with brokers, a policy administration agency, other PEF insurance teams and prospects. This last term is used to describe companies whose risks might be underwritten by the PEF team. Therefore it includes all those who have proposals that are currently being evaluated and those who have policies with PEF at present (i.e. are *prospects* for renewal).

The ellipses represent agents. Each link denotes the relationship *interacts with*. The diagram also shows cardinality. Double ellipses denote *one or many*. Single ellipses denote *one*. For example, there is one PEF Corporate Team and one or many brokers.

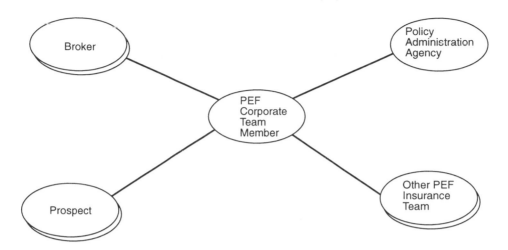

Fig. 11.1 The PEF Corporate Team Context Model

It is through the study definition (Chapter 6) that the purpose of the modelling work is discussed and declared. In our case the purpose is to support the underwriting process. This will involve looking at the interaction of the PEF corporate team with brokers. A second model in Figure 11.2 is used to make this scope absolutely clear.

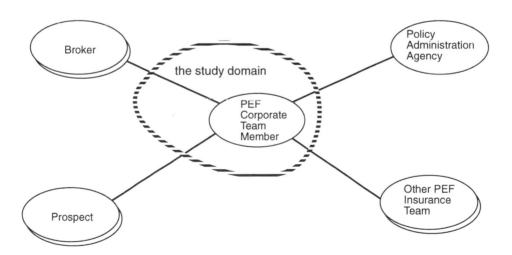

Fig. 11.2 The PEF Corporate Team Context Model and the Study Domain

In the following sections a number of further models are presented. These describe sub-systems of the above (Figure 11.2). The sub-systems described are as follows:
• Interaction of Administrator, Broker, Underwriter.
• Broker interacts with Underwriter.
• Administrator interacts with Underwriter.
• Interaction of Administrator, Underwriter, other Administrator.
Through the development of these sub-systems we will see how models of goals, models of

method and active models can be developed.

11.4 Interaction of Administrator, Broker, Underwriter

11.4.1 The Model of the System

The relationship between Administrators, Brokers and Underwriters is a system of interest to us. How do we arrive at this conclusion? Well, it is through our process of interviewing and finding out information that we begin to focus upon certain sets of interactions (see Chapter 7). We cut up the domain of interacting agents in any way which we find useful to describe behaviour. We are also, of course, thinking about goals as we progress.

Figure 11.3 can be thought of as representing a sub-system of Figure 11.1.

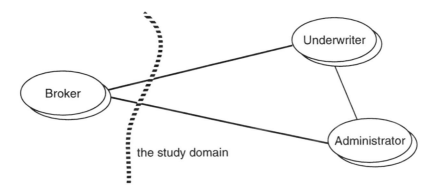

Fig. 11.3 Interaction of Administrator, Broker, Underwriter

The business of the brokers themselves are shown as being beyond the scope of the study whilst clearly their interactions are inside the scope. Therefore the business of brokers is understood to be a *black box* which PEF personnel may interact with but yet have no need to understand its intricate, internal workings. PEF team members do not necessarily understand how the brokers' businesses operate, but they do seek to understand how to coordinate with them.

11.4.2 The Model of Goals

The following model in Figure 11.4 shows a set of operational goals which are held by the broker, underwriter and administrator. They have been described as 'Giving, Logging and Evaluating Proposals'. Thus, the model describes a set of behaviours wherein administrators log risk proposals, underwriters give decisions on them and brokers utilize these decisions.

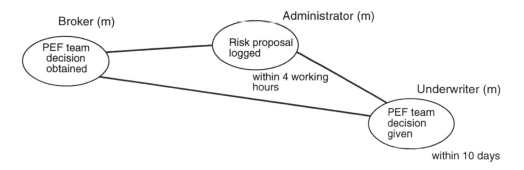

Fig. 11.4 Giving, Logging and Evaluating Proposals

Figure 11.5 shows a different *why* model developed from the same *what* model. It describes the interactive behaviour between brokers, administrators and underwriters through which a risk is formally underwritten by the PEF corporate team. Considering the goals in a random order we note:

• An administrator seeks to log the fact that the business is underwritten by the PEF corporate team and to create a draft policy document.
• An underwriter seeks the production of an authorized policy document. A non-functional goal of achieving this within twenty-one days is noted.
• A broker seeks to have a risk underwritten by the PEF corporate team.
  The label that is chosen to describe the model is 'Formally underwriting the risk'.

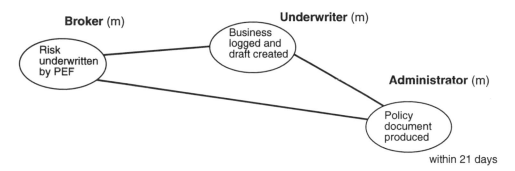

Fig. 11.5 Formally Underwriting the Risk

11.4.3 The Model of Method

If things are as they usually are, then an early attempt at expressing *why* agents interact will quickly be followed by the creation of a *how* model. This helps the modeller to understand the validity of the *why* model and informs the creation of the active model (i.e. *doing* model). The *how* model gives the first opportunity to express in some depth the behaviour of the system under investigation.

The *how* model, the model of method, is thus about understanding and validating. Those presented here are the fruits of a process of development. This has been described before as a series of dialectics.

There are two *why* models which can be developed as *how* models. These are Figure 11.4 and Figure 11.5. First we consider the mapping of Figure 11.4.

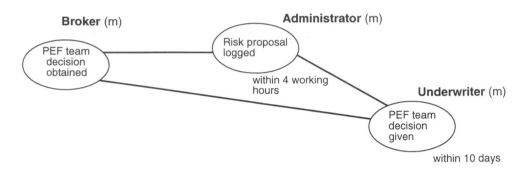

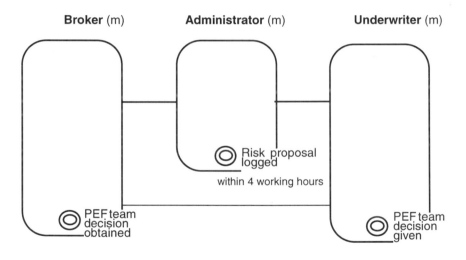

Fig. 11.6 For Purposes of Illustration: the Mapping of Figure to a Model of Method

The method for attaining each operational goal is expressed as a role. It follows that each role will at some state achieve the operational goal. The non-functional goals are applied to the roles. It is known that the roles must interact but the detail of these interactions is not yet understood.

A detailed *how* model is given in Figure 11.7.

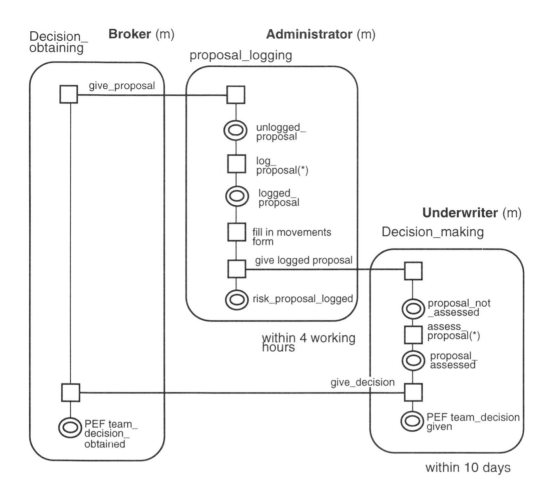

Fig. 11.7 Giving, Logging and Evaluating Proposals (Method 1)

Note that the asterisk (*) notation indicates that certain activities are expressed as sub-roles. These are shown later in Section 11.8. It should also be noted that as the scope of the study is confined to the PEF corporate team, the activities that brokers undertake are beyond the scope of the study. Only the interactions are shown.

Figure 11.8 describes a method for achieving the goals expressed earlier in Figure 11.5 ('Formally Underwriting the Risk').

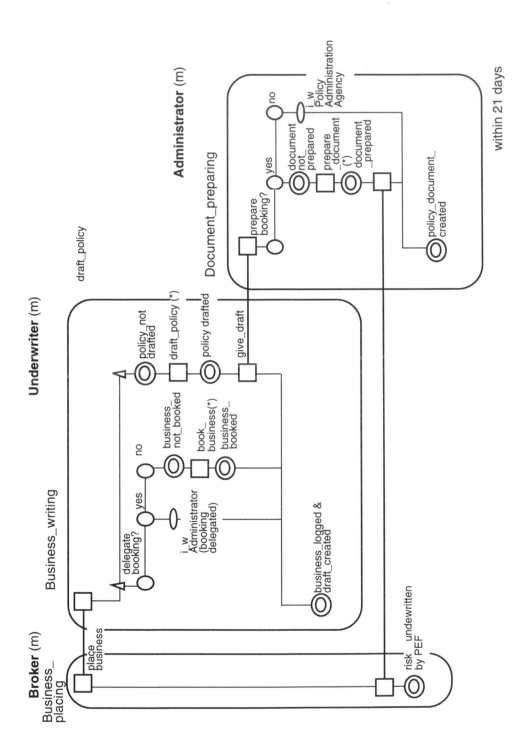

Fig. 11.8 Formally Underwriting the Risk (FUR) (Method 1)

It is time to think again about the scope of a system under investigation and the way in which a pattern of interactions knit together in a process. Figure raises two cases:

- In the 'Business writing' role, under the 'delegate booking?, yes' thread, an ellipse denotes an interactive behaviour which is described elsewhere. The label gives some information. The underwriter will interact with an administrator with the goal of having the 'booking delegated'. Thus in describing how a set of goals is achieved we uncover the need to describe a new set of goals. This is done in Figure 11.17. This is an example of how an apparently fragmented view of activity at the system level connects together when we consider the method by which goals are achieved.
- In the 'Document preparing' role under the 'No' condition, an ellipse marks a need to interact with the Policy Administration Agency. This agency creates standard policies on behalf of insurance companies so saving them administrative time and costs. The interaction has been shown in the system model in Figure 11.2. The model has not been further developed to describe the interactive behaviour because the Policy Administration Agency is outside the scope of the study. Therefore the ellipse is labelled simply by 'interact with Policy Administration Agency'.

11.4.4 The Library

The models we have created up to this point are identified in the table below.

Model	No.	Description
System (*what*)		The PEF corporate team context
System (*what*)		Interaction of Administrator, Broker, Underwriter
Goal (*why*)	1	Giving, Logging and Evaluating Proposals
Method (*how*)	1	Giving, Logging and Evaluating Proposals
Goal (*why*)	2	Formally Underwriting the Risk
Method (*how*)	1	Formally Underwriting the Risk

Table 11.1 Library of models created for (1) the PEF corporate team context and (2) Interaction of Administrator, Broker, Underwriter

11.4.5 The Active Model

The active model of coordination can be created by mapping from the *why* model into the structures of an executable language, in this case PML. Where role boundaries are retained between the two models (see Chapter 7), the commitment made is that the executable role is used to attain the goal described in the *why* model. By doing this the executable takes a structural form which is meaningful to the PEF team. The *how* model is then used to further inform the creation of the executable by describing the activities that the users seek to carry out. In the examples that follow in Figure 11.9 and Figure 11.10 the executable roles of the active model map back to the *why* model in Figure 11.4. In this example the activities described are actually common to the *how* model and the active model.

```
Proposal_Logging isa Role with

resources !**the resources of the role
        intrayentry : InTrayEntry
        referproposal : giveport InTrayEntry
        referproposal : giveport InTrayEntry
        proposal_logged : Bool {false}

actions !**the activities that the role can execute

        log_proposal :
        {UserAction (agendaLabel = 'Log this proposal');
        ViewObjectNow (object = 'Sorry sub-role not implemented yet!')}
        when log_proposal = nil

        allocate_logged_proposal :
        {UserAction (agendaLabel = 'Refer submission to underwriter');
        Give (interaction = referproposal, gram = intrayentry);
        proposal_logged := true}
        when log_proposal ~= nil
termconds proposal_logged
end with !* Proposal_Logging
```

Fig. 11.9 PML for the 'Risk Proposal Logged' Goal

This is compilable code but of course in the creation of the full executable, additional coding would be required to implement aspects not described in the *what*, *why* and *how* models.

Another illustration is given in Figure 11.10. This is the active model for the 'PEF decision given' role. Again, the activities represented in the *how* model in Figure 11.7 have been retained.

```
Decision_Making isa Role with

resources !** the resources of the role
        intrayentry: InTrayEntry
        takereferral: takeport InTrayEntry
        pef_decision_given: Bool {false}


actions !** the activities that the role can execute

        loggedproposalallocated:
        Take (interaction = takereferral, gram= intrayentry)
        when loggedproposalallocated = nil

        assess_proposal:
        {UserAction (agendaLabel = 'Assess this proposal');
        ViewObjectNow (object = 'Sorry sub-role not yet implemented!');
        QueryAlertNow (question = 'Have you finished assesing this proposal?'
        answer = pef_decision_given)}
        when loggedproposalallocated~ = nil
```

```
termconds pef_decision_given = true

end with !*Decision_Making
```

Fig. 11.10 PML for 'PEF Team Decision Given' Goal

Using these examples, we can imagine what the code created to support the achievement of the goals in Figure 11.5 would look like. The mapping shown in Figure 11.11 infers that two variables will be used to determine the achievement of the goal 'Business logged and draft created'.

```
Business_Writing isa Role with
resources !**the resources of the role
        business_logged: Bool {false}
        draft_created: Bool {false}

        .....insert executable code created to help achieve the goal....

termconds business_logged = true & draft_created = true

end with !* Business_Writing
```

Fig. 11.11 Active Model Mapping: PML for 'Business Logged and Draft Created' Goal

11.5 Broker Interacts with Underwriter

11.5.1 The Model of the System

Figure 11.12 represents another sub-system of interest to the system modelled in Figure 11.1.

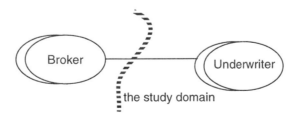

Fig. 11.12 Broker Interacts with Underwriter

Remember, the decisions on what sub-systems interest us are guided by the information gained as the investigation progresses. As has been demonstrated already, the sub-systems start to connect to one another when we create *how* models. Of course, there is no magic involved and it is important to constantly seek to create valid and meaningful models.

11.5.2 The Model of Goals

Figure 11.13 shows a *why* model development of Figure 11.12. It describes the broker seeking to obtain a decision of the PEF corporate team upon a risk proposal. The underwriter seeks to give a decision and is committed to achieve this within ten days (a non-functional goal). The label used to describe this diagram is simply 'Obtaining and Giving Decisions'.

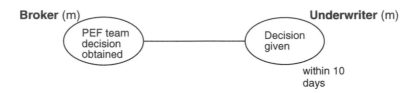

Fig. 11.13 Obtaining and Giving Decisions

11.5.3 The model of method

The diagram in Figure 11.14 shows how the operational goals of Figure 11.13 might be achieved.

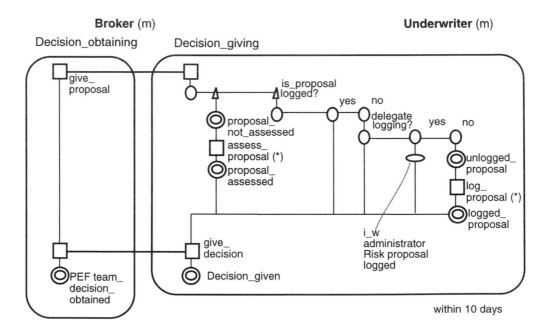

Fig. 11.14 Obtaining and Giving Decisions (Method 1)

The model describes the underwriter receiving a proposal from a broker. The underwriter will then proceed to assess it as well as having it logged on to the PEF team database. This can be done by the underwriter or by interacting with an administrator. If the underwriter chooses to delegate the logging to an administrator, this will be done by taking part in the interactions which are shown later in Figure 11.18. There are two examples of sub-role calls. One is at 'assess proposal'. the other at 'log proposal'. The detail is given in Section 11.8.

11.5.4 The Library

The models created of the system 'Broker interacts with Underwriter' are identified in the table below.

Model	No.	Description
System (*what*)		Broker interacts with Underwriter
Goal (*why*)	1	Obtaining and Giving Decisions
Method (*how*)	1	Obtaining and Giving Decisions

Table 11.2 Library of models created for Broker interacts with Underwriter

11.6 Underwriter Interacts with Administrator

11.6.1 The Model of the System

As with brokers and underwriters, so too interactions between underwriters and administrators are of interest. The model is just as simple.

Fig. 11.15 Administrator Interacts with Underwriter

So far so good, progress could hardly be easier; but think for a moment about what has been achieved. By declaring Figure 11.1 to be of interest to us, we were actually saying that we are interested in the system described by it. In other words, we are interested in the PEF corporate insurance system which, at a level of abstraction, reveals the PEF corporate insurance team to interact with brokers, prospects, other PEF insurance teams and a policy administration agency. Next we say, 'OK, we are interested in this system, but this study will focus only on the interactions of the members of the PEF corporate team and brokers.' Hence we have Figure 11.2. Then, progressing between Figure 11.1 and Figure 11.15, we have actually looked at this system from three viewpoints. We have defined the scope in three ways. Each represents a subsystem of that in which we originally declared an interest in Figure 11.1.

11.6.2 The Model of Goals

A *why* model development of Figure 11.15 is shown below in Figure 11.16. The label 'Getting the proposal logged' has been chosen to describe it. We have seen the goals described already in the *how* model in Figure . The model has been constrained to show a dependency. This is indicated by the arrow head pointing from left to right. Therefore any developments of it must show the underwriter as initiator and the administrator as responder. The underwriter and the administrator both seek to see a risk proposal logged. The model records that the administrator is required to act within a time-span defined by the underwriter.

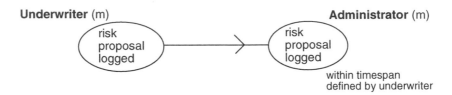

Fig. 11.16 Getting the Proposal Logged

The *why* model in Figure 11.17 describes the underwriter seeking to delegate the booking of a risk and an administrator seeking to book the risk. In the parlance of the PEF corporate team, the verb *to book* refers to the logging of some underwritten risk into the 'Business' database. The label 'Delegating the booking task' is used to describe it.

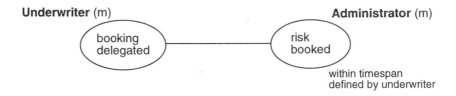

Fig. 11.17 Delegating the Booking Task

11.6.3 The Model of Method

The following Figure 11.18 depicts a method by which the goals of Figure 11.16 can be achieved. Note the call to the sub-role 'log proposal' which has already been seen in Figure 11.7 and Figure 11.14. Sub-roles are useful because they allow a common functionality to be described once and reused. They allow the actions by which agents coordinate (e.g. as represented by Figure 11.7, Figure 11.14 and Figure 11.18) to be distinguished from the functions that they perform.

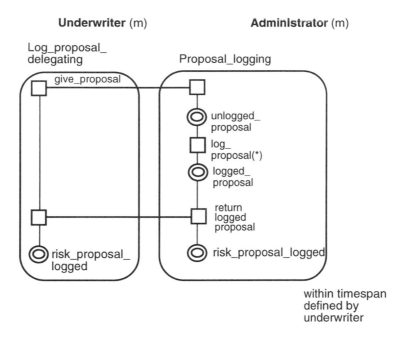

Fig. 11.18 Getting the Proposal Logged (Method 1)

At Figure 11.19 a *how* model development of Figure 11.17 is given.

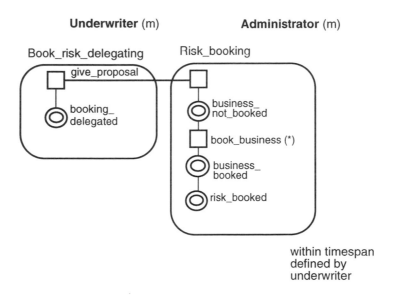

Fig. 11.19 Delegating the Booking Task (Method 1)

Throughout it has been emphasized that alternative *how* models can be created for the same *why* model. This is now illustrated. If a booking is considered to have been *successfully* delegated only when the task has been completed, the next model would be appropriate. Figure 11.20, like Figure 11.19, is a valid development of Figure 11.17.

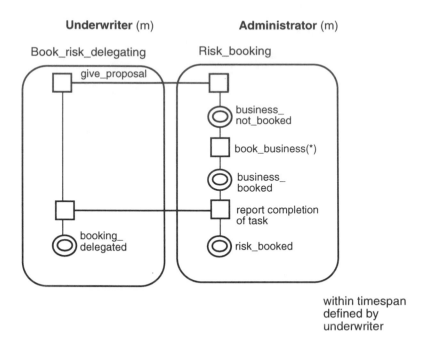

Fig. 11.20 Delegating the Booking Task (Method 2)

11.6.4 The Library

The models created of the system Underwriter interacts with Administrator are identified in the table below.

Model	No.	Description.
System (*what*)		Underwriter interacts with Administrator
Goal (*why*)	1	Getting the proposal logged
Method (*how*)	1	Getting the proposal logged
Goal (*why*)	2	Delegating the booking task
Method (*how*)	1	Delegating the booking task
Method (*how*)	2	Delegating the booking task

Table 11.3 Library of models created for Underwriter interacts with Administrator

11.7 Interaction of Administrator, Underwriter, Administrator

11.7.1 The Model of the System

The following example develops another view of the interacting system introduced in Figure 11.1. It describes administrators interacting with each other and with underwriters. This is shown below in Figure 11.21.

In Chapter 7, the basic constitution of the role was introduced. The basic constitution describes certain behaviours which we can assume to be common to different roles. It means that it is not necessary to concern ourselves with declaring these behaviours explicitly except when it is necessary to prohibit them. The two rights conferred by the basic constitution of roles in the PEF example are as follows. First, any particular role that is assigned to an agent with a multiple cardinality, can be reassigned to a similar agent. Secondly, a role can fail to complete the behaviour described in the role. This means that a role can be exited at any point (e.g. an underwriter can decide not to continue with the assessment of a submission before he has completed it).

The first right means that there is no need to model the reassignment of a role between similar agents where there is a multiple cardinality. For example, we can assume that an Administrator undertaking 'risk booking' can reassign the role to another administrator (see Figure 11.20). Here (Figure 11.21 and Figure 11.22) the concern is also with an interactive behaviour between Administrators, but it is not a simple, straightforward case of reassignment.

Consider the maintenance of a system for tracking the fortunes of different companies and industrial sectors. In the PEF team this is currently known as the Industry Prospects System (IPS). The work of maintaining the IPS involves interaction between administrators and between administrators and underwriters. The following model of a system has been created.

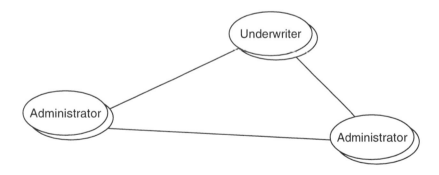

Fig. 11.21 Interaction of Administrator, Underwriter, Other Administrator

11.7.2 The Model of Goals

The following *why* model develops the *what* model to describe the goals involved in the maintenance of the IPS. An administrator seeks to bring the IPS information profiles up to date. Another administrator seeks to give new information to the administrator who updates the IPS. A number of underwriters similarly give information for inclusion in the IPS. The operational goals are represented in Figure 11.22. Note that the modeller has described one Administrator as an 'IPS' Administrator and the other as 'Sources'. These informal qualifiers help to make sure that the diagram is clear.

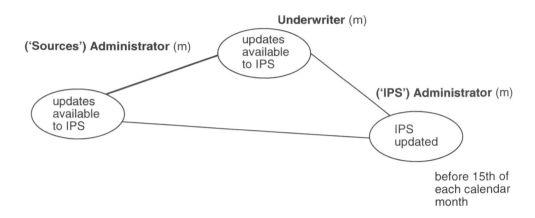

Fig. 11.22 The Updating of the IPS

11.7.3 The Model of Method

The *how* model describes how an administrator takes information from various sources and puts it together in an IPS file and a database. Underwriters are one source. As part of their everyday work they may come upon information which they feel will be usefully shared throughout the team in the IPS. Another source is the administrator specifically tasked with gathering information about industry prospects (e.g. from market reports, industry sources and newspapers). The aim is to maintain the IPS with up-to-date information. The task is to be completed before the 15th of each month. The routine updating of the IPS according to this time scale is important because the underwriters may find it useful to keep abreast of development in certain companies or industry sectors as a whole. Such contextual information that may affect an underwriter's appraisal of a particular industry type or company. For example, a newspaper reports that the Finnegan & Henchy hotel group have commissioned a famous architect to design new high tech, gothic hotels for sites in Audenshaw, Rotterdam, Lvov and St Petersburg. This is a departure for Finnegan & Henchy who have traditionally specialized in small and medium size countryside hotels in the North West of Europe. The 'IPS' administrator will record this information in a database under 'Finnegan & Henchy' and under 'hotels'.

The *how* model is shown in Figure 11.23.

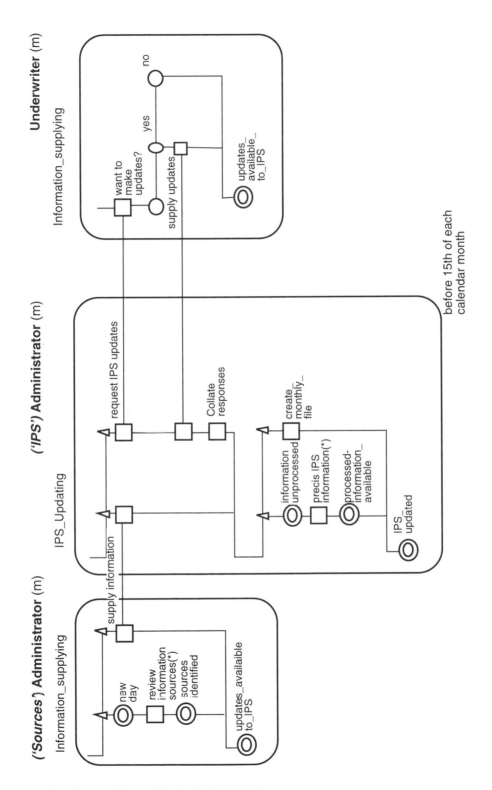

Fig. 11.23 The Updating of the IPS (Method 1)

11.7.4 The Library

The models created of the system Administrator interacts with Underwriter interacts with Administrator interacts with Administrator are identified in the table below.

Model	No.	Description
System (*what*)		Interaction of Administrator, Underwriter, other Administrator
Goal (*why*)	1	Updating the IPS
Method (*how*)	1	Updating the IPS

Table 11.4 Library of models created for interaction of Administrator, Underwriter, other Administrator

11.8 Sub-Roles

In the models of method shown in this chapter, it has been the general policy to try and use sub-roles as often as is practicable. Sub-roles expand out the detail of some of the functionality of the role to which they relate. They do not contain interactions in the same way that other roles do. They express functions. Using sub-roles helps to keep the top level roles simple. They are easier to read. They are also easier to create. It also introduces a modularity to our thinking and design as they are potentially common to many roles. If we are strict about the use of sub-roles, they also help us to distinguish coordinative activity between agents from that carried out by agents in their everyday tasks.

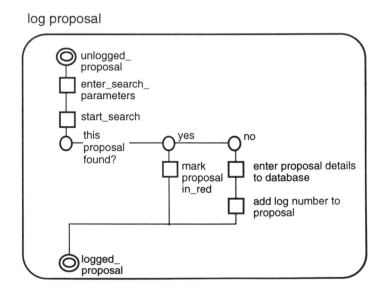

Fig. 11.24 Sub-Role 'Log Proposal'

The sub-roles used in the how models between Figure 11.7 and Figure 11.23 are all given in this section. First shown is 'log proposal' in Figure 11.24. This describes how an agent searches a database to find out if a proposal has been registered already. Those proposals that have already been registered are marked in *red*. Others are added to the database.

The sub-role 'log proposal' is used by 'Giving, Logging and Evaluating Proposals (Method 1)' in Figure 11.7, and 'Obtaining and Giving Decisions (Method 1)' in Figure 11.14, and 'Getting the Proposal Logged (Method 1)' in Figure 11.18.

Figure 11.25 ('assess proposal') describes the activities undertaken by an agent when evaluating the risk associated with a particular project. It has been annotated with the names of some of the technology used.

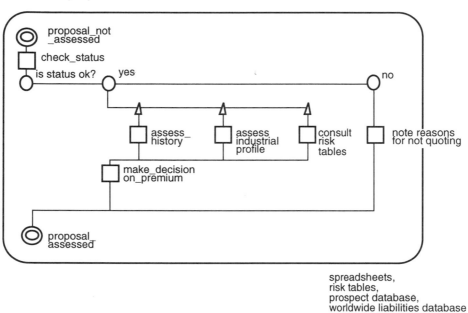

Fig. 11.25 Sub-Role 'Assess Proposal'

The sub-role 'assess proposal' is used by 'Giving, Logging and Evaluating Proposals (Method 1)' in Figure 11.7 and 'Obtaining and Giving Decisions (Method 1)' in Figure 11.14.

draft policy

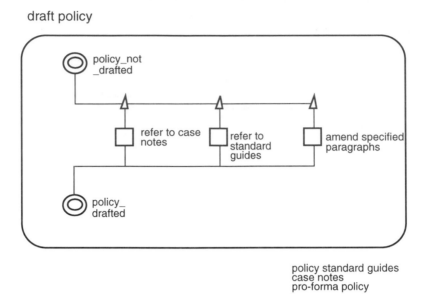

Fig. 11.26 Sub-Role 'Draft Policy'

Figure 11.26 ('draft policy') describes how a policy is created by referring to certain documents and amending specified paragraphs on a pro-forma policy. It is used by 'Formally Underwriting the Risk (FUR) (Method 1)' in Figure 11.8.

Figure 11.27 describes the preparation of other documents from pro-forma templates. It is used by 'Formally Underwriting the Risk (FUR) (Method 1)' in Figure 11.8.

prepare document

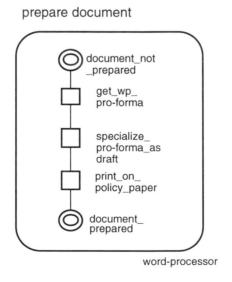

Fig. 11.27 Sub-Role 'Prepare Document'

Figure 11.28 describes another simple set of activities. It is concerned with the formal record-ing of a policy when the decision has been taken to underwrite the risk. This recording is known as 'booking'. The sub-role is used by 'Formally Underwriting the Risk (FUR) (Method 1)' in Figure 11.8, 'Delegating the Booking Task (Method 1)' in Figure 11.19 and 'Delegating the Booking Task (Method 2)' in Figure 11.20.

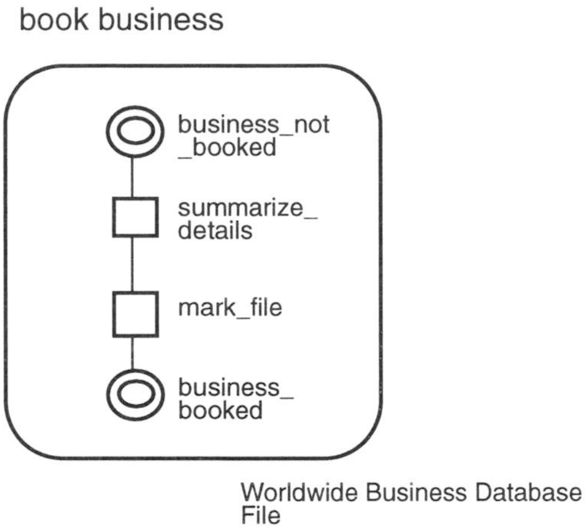

book business

business_not
_booked

summarize_
details

mark_file

business_
booked

Worldwide Business Database
File

Fig. 11.28 Sub-Role 'Book Business'

The following two sub-roles all relate to 'The Updating of the IPS (Method 1)' in Figure 11.23. The sub-role 'Review information sources' is used by the role 'Information Supplying'.

review information sources

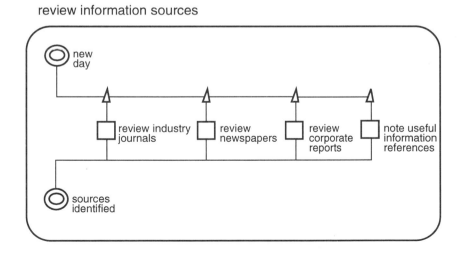

new
day

review industry
journals

review
newspapers

review
corporate
reports

note useful
information
references

sources
identified

Fig. 11.29 Sub-Role 'Review Information Sources'

The sub-role 'precis IPS information' is used by the role 'IPS Updating'. The 'Profiles' da-tabase is used to store summaries and reference addresses of IPS information.

precis IPS information

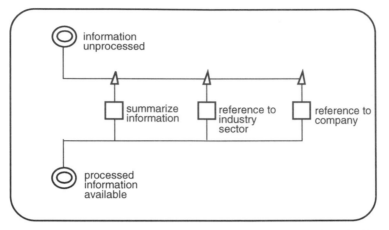

Profiles database

Fig. 11.30 Sub-Role 'Precis IPS Information'

11.9 Conclusion

Stop Press: The description that you have just read of the Parker, Ellington and Fitzgerald corporate insurance team is no longer valid. The whole process has been reinvented and marketed under the label *Blue Sky Directory*. For details refer to Chapter 8.

...well, it was only ever a snapshot. The organization has to be free to live, to adapt and to progress. In some ways the model being out of date so quickly has done us a favour, for it has reminded us of the intrinsic dynamism of organizations. Obviously, the way in which *the organization changes* is crucial, but it is not just that. The act of creating models is *itself dynamic* and uncertain. They are unlikely to take a sustainable form straight away. They are shaped throughout the modelling process, each phase introducing a new dialectic. The status they attain might be described as sustainable, or as plausible, but never as inviolable. We believe the model to be valid for as long as it is believable. Then we reflect upon it, refine it or reinvent it. We learn.

Looking over the models that have been presented in this chapter it would be easy to pay too little attention to the dynamic character of their creation. They sit there, on the page, and would look no different had they been proven by the testimony of generations. Software can be a little like this too. If we look over the functions of almost any executing system in an organization today, we observe that it runs down tramlines however sophisticated the logic of the junction boxes may be. It is easy for users (i.e. everyone, managers as well as clerks) to believe that its form is preordained, rationalized and there to be obeyed. This might sometimes be a good thing, but often it is a problem. The organization might want to move to plan B.2 whilst the software is still stuck on plan A.0. To change this situation it is necessary to appreciate the process of creation of software systems. This is a modelling process. We need the templates and the reference points. We need to be able to change the models.

12

Conclusion

This chapter brings the book to a close by returning to the organizational agenda that was established at the start. It emphasizes the value of a problem focus that draws upon and relates to different disciplines. The chapter then summarizes the focus of a process approach to business information systems. A review of the chapters of the book is provided and, finally, some thoughts are set out on the further development of this process approach.

12.1 Organizations and their Software

At the start of this book it was stated that the broadest aim is to make a contribution to organizations. There followed from this a serious and, it is to be hoped, interesting investigation of the nature of organizations. All the while that this agenda was being developed, another was also being recounted. This second agenda was more technical, involving a review of software engineering research and leading through ideas about architecture to an account of process support technology.

It may be recalled how in Chapter 2 it was noted that the direct lineage of this work lies with software engineering research. In particular, the contributions of the IPSE 2.5 project, concepts of evolutionary systems and software process research have all been described.

Thus the book has entertained both an organizational agenda and a technical agenda. This gives it a dual presence wherein organizational and technical interests coexist and shape each other. A fascination for organizational problems helps to shape the technical agenda. Equally, a fascination for technical possibilities helps to redefine organizational expectations. This duality, which is essentially a determination to bring technical expertise to life in real, human settings, is a characteristic of much engineering work. For example a professional architect who is asked to design a school might be enthralled by the challenge. The successful completion of the project will require that an understanding of the human requirements are met by a technical act of assembling steel, stone and glass.

The work of the architect gains its cohesion from its problem focus. The problem is one of building design and development for human use; a task which may require the architect to refer to skills in structural engineering, art, psychology, sociology, economics and other areas. Each of the disciplines that is referred to, both contributes to architecture and is informed by architecture. In an area as old and well-established as architecture the interdisciplinary relationships are, for the most part, symbiotic.

So too, when a problem focus is taken in the domain of organizations and their software, the result is that many disciplines are called upon to contribute to the understanding and resolution of the problem. Hence, in this book, software engineering research has sat alongside information systems research, systems thinking and other work. In an area as new as the task of developing software systems for organizations, the inter-disciplinary relationships should, it is to be hoped, become increasingly symbiotic.

12.2 A Process Approach

Hence, the will to grapple with the reality of organizational life has informed this work at every stage. The reality of this organizational life has repeatedly challenged methodological and technical assumptions. In the IPSE 2.5 project the work was challenged by the needs of software developers; subsequently, as the research agenda matured, insurance companies, health care organizations, government departments and manufacturing companies have been amongst those asking the questions.

The process approach espoused in this book is thus a product of thinking *very hard* about organizations. Systems theory has informed this thinking. The linkage of systems and processes has been examined in Chapter 2. This debate has given ways of thinking about organizations, of understanding the relationship of structure and process, and of accounting for organizational reality as it seems to be.

The process approach developed in this book rests upon two observations about organizational life:
• Organizations are essentially interactive. They are composed of elements which interact with each other.
• Organizations are essentially dynamic. The elements and interactions of an organization change. We can call this phenomenon evolution.

The resulting patterns of behaviour (interactive and evolutionary) can be described as processes. The task of process modelling is to observe and represent these patterns of behaviour. This gives us some capability to both reflect upon and to shape behaviour in the real world. It follows that process modelling is a way of analyzing and designing the behaviour of systems. This takes place, as has been said, on both an operational level (elements coordinating with each other) and a meta level (changes to these patterns of interaction).

Therefore, in its broadest sense process modelling is a very general technology. It is applicable to many different problem areas. Of course, the focus of this book is upon the contribution of software systems to organizations, i.e. the use to which process modelling is put, in this book, is to inform the development of software systems.

12.3 Review

Chapter 1 sets the scene for the book by introducing the topic of organizations and their software. It then sets out a map of how the rest of the book would try to address these concerns through its two parts, Concepts and Practice.

Chapter 2, Positioning sets the work amongst other research. It utilizes systems theory as a way of thinking about the nature of organizations. In Positioning, a process approach is promoted. At its most simple, this can be understood as giving a way of studying the behaviour of systems. Through process modelling the approach looks at interactions, the goals they serve and the way in which these goals are fulfilled. Two themes are presented; interaction and evolution. These are patterns of behaviour (processes), the investigation of which has been the subject of each of the following chapters.

Chapter 3, Process Concepts responds to the need to understand the nature of processes. It seeks to promote a cohesive and comprehensive grounding for a process approach. The chapter has a necessary breadth. The concepts contribute to the ongoing understanding of processes as well as providing the basis for the modelling methods which are introduced in Part 2. The chapter focuses upon understanding the relationship between goal, activity and interaction in organizations. This leads to a description of different kinds of models. The concept of an active model is introduced and the reader is encouraged to think about IT systems using this idea. It emphasizes the issue of the validity of the model. The notion of process domains is then introduced. The chapter concludes with a brief introduction to the concept of the meta-process.

Chapter 4, Engineering of Processes is concerned with how we find solutions. It introduces the essentials of an engineering approach to problem-solving through process modelling. It discusses the characteristics of such an approach, some relevant issues, and its limitations. Particular attention is focused on the design activity and how it might be structured.

Chapter 5, Nature of the Method serves as a bridge between the two parts of the book. Its illustrates how thinking about organizational systems can be utilized in the design of software support systems. It introduces the case study of the PEF corporate insurance team. Three important implementation concepts are introduced. These are the Organizational Process Modelling (OPM) method, the architectural concept of the coordination layer and the P2E meta-process model. Each of these can be understood to be a pillar upon which the particular process approach espoused in this book is founded.

Chapter 6, Process Contexts commences the description of the Organizational Process Modelling Method (OPM). The initial focus is to develop an analysis of the problem domain in which it is applied. This is done by focusing on two specific views. The first is the context of the intervention which aims to solve some problem. The second is the context of the problem process itself.

Chapter 7, Process Capture describes how OPM is used to model organizational processes. The basis of the approach is to identify interacting agents and then to describe their goals and how they achieve these goals. The three simple descriptions that result are known as the model of the system, the model of goals and the model of method. These are graphical, *passive* models which aid in the process of learning about the subject organization. The creation of these models requires a high level of dialogue with the people whose work it is that we are seeking to represent. The end result is a modularization of the problem domain and useful descriptions of organizational behaviour.

Chapter 8, Process Design extends OPM by utilizing it to develop executable support for coordination. The modeller is required to think about the issues that arise when seeking to move beyond the passive model, to make the model *active*. In so doing the modeller shapes the new behaviour of the organization itself. The chapter progresses by describing a number of design examples from the PEF case study.

Chapter 9, Process Managing returns to the observation that organizational process are not insulated from their environments. They are subject to influences from many sources and, as a result, every process is subject to change. The chapter then takes the modelling process another step further on. It asks what must be done to make the model *evolvable*. The Process for Process Evolution (P2E) meta-process model serves as the vehicle for this. An example of process change using P2E is developed from the PEF case study.

The organizational analysis set in train in Chapter 2 asks fundamental questions about the nature of IT systems. Through the following chapters some important ideas about IT emerge as the organizational agenda provokes a technical agenda. This can be seen in Chapter 8 where the coordination layer is utilized and there are examples of close mappings between the simple models created in an organizational investigation and executable code. In Chapter 9 the use of the P2E develops the idea of structuring a system through a recursive network which relates methods to objectives. Then in Chapter 10, Process Support Technology, the technical agenda is explored more fully. This is done by reference to candidate technologies with a particular emphasis given to Process*Web*. The chapter records that an ideal technology would enable a clear mapping between the models drawn at the design stage and the active model. It would offer excellent facilities for integrating other software tools to the active model, and include the ability to respond to change by evolving active models.

Chapter 11 brings together the model created for the PEF corporate case study. It serves as a reference for the OPM method as it shows the various parts of the model and how they relate to one another.

This review shows how the concerns of the book are developed through both theory and practice. The Practice part of the book applies ideas from the Concepts part to the problem domain of modern organizations and their software systems. This application yields experience which, of necessity, should drive the process approach onward.

12.4 A Way Forward

Early on, we were reminded of the facts of life for the many who inhabit modern organizations. Organizational life can be an exhilarating, frightening or turgid experience. Increasingly, the will to innovate and the ability to adapt are the acid test of successful enterprises. Modern organizations constantly strive to maintain or improve their position, to eradicate threats, to differentiate themselves and to extemporize. It follows that in this context a process approach, *any process approach*, should be a platform for investigation of how best to build systems for these adapting and heterogeneous organizations. It should encourage and facilitate managers and software engineers as they seek to address the real issues affecting their organization.

This book has sought to show the feasibility and usefulness of a process approach to software development. It has not sought to monopolize the idea of a process approach per se. It has been stressed that this is *a* process approach, not *the* process approach.

Moreover, it should be emphasized also that the further development of this work should continue to draw upon work carried out in different spheres. Information systems research and systems theory are obvious reference points. The problem focus will ensure that cohesion is maintained. Similarly, process approaches should continue to inherit the concerns of good engineering practice that have been developed throughout the lifetime of software engineering. Thus, once the usefulness and feasibility of the approach are established, new efforts in the effective engineering of process solutions should become increasingly prominent. It is to be hoped that in the future the process platform will accommodate a renewed emphasis upon the verification of models alongside the emphasis this book has given to validation.

References

Ackoff, R.L., (1976). 'Towards a System of Systems Concepts', in Beishon, J., and Peters, G., (eds.), *Systems Behaviour*, Second Edition, The Open University Press, London: Harper and Row.

Ackoff, R.L., (1981). *Creating The Corporate Future,* Chichester: John Wiley & Sons.

Alexander, C., (1964). *Notes on the Synthesis of Form*, Harvard University Press.

Bank, J., (1993). *The Essence of Total Quality Management*, Prentice Hall.

Basili, V., Caldiera, G., McGarry, F., Pajerski, R., Page, G., and Waligora, S., (1992). 'The software engineering laboratory: an operational software experience factory', in *Proceedings of the 14th International Conference on Software Engineering*, Melbourne, Australia: IEEE.

Bauer, M., Kohl, C., and Mayr, H., (1994). 'Enterprise Modeling Using OOA Techniques', in Chroust, G., and Benczur, A., (eds.), *Workflow Management: Challenges, Paradigms and Products. Conference Proceedings of CONnectivity '94*, Oldenburg: Verlag.

Beer, S., (1974). *Designing Freedom*, Chichester: John Wiley & Sons.

Beer, S., (1979). *Heart of Enterprise*, Chichester: John Wiley & Sons.

Beishon, J., and Peters, G., (1976). 'Introduction', in Beishon, J., and Peters, G., (eds.), *Systems Behaviour*, Second Edition, The Open University Press, London: Harper and Row.

Belady, L.A., and Lehman, M.M., (1985). *Program Evolution*, APIC Studies in Data Processing: Academic Press.

von Bertalanffy, L., (1971). *General System Theory: Foundations, Development, Applications*, London: Penguin.

Biddle, B., and Thomas, E., (eds.) (1966). *Role Theory: Concepts and Research*, John Wiley.

Blockley, D., (1992). 'Engineering from Reflective Practice', *Research in Engineering Design*, 4.

Bruynooghe, R.F., Greenwood, R.M., Robertson, I., Sa, J., Snowdon, R.A., and Warboys, B.C., (1994). 'PADM: Towards a Total Process Modelling System', in (Finkelstein, A., Kramer, J., and Nuseibeh, B., (eds.) 1994), pp. 293–334.

Buxton, J.N., and Randell, B., (1970). 'Software Engineering Techniques', Report on a Conference Sponsored by the NATO Science Committee, Rome, Italy, 1969, Brussels: NATO Science Committee.

Capra, F., (1996). *The Web of Life,* London: Flamingo.

Checkland, P., (1981). *Systems Thinking, Systems Practice*, Chichester: John Wiley & Sons.

Checkland, P., and Scholes, J., (1990). *Soft Systems Methodology in Action*, Chichester: John Wiley & Sons.

Chen, P.P-S., (1976). 'The Entity-Relationship Model: toward a unified view of data', *ACM Transactions on Database Systems,* 1 (1), pp. 9–36.

Codd, E.F., (1970). 'A Relational Model of Data for Large Shared Data Banks', *Communications of the ACM*, 13 (6), pp. 377–387.

Coyle, R., (ed.) (1996). *Systems Dynamics Modeling*, Chapman and Hall.

Conradi, R., Fernström, C., and Fugetta, A., (1994). 'Concepts for evolving software processes', in (Finkelstein, A., Kramer, J., and Nuseibeh, B., (eds.) 1994), pp. 9–32.

Curtis, B., Kellner, M., and Over, J., (1992). 'Process Modeling', *Communications of the ACM*, 35 (9), pp. 75–90.

Dasgupta, S., (1991). *Design Theory and Computer Science*, Cambridge: Cambridge University Press.

Davenport, T. H., (1993). *Process Innovation – Reengineering Work Through Information Technology*, Harvard Business School Press.

Derniame, J.-C., Kaba, A.B., and Wastell, D., (eds.) (1999). *Software Process: Principles, Methodology, and Technology*, volume 1500 of *Lecture Notes in Computer Science*: Springer Verlag.

Dowson, M., (1993). 'Software Process "Themes and Issues"', in *Proceedings of the 2nd International Conference on the Software Process*, Berlin, Germany: IEEE Computer Society Press, pp. 54–62.

Dowson, M., and Fernström, C., (1994). 'Towards requirements for enactment mechanisms', in (Warboys, B.C., (ed.) 1994), pp. 90–106.

Eden, C., (1989). 'Using strategic mapping for strategic options development and analysis', in Rosehead, J., (ed.), *Rational Analysis for a Problematic World*, John Wiley & Sons.

Emery, F.E., (1959). *Characteristics of Sociotechnical Systems,* London: Tavistock Institute, Document No. 527.

Espejo, R., and Harnden, R., (eds.) (1989). *The Viable System Model,* John Wiley & Sons.

Feiler, P., and Humphrey, W., (1993). 'Software Process Development and Enactment: Concepts and Definitions', in *Proceedings of the 2nd International Conference on the Software Process*, Berlin, Germany: IEEE Computer Society Press, pp. 28–40.

Fernström, C., (1992). 'Computer Aided Process Support: State-of-the-Art and State-of-the-Market', *Proceedings of EUROCON'92*, Zurich: IEEE Press.

Fernström, C., (1993). 'Process WEAVER: Adding Process Support to UNIX', in *Proceedings of the 2nd International Conference on the Software Process*, Berlin, Germany: IEEE Computer Society Press, pp. 12–26.

Finkelstein, A., Kramer, J., and Nuseibeh, B., (eds.) (1994). *Software Process Modelling and Technology*, Taunton: Research Studies Press.

Fischer, L., (ed.) (1995). *New Tools for New Times: The Workflow Paradigm*, Future Strategies.

Flood, R.L., and Jackson, M.C., (1991). *Creative Problem Solving, Total Systems Intervention*, Chichester: John Wiley & Sons.

Follett, M. (1941). 'The psychology of control', in Metcalf, H., and Urwick, L., (eds.), *Dynamic Administration: The Collected Papers of Mary Parker Follett*, London: Pitman.

Fowler, M., and Scott, K., (1997). *UML Distilled,* Reading, Massachusetts: Addison-Wesley.

Greenwood, R.M., Guy, M.R., and Robinson, D.J.K., (1992). 'The Use of a Persistent Language in the Implementation of a Process Support System', *ICL Technical Journal*, 8 (1), pp.108–130.

Greenwood, R.M., Robertson, I., Snowdon, R.A., and Warboys, B.C., (1995) 'Active Models in Business', in *Proceedings of the 5th Annual Conference on Business Information Technology (BIT'95)*, Department of Business Information Technology, Manchester Metropolitan University, pp. 141–152.

Greenwood, R.M., Warboys, B.C.., and Sa, J., (1996). 'Cooperating Evolving Components – A Rigorous Approach to Evolving Large Software Systems', in *Proceedings of the 18th International Conference on Software Engineering ICSE'18,* Berlin, Germany: IEEE Computer Society Press, pp. 428–437.

Gruhn, V., (ed.) (1998). *Proceedings of the 6th European Workshop on Software Process Technology EWSPT'98*, volume 1487 of *Lecture Notes in Computer Science*: Springer Verlag.

Gruhn, V., (1994). 'Software Process Management and Business Process (Re-)Engineering', in (Warboys, B.C., (ed.) 1994), pp. 250–253.

Halé, J., (1995). *From Concepts to Capabilities*, John Wiley & Sons.

Hammer, M., (1990). 'Re-engineering Work: Don't Automate, Obliterate', *Harvard Business Review*, July-August, pp. 104–112.

Hammer, M., (1995). *The Reengineering Revolution*, Harper Business.

Hammer, M., and Champy, J., (1993). *Reengineering the Corporation*, London: Nicholas Brealey Publishing.

Harrington, H.J., (1991). *Business Process Improvement*, New York, McGraw-Hill.

Hirscheim, R., and Klein, H., (1989). 'Four Paradigms of Information Systems Development', *Communications of the ACM*, 32 (10), pp. 1199–1214.

Holt, A.W., Ramsey, H.R., and Grimes, J.D., (1983). 'Coordination System Technology as the Basis for a Programming Environment', *Electrical Communication*, 57 (4), pp. 308–314.

ICL, (1996). *ProcessWise Integrator PML Reference Manual*, ICL/PW/635/01, issued with release 4.1.

ICSM, (1999). *International Conference on Software Maintenance ICSM'99, Oxford*: IEEE.

ICSP, (1996). *Proceedings of the 4th International Conference on the Software Process ICSP '96*. IEEE Computer Society.

IDEF0, (1993). *Integration Definition for Function Modeling (IDEF0)*, U.S. Department of Commerce, Technology Administration, National Institute of Standards and Technology, Federal Information Processing Standards Publication, Report No. FIPS PUB 183.

IEEE, (1990). *IEEE Standard Glossary of Software Engineering Terminology.* ANSI/IEEE Std. 610.12-1990, Piscataway, N.J.: IEEE.

ISPW, (1998). *Proceedings of the 10th International Software Process Workshop ISPW-10*, IEEE Computer Society.

Jackson, M., (1994). 'Problems, methods and specialisation', *Software Engineering Journal*, pp. 249–255.

Katz, D., and Khan, R., (1978). *The Social Psychology of Organizations*, Wiley.

Kawalek, P., and Leonard, J., (1996). 'Evolutionary Software Development to Support Organizational and Business Process Change: A Case Study Account', *Journal of Information Technology*, 11, pp. 185–198.

Keen, P., (1997). *The Process Edge*, Boston: Harvard Business School Press.

Koestler, A., and Smythies, J.R., (eds.) (1969). *Beyond Reductionism*, London: Hutchinsons.

Lawrence, P., (ed.) (1997). *Workflow Handbook 1997*, published in association with the Workflow Management Coalition, Chichester: John Wiley & Sons.

Lehman, M.M., (1980). 'Programs, Life Cycles, and the Laws of Software Evolution', *Proceedings of the IEEE*, 68 (9).

Lehman, M.M., (1987). 'Process Models, Process Programs, Programming Support' – invited response to keynote address, *Proceedings of the 9th International Conference on Software Engineering ICSE'9*, Monterey: IEEE Computer Society.

Lehman, M.M., (1989). 'Uncertainty in Computer Application and its Minimisation Through the Engineering of Software', *Software Maintenance Research and Practice*, 1 (1), pp. 3–27.

Lehman, M.M., (1991) 'Software Engineering, the Software Process and their Support', *Software Engineering Journal*, 6 (5), pp. 243–258.

Lehman, M.M., (1992). 'Evolution of Processes and Process Models', *IOPener, the Newsletter of the IOPT Club*, Bath: Praxis Systems Ltd., 1 (4), p. 4.

Leintz, B., and Swanson, E., (1980). *Software Maintenance Management*, New York: Addison Wesley.

Lewis, P., (1994). *Information-Systems Development*, London: Pitman Publishing.

Li, E.Y., and Rogers, J.C., (1991). 'An Information System Profile of U.S. Companies,' *Information and Management*, 21, North-Holland.

Lonchamp, J., (1993). 'A Structured Conceptual and Terminological Framework for Software Process Engineering', *Proceedings of the 2nd International Conference on the Software Process*, Berlin, Germany: IEEE Computer Society Press, pp. 41–53.

London Ambulance Service, (1993). *Report of the Inquiry into the London Ambulance Service*, public domain.

Madhavji, N., (1991). 'The Process Cycle', *Software Engineering Journal*, 6 (5), pp. 234–242.

Madhavji, N., Gruhn, V., Deiters, W., and Schäfer, W., (1990). 'Prism = Methodology + Process-oriented Environment', in *Proceedings of the 12th International Conference on Software Engineering ICSE'12*: IEEE Computer Society Press.

Maturana, H.R., and Varela, F., (1980). *Autopoiesis and Cognition: The Realization of the Living*, Reidel: Dordrecht.

Miers, D., (1994). 'Use of Tools and Technology within a BPR Initiative', in Coulson-Thomas, C., (ed.), *Business Process Re-engineering: Myth & Reality*, London: Kogan-Page.

Morgan, G., (1986). *Images of Organizations*, London: Sage Publications.

Mumford, E., (1981). 'Participative Systems Design: Structure and Method', *Systems Objectives, Solutions*, 1, pp. 5–19.

Mumford, E., and Wier, M., (1979). *Computer Systems in Work Design: The Ethics Method*, New York: John Wiley & Sons.

Naur, P., and Randell, B., (1969). 'Software Engineering', Report on a Conference Sponsored by the NATO Science Committee, Garmisch, Germany, 1969, Brussels: NATO Science Committee.

Oakley, B., and Owen, K., (1989). *Alvey Britain's Strategic Computing Initiative*, MIT Press.

Osterweil, L.J., (1987). 'Software Processes are Software too'. In *Proceedings of the 9th International Conference on Software Engineering ICSE'9*, Monterey: IEEE Computer Society.

Ould., M.A., (1995). *Business Processes: Modelling And Analysis For Re-engineering And Improvement*, Chichester: John Wiley & Sons.

Oxford, (1990). *Oxford Dictionary of Computing*, Third Edition, Oxford: Oxford University Press.

Pasmore, W., (1988). *Designing Effective Organizations*, John Wiley & Sons.

Paulk, M., Curtiss, W., Chrissis, M., and Weber, C., (1993). *Capability Maturity Model for Software, Version 1.1*, Technical Report CMU/SEI-93-TR-24, DTIC ADA263403, Software Engineering Institute, Carnegie Mellon University, Pittsburg, U.S.A.

Platt, D., (1994). *Process Modelling and Process Support Environments for Design Management*, PhD thesis, University of Bristol, Faculty of Engineering, Department of Civil Engineering.

Robertson, I., (1998). 'Evolution in Perspective', *Proceedings International Workshop on the Principles of Software Evolution at the 20th International Conference on Software Engineering*, Kyoto, Japan, pp. 172–176.

Rodden, T., King, V., Hughes, J., and Sommerville, I., (1994). 'Process Modelling and Development Practice', in (Warboys, B.C., (ed.) 1994), pp 59–64.

Rotter, J.B., (1966). 'Generalized Expectancies for Internal versus External Control of Reinforcement', *Psychological Monographs*, 30 (1), pp. 1–26.

Sa, J. and Warboys, B.C., (1994). 'Modelling Processes Using a Stepwise Refinement Technique', in (Warboys, B.C., (ed.) 1994), pp. 40–58.

Schön, D. (1983). *The Reflective Practitioner*, Basic Books.

Scott Morton, M., (ed.) (1991). *The Corporation of the 1990s: Information Technology and Organizational Transformation*, Oxford University Press.

Shaw, M., (1990). 'Prospects for an Engineering Discipline of Software', *IEEE Software, 7 (6)*, pp. 15–24.

Simon, H.A., (1962). 'The architecture of complexity', reprinted in (Simon, H.A., 1981).

Simon, H.A., (1976). *Administrative Behaviour*, Macmillan.

Simon, H.A., (1981). *The Sciences of the Artificial*, Second Edition, London: MIT Press.

Sommerville, I., and Monk, S., (1994). 'Supporting informality in the software process', in (Warboys, B.C., (ed.) 1994), pp. 114–118.

Snowdon, R.A., (1989). 'An Introduction to the IPSE 2.5 Project', *ICL Technical Journal*, 6 (3), pp. 467–478.

Suchman, L. (1983). 'Office Procedures as Practical Action', *ACM Transactions on Office Information Systems*, 1, pp. 320–328.

Taylor, F. W., (1911). *Principles of Scientific Management*, New York: Harper & Row.

Turski, W., (1991). 'Prescribing Behaviours', *Theoretical Computer Science*, 90, pp. 119–125.

Walsham, G., (1993). *Interpreting Information Systems in Organisations*, Chichester: John Wiley & Sons.

Warboys, B.C., (1990). 'The IPSE 2.5 project: process modelling as the basis for a support environment', in *Proceedings of 1st International Conference on Software Development, Environments and Factories*, Berlin: Pitman Publishing.

Warboys, B.C., (1991). 'The Practical Application of Process Modelling: Some Early Reflections', *Proceedings of the 1st European Workshop on Software Process Technology*, Milan: AICA Press.

Warboys, B.C., (ed.) (1994). *Proceedings of the 3rd European Workshop on Software Process Technology EWSPT'94*, volume 772 of *Lecture Notes in Computer Science*: Springer Verlag.

Warboys, B.C., (1995). 'The Software Paradigm', *ICL Technical Journal*, 10 (1).

Wardman, K.T., (1994). 'From Mechanistic to Social Systemic Thinking': A Digest Of A Talk Given By Russell L. Ackoff, *The Systems Thinker*, 5 (1): Pegasus Communications Inc.

Wastell, D., and Arbaoui, S., (1999). 'Human Dimensions of the Software Process', in (Derniame, J.-C., Kaba, A.B. and Wastell, D., (eds.) 1999).

Wastell, D., White, P., and Kawalek, P., (1994). 'A Methodology for Business Process Redesign: Experiences and Issues', *Journal of Strategic Information Systems*, 3 (1).

Weiss, P.A., (1969). 'The Living System: Determinism Stratified', in Koestler, A., and Smythies J.R., (eds.) *Beyond Reductionism*, London: Hutchinsons.

White, P.R., and Kawalek, P., (1993). *A Framework for Business Process Management*, Report of the Informatics Process Group, Department of Computer Science, University of Manchester, UK.

Wiener, N., (1950). *The Human Use of Human Beings*, reprinted 1989, London: Free Association Books.

Wiener, N., (1961). *Cybernetics*, Second Edition, London: MIT Books.

Wilson, B., (1990). *Systems: Concepts, Methodologies and Applications*, Second Edition, Chichester: John Wiley & Sons.

Winter, M.C., and Brown, D.H., (1994). *Thinking Systemically: Information Systems Development, Redressing the Balance*, Second Conference of the BCS Information Systems Methodologies Special Interest Group, Edinburgh, UK.

Winter, M.C., Brown, D.H., and Checkland, P., (1995). 'A Role for Soft Systems Methodology in Information Systems Development', European Journal of Information Systems, 4, pp. 130–142.

Wood-Harper, A.T., and Fitzgerald, G., (1982). 'A Taxonomy of Current Approaches to Systems Analysis', *The Computer Journal*, 25 (1).

Wynne, E., (1979). 'Office Conversations as an Information Medium', Ph.D Thesis, University of California at Berkeley.

Yeomans, B.S., (1997). 'A Process-Based Environment for the Evolutionary Development of Large Software Systems', M.Res. Thesis, University of Manchester, UK.

Index